ECONOMIC GROWTH IN BRITAIN

ECONOMIC GROWTH IN BRITAIN

Edited by
P. D. Henderson

WEIDENFELD AND NICOLSON
5 Winsley Street London W1

Printed in Great Britain by
Western Printing Services Ltd, Bristol

CONTENTS

PREFACE

Each of the chapters in this book was read by all the contributors, and in every case the resulting comments and suggestions led to amendments, some of which were substantial. However, the responsibility for the eventual form of each chapter, and for the opinions expressed, is that of the individual author alone.

Although much of the argument of the book is unavoidably technical, we have tried to write for a wider audience than our fellow-economists. In pursuit of this aim, we have kept down the number of references and dispensed entirely with footnotes. However, an annotated reading list is appended to each chapter.

Since the commitment to write the book was undertaken, in the summer of 1964, some of the co-authors have accepted temporary posts in Government departments. The opinions expressed in their respective chapters are purely personal, and should not be taken as in any way reflecting the official views of the departments concerned. The chapters were either wholly or substantially completed before any question of working for a department had arisen.

The editor wishes to thank the Warden and Fellows of Nuffield College for the help and facilities which they generously gave him during the academic year 1963–64, and which among other things greatly assisted the task of preparing this book. In particular, he is grateful for the expert and patient secretarial work of Miss Jean Brotherhood.

I

INTRODUCTION

Ten years ago the publication of a book on economic growth in Britain would have been a rather surprising event. Today this seems an obvious subject to choose, and there are a good many recent publications which deal with it. The explanation of this contrast is to be found in a gradual change of emphasis in economic thinking, and in the mental attitudes of those concerned with economic policy, a change which has been brought about by a number of related influences. A good illustration of it can be found in the changing content of economic textbooks. For example, in the first edition of Professor Samuelson's excellent and widely used introductory text, there was no section which was specifically devoted to economic growth, while in the current (sixth) edition there are three substantial chapters.

At first sight it may seem odd that a subject so important as the rate of economic growth should not have been continuously in the forefront of analysis and discussion. To understand this, and to account for the change that has taken place, it is necessary to look at the historical evolution of economic thought, and of the events which have influenced its content and direction, over the past twenty years or so.

At the end of the second world war the main single preoccupation of British economists was gaining acceptance for Keynesian ideas, and for policy measures derived from those ideas. This was both inevitable and entirely justified. At the present time, when lengthy sections on macroeconomics are a standard ingredient of every textbook of economics, and after twenty-five years of continuous full employment in Britain and with no serious recession in world output and trade, it is easy to take the Keynesian revolution for granted. But in the early nineteen-forties none of this could be regarded as inevitable, or even perhaps as probable. At the outbreak of war in 1939

9

British administration and business had been little affected by the new ways of thinking. Even in university departments the revolution, though well under way, was by no means fully accepted and had not yet consolidated its gains. (A comparative historical study of the syllabuses and examination papers for degree courses in economics would make an interesting chapter in the history of economic thought.) Given this situation, and considering also the prolonged and acutely depressing inter-war history of instability, unemployment, and the failure of advanced industrial countries to achieve full utilisation of their productive potential, it was quite natural that at the end of the war the Keynesian system and its implications should be the central topic of discussion.

Thus attention was largely concentrated on the economics of full employment – that is, on the general principle of maintaining and controlling the level of aggregate demand in order to ensure that the full productive potential of the economy was realised, and on the various instruments of policy by which this objective might be attained. As it proved, the immediate need in the post-war years was to restrain rather than stimulate demand, but essentially the same analytical scheme and the same instruments of policy were relevant.

Once the government had accepted responsibility for controlling the level of demand with the object of avoiding either unemployment or inflation, a number of complex problems presented themselves. First, there was the need to build up a comprehensive and detailed set of national accounts. Second, there was the problem of finding the best combination of policy instruments to control demand, and of analysing the probable effects of different combinations. This is a subject in which, after twenty years of actual experience, there is still considerable scope for disagreement and for further research. Third, there was the related question of how to reconcile internal and external policy objectives, and to try to ensure that policy measures designed to maintain demand would be consistent with achieving a reasonable surplus in the balance of payments. All these were comparatively novel problems, on which not much previous work had been done. Moreover, the past experience of economies in which the level of demand had been largely uncontrolled necessarily provided very limited guidance.

With a difficult agenda of this kind, and given also the very serious short-term problems which affected the British economy in the early post-war years, it is not surprising that the subject of economic growth was comparatively neglected.

There were also other factors which contributed to this result. First, the rates of growth which it seemed reasonable at the time to project appeared rather unglamorously low: it was commonly assumed that the British economy would continue to grow at something close to what was believed to be the pre-war rate of growth of output per man, of $1\frac{1}{2}$ per cent per annum. It was sometimes suggested – for example, by Mr Nicholas Kaldor in his appendix to Beveridge's study, *Full Employment in a Free Society* (published in 1944) – that the maintenance of full employment would itself provide a stimulus to productivity growth, so that one could reasonably hope for some improvement on past performance. (Kaldor himself suggested a rate of growth in output per man-hour of 2 per cent per annum, which has in fact proved to be a good forecast.) But even given acceptance of such an assumption, it was obvious that uncontrolled fluctuations in demand might lead to year-to-year changes in output and income which would be large in comparison with the long-term trend rate of growth. Between the years 1929 and 1933 the gross national product of the United States fell by more than one-third; as between the two adjacent calendar years of 1931 and 1932, the fall was 15 per cent. Thus it was apparent that failure to avert depression could lead to a fall in output, over quite a short period, which would be equivalent to perhaps a decade or more of growth at the trend rate. It is easy to see why people should have been more concerned with how to prevent a recurrence of such disasters than with the prospects of raising what might well appear to be insignificant-looking rates of growth in output per man.

A second additional factor was that some of the main determinants of growth – in particular, population growth and technical progress – were often held or assumed to be largely unamenable to explanation in terms of economic variables. Thus in the systems of thought or models which economists used as their intellectual frames of reference, these determinants of growth were often treated as something which had to be taken into account – at any rate in a long-term view – but which it was not necessarily the responsibility of the economist to analyse or account for. In technical language, they were treated as exogenous rather than endogenous variables. There was nothing inevitable about this. The frontiers which separate economics from neighbouring fields of inquiry – such as history, demography, sociology or engineering – are disputable, and best left ill-defined. Earlier economic models had tried to incorporate population changes (where Malthus's system is the best-known example) or technical progress (where Schumpeter is the outstanding instance) as variables which were explained within the model, rather than being treated as largely external influences. But it can easily be seen that this is a more daring enterprise for an economist to attempt than trying to explain changes (say) in the demand for coal or the volume of consumers' expenditure. Partly because of the preoccupations which we have already referred to, the prevailing climate of opinion among economists in the nineteen-forties favoured a rather modest conception of the economist's role in explaining growth.

This tendency was reinforced by a further additional factor, namely the comparative poverty, by present standards, of statistical evidence on economic growth. Although absence of data has not always inhibited economists from drawing firm conclusions, availability of data is itself a stimulus to inquiry. Since the war, partly as a result of Keynesian ideas and policies, and partly because of the growing interest in the analysis of economic growth over longer periods, the amount of information available has enormously increased. Much further work has been undertaken on historical data, producing new series and refining previously existing ones; and in addition, increasingly detailed and consistent figures have been produced for the current national accounts of different countries. Thus the quantity, quality and international comparability of growth statistics have been greatly improved. Although this is in part the result of an increasing interest in growth problems, it has naturally helped to stimulate and sustain that interest.

Finally, during the first five to ten years after the war, attention was to some extent distracted from the analysis of economic growth, not merely because other questions seemed relatively more important and more urgent, and because economists had good reason for diffidence about their ability to explain the process of growth, but also because the rate of growth in Britain seemed reasonably satisfactory. Although there was a good deal of general concern about raising productivity, which was stimulated by comparative studies of British and US output per man in particular industries, there was no reason to feel that by historical standards, or by comparison with other countries, the overall rate of growth of the economy was seriously disappointing.

Thus a variety of factors combined in causing growth problems to remain on the fringe of analysis and discussion, rather than in the centre. In the course of the nineteen-fifties each one of these factors disappeared.

In the first place, both the extent of acceptance and the degree of success achieved by Keynesian policies were unexpectedly great. The results of this were twofold. First, the intellectual energies released from the task of proselytising, and from the analysis of what as time went on appeared to be increasingly remote problems such as the 'pure' business cycle, could be turned to refining and extending economic models to encompass new problems. This helps to explain the increasing attention given to growth in economic theory, though this was in part the natural result of attempts to generalise the original and largely static Keynesian models. Second, as full employment and comparative stability of output come increasingly to be taken for granted, the relative importance of raising the rate of growth naturally appeared larger. When the national product cannot be significantly raised by increasing demand, and (as in Britain) fluctuations in output have in total been very small, an increase in the rate of growth of productivity from (say) 2 per cent to 3 per cent no longer seems a small matter. Thus despite the growing interest in methods of controlling the economy in the short term, there was also a predictable trend towards the analysis of growth. Indeed, as will be seen, the earlier tendency to separate short-run and long-run problems into distinct analytical compartments became increasingly outmoded.

The most important factor, however, was a growing realisation that there were considerable differences in international rates of growth, and that in comparison with other countries British economic performance seemed a good deal less satisfactory than it had been previously thought to be. During the nineteen-fifties the United Kingdom rates of growth, both of total output and of output per person employed or per man-hour, were the lowest in Western Europe. In the first part of the decade, it was widely believed that this was a natural result of exceptionally high rates of growth in Europe – particularly in Western Germany – which were a strictly temporary phenomenon associated with recovery from war. It is still argued by some that temporary factors were mainly responsible, and that a reversion to rates of growth more in line with long-term historical trends can be expected. As time went on, however, this doctrine (which is referred to – and rejected – in Chapter 3 of this book) began to lose adherents, and it was increasingly argued that the relatively poor performance of the British economy might be neither temporary nor inevitable.

The effect of this slower rate of growth, over a substantial period, has naturally been a relative fall in the British material standard of living as compared with that of other industrial countries. In 1950 this country was quite clearly one of the richest in Western Europe, with a level of output per head surpassed only by Sweden and Switzerland. By 1963, the latest year for which comparable data are available, Britain had become one of a group of several nations, all of them below Sweden and Switzerland, which had much the same income per head. If the rates of growth of output per head of population which were attained in the nineteen-fifties by France, Germany and Britain are projected from 1963 to 1970, then by that time French output per head will be over 10 per cent higher than ours, and the German figure over one-third higher. A particularly disturbing feature of the present British situation is that output per head in manufacturing seems now to be considerably lower than in many European countries, including France and Germany. Whatever the explanation of these changes in the relative position of Britain, they are too important to be treated as a minor or secondary problem.

Thus the conjunction of world prosperity and wide differences in national growth rates has naturally led to an increasing concern with the analysis and explanation of growth. There has been a general acceptance by governments of the need to attain high rates of growth, and as a corollary more attention is being given to the means by which this aim might be realised. At the same time, and partly in consequence, we have seen that the data that are available for recording and analysing the process of growth have been greatly improved. It is thus not surprising that some earlier inhibitions and reservations about the competence of economists to explain the phenomena of growth, which were referred to above, have been gradually weakened or set aside; and that the quantity and scope of publications devoted to this topic have grown in a remarkable way.

Despite all that has been done, however, our understanding of the nature and causes of economic growth remains very limited. Some people have been tempted to attribute this unsatisfactory state of affairs to the stupidity or perversity of economists, but unfortunately this simple diagnosis is at fault. (If it were correct, a quite small investment in improving the quantity and quality of economists would yield spectacularly high returns to society.) The problems of analysing growth are exceedingly complex, and the evidence is fragmentary and difficult to interpret. Thus it is not surprising that the conclusions of some recent studies of growth problems have been negative or agnostic, nor that when positive conclusions have been reached they have almost always proved to be controversial.

Although any simple classification of views is necessarily arbitrary, a useful initial distinction can be made between what may be called a fatalist school of thought, on the one hand, and a more pragmatic approach on the other. Economists who fall into the first group have been strongly impressed by two related phenomena which they regard as reasonably well established: first, the comparative stability of individual national growth rates over long periods of time; and second, the difficulty or impossibility of doing much to raise the underlying rate of growth of a country over a short period of time. In the British context, such a view leads to two conclusions, one consolatory and the other depressing. The first is that, judged by past historical performance, the recent British rate of growth has not been low; and the apparently better results achieved by other industrial countries can in many cases be explained as a temporary matter, associated with making up ground which was lost in the depression or the war or the early post-war periods, when the rate of growth in these countries was well below the long-term underlying trend. The second conclusion is that there is not a great deal that governments can do to bring about any rapid and significant increase in the future rate of growth. To say this is not to deny that government policies may affect economic growth, both favourably and un-favourably; nor does it imply that suitably chosen measures to stimulate growth will not succeed. But as Denison has put it in his study of economic growth in the United States, 'We should not be surprised, or disappointed, to find that measures to alter the growth rate by 1 or 2 percentage points would have to be very big measures – if, indeed, they exist at all.' This conclusion was reached for the United States, and was not intended by the author to apply to other less advanced industrial countries in which, precisely because of their lower output per head, there may be greater opportunities for achieving higher growth rates. Other economists, however, would probably be ready to give the argument a wider application.

By contrast, the pragmatic view is sceptical about the per-sistence (or even the existence) of underlying trends in national growth rates. The high rates recently achieved by many West-ern European countries and by Japan are explained mainly by reference to the success with which high levels of demand and employment have been maintained in these countries and in the industrial world as a whole, and to peculiar features of indivi-dual economies which result, not from given and largely un-alterable historical circumstances, but from a complex of inter-related factors which government policy can influence if not determine. It would be misleading to suggest that there is a single unified body of doctrine here. But a number of recent studies of economic growth in Europe have a close family resemblance; and they conclude, or suggest by implication, that better management of the United Kingdom economy would have led to a higher rate of growth in the past, and could do so in the future.

One common feature that emerges from these studies is the notion of a virtuous or vicious circle in the process of growth;

thus a high rate of growth or a low rate, once maintained over a period, may become self-perpetuating. (An argument of this type is developed in Chapter 3 below.) Rapid growth is associated, as both cause and effect, with high rates of investment, a high yield of investment in terms of output potential, more rapid introduction of technical and organisational improvements, a slower rate of increase in prices, a more favourable international competitive position, and a climate of business expectations and social attitudes which is favourable to growth. A corresponding network of causal relations may explain the persistence of a low rate of growth. What we have termed the fatalistic school of thought is inclined to emphasise the importance of human factors in economic growth: the spread of education and skill; the development of social attitudes and values favourable to innovation and change; and the advancement of technical knowledge. These underlying determinants of growth (it is argued) can be changed only very gradually; while the influence of more strictly economic variables, such as the level of demand or the rate of investment, is relatively small. By contrast, the pragmatic view, while not necessarily denying the importance of non-economic factors, regards some of these at least as subject to more direct and immediate influence by the rate of growth itself, and thus by economic measures which would contribute to accelerating growth.

Acceptance of this view implies that with suitable policies an improvement in the British rate of growth might be achieved over a relatively short period; and it suggests at any rate the broad outlines of a strategy which might enable the United Kingdom economy to escape from the vicious circle that seems to have been established. However, detailed diagnosis and prescription still remain complex and highly controversial matters; and it does not need to be argued in 1965 that there is no obvious combination of policies to hand which is free from difficulties and objections.

In so far as any single factor can be held to account for the failures of the past, the balance of payments is the most widely accepted choice. There is a good deal of agreement that British balance of payments problems, and the periodic imposition of restrictive policies in order to deal with them, have been largely or partly responsible for holding back growth. In some formulations, this line of argument had led to a rather simple basic programme designed to improve British performance: governments should change the relative importance they have given to conflicting objectives, and should be ready to sacrifice external objectives – such as exchange stability – for higher growth; by doing so they would avoid the need to resort to 'stop-go' policies; and this in turn would ensure, either in itself or in conjunction with other measures, a much higher rate of growth.

Such an analysis can be attacked head-on, for example by denying that temporary short-term restrictions have affected the underlying rate of growth of the economy, or by arguing that in the British case exchange stability is a precondition of a high rate of growth rather than an obstacle to it, or that international obligations and the status of sterling as a reserve currency preclude the notion of an overriding commitment to growth. Even if one rejects such arguments, however, the analysis is unacceptable, at any rate it is in its simpler forms, because it seriously over-simplifies the issues in two respects. Both weaknesses derive from the neglect of the basic distinction, which is also referred to later in this book, between the rate of growth of actual output and of the output potential of the economy.

The actual output of an economy in a given period will depend on two things: the maximum output potential at that time; and the extent to which that potential is realised, which in turn can be said to depend on the pressure of demand. Over long periods of time – twenty years or more – the rate of growth of actual output will be very largely determined by the growth of output potential; by comparison, changes in the pressure of demand will have little effect. But over short periods, of five years or less, changes in the pressure of demand may have a dominant influence on the rate of growth of actual output, which because of such changes may grow at a considerably faster or slower rate than the underlying rate of growth of output potential. Thus when it is alleged that 'stop-go' policies have slowed down the rate of growth, it is important to distinguish between their effects on the pressure of demand and on the underlying rate of growth.

In any economy in which the government tries to control the level of total demand, the need to restrain demand as well as to stimulate it may clearly arise. Further, if over a period the rate of growth of actual output considerably exceeds the growth of potential output, restraints will eventually be needed quite independently of the state of the balance of payments. To this extent, what can broadly be described as 'stop-go' policies are not in the least undesirable, but are indeed a necessary ingredient of economic policy. It is true that the restrictions imposed on each of three past phases of British economic expansion were affected, as to their timing, content and severity, by the state of the balance of payments. But it is also true that in each of these booms – in 1954–55, in 1959–60, and in 1963–64 – the rate of growth of output rose at a rate which could not have been sustained for long, even had balance of payments difficulties not arisen.

Thus it is a mistake to attribute the restrictive measures that were taken to external factors alone (though this is a fair point to make in relation to the events of 1957, when the pressure of demand was not high and was falling). The criticism of policy that emerges from an analysis of this experience is not that growth was sacrificed to the supposed needs of the balance of payments, but rather that the economy was allowed to expand too fast. Not only was this rate of expansion harmful to the balance of payments, but even apart from this it made corrective measures inevitable. The chief moral to be drawn from the experience is that, in its short-term stabilisation measures, the government should try to ensure that the rate of expansion of demand should be more gradual, and closer to the rate of increase in potential output. This in turn would help to ensure avoidance of the more hasty and drastic forms of 'stop-go', which may well have had adverse effects on the long-term rate of growth of output.

The second weakness of the analysis is that there is no necessary antithesis between a higher rate of growth and an improvement in the strength of sterling. An increase in output associated with a rise in the pressure of demand, so that actual output is growing faster than the output potential of the economy, is very likely to worsen the current account balance; but a higher rate of growth in the longer period, in line with potential output, may well have favourable effects. The argument of Chapter 3 suggests that the low rate of growth in Britain may have been in part the cause as well as the effect of deteriorating international competitiveness and poor export performance. In this respect, the suggestion that past policies have failed by putting external objectives before growth is something of an over-simplification.

On closer inspection, therefore, the apparent consensus of opinion about the relation between growth and the British balance of payments turns out to be partly illusory. Nevertheless, there are good reasons for believing that if the balance of payments had been less troublesome, or if the problems it presented had been differently handled, the effects on growth would have been favourable. The issue is discussed at the beginning of Chapter 4 of this book, which also draws on the argument of the previous chapter; and it is concluded there that specific measures to improve the balance of payments might enable the rate of growth of output to be increased. However, it is clear that other measures of policy may affect both the rate of growth and the balance of payments – which are themselves causally related; so that in the more general analysis of economic growth, there has been an increasing tendency to emphasise the interdependence of short-term policies and the rate of growth over longer periods.

The most obvious form of interdependence that may exist is between employment policy and growth. The object of policy here is to control the level of demand in such a way as to maintain the pressure of demand – and with it the rate of unemployment – at what is regarded as the right level. This at once raises the question of how one determines the right level. In particular, the problem arises of whether the maintenance of a higher or lower pressure of demand will significantly affect the rate of growth of productivity and potential output.

Even if one simplifies the issue by leaving aside the effects of the pressure of demand on prices and the balance of payments, this remains a disputed question. Moreover, in the British case these effects cannot be ignored. Thus it becomes necessary to form a view about the relations between the pressure of demand, the price level, the rate of growth, and the balance of payments. If for example one believes that a high pressure of demand is favourable to productivity growth and has little effect on the rate of increase in money incomes, then its effects on competitiveness and the balance of payments can be presumed to be favourable. If on the contrary one believes that wage and salary rates are sensitive to the pressure of demand, and that the long-run growth of output potential is unaffected by it, then there appears to be a strong case for running the economy at a lower pressure. Basic disagreements on this issue are often widened still further by different opinions or presuppositions about the freedom of action available to the United Kingdom in framing its external policies, and in particular, about the feasibility and potential usefulness of variations in the exchange rate.

A further complication is introduced if we consider the possible effects on the price level of a prices and incomes policy. Here it can be argued that a high pressure of demand will be favourable to the acceptance and operation of such a policy, and will therefore help to keep down prices quite apart from stimulating productivity growth. The contrary view is that with a high pressure of demand money incomes will be pushed up by labour scarcity; that a prices and incomes policy in such a situation must be ineffectual if not farcical; and that with a lower pressure of demand the apparent need for such a policy might disappear. Not surprisingly, opinions on this question are strongly affected by judgements about whether people could actually be persuaded to adopt an incomes policy, and whether if they did it would be a good thing.

Further complexities arise if we look not merely at the level of the pressure of demand, but at its rate and direction of change. It has been seen that in the United Kingdom the recent periods of expansion have been marked by a rather fast growth in output. Conversely, the growth of output in other years has been well below the rate of growth of output potential. This instability may have been harmful to the long-term growth of productivity. Again, the analysis of Chapter 3 suggests that confident expectations of a steady growth in demand may be necessary, or at least highly favourable, to a fast rate of growth over time. One might argue from this that even if a lower pressure of demand consistently maintained would not in itself be unfavourable to growth, the process of transition from a higher to an appreciably lower level would seriously damage expectations and bring down the future rate of growth.

Employment policy may also affect growth through the choice of particular instruments of policy to control the level of demand. For example, British governments have made considerable use over the past fifteen years of monetary policies, and have also held back demand by restrictions on public investment. It has been argued that a greater reliance on fiscal measures, with the object of influencing consumers' expenditure, would have produced better results. On this view, restrictions would have fallen less heavily on investment, and this would have been favourable to productivity growth. In addition, the greater uncertainty of the effects of monetary as opposed to fiscal measures, as to both magnitude and timing, may have led governments into decisions which increased the instability of demand, with consequences which have already been noted.

Even from these summary illustrations, it can be seen that the construction of a suitable explanatory model for analysing the effects of economic policies, and the ways in which different policy measures and objectives may interact, is very far from being a simple or uncontentious matter. Moreover the choice of objectives, and the assignment of weights to different objectives which may conflict, clearly depend on a system of value judgements and preferences which may not be acceptable to others: this subject is taken up in the following chapter. It is therefore not surprising if economists often seem to resemble the three philosophers in Peacock's *Headlong Hall*, who drew respectively, from identical evidence and experience, the conclusions (a) that the state of mankind and the world was steadily improving over time; (b) that it was steadily deteriorating; and (c) that while there was much to be said on both sides, on the whole it was remaining about the same. Nevertheless, the development of a more complete system of analysis, in which the possible interdependence of economic policies is more fully recognized, is a step forward. At worst, it has led to a greater and more sophisticated awareness of possibilities. On a more hopeful view, it has not only increased our understanding of how the economic system works, but has suggested new and better ways of securing the fuller realisation of economic objectives.

.   .   .

The first four of the eight chapters which follow are linked with each other, and deal for the most part with the broader aspects of policies for economic growth. Since a high rate of growth is only one of the goals which a community may adopt, the effects of pursuing it have to be considered in relation to the achievement of other and possibly conflicting aims. This theme is developed in Chapter 2. Particular attention is given to the consistency of different policy objectives, and to the issues which arise when conflict is inevitable.

Chapter 3 outlines a general analysis of the factors determining the rate of growth in a modern advanced society, which draws on (and helps to explain) the recent experience of growth in Western countries. This analysis leads to some broad conclusions about the relative effectiveness of different types of policy measures designed to raise the rate of growth. Since a good deal of emphasis is laid on competitiveness and on the growth of exports, and also on expectations about the future growth of total demand which in Britain have been affected both directly and indirectly by the state of the balance of payments, this leads naturally to the discussion of the balance of payments in Chapter 4. This starts from the proposition that measures to improve the balance would be favourable to growth, and considers the alternative ways in which one could try to bring about such an improvement. Chapter 5 is concerned with the interactions of demand, money incomes and prices. It reviews the factors affecting prices, the control of the price level as an object of policy (a matter which is also raised in Chapter 2), the means by which control can be attempted, and the possible interconnections of inflation and growth.

The next three chapters are concerned with more specific aspects of growth policy, and have no particular connection with each other (though the argument of Chapters 6 and 7 relates at various points to earlier chapters). Chapter 6 examines the scope for improving growth performance by means of taxation policies. It deals with the uses and limitations of fiscal policy as a means of controlling demand, and the connection between fiscal policies and the efficient working of the economy over the longer period. Chapter 7 considers, in the light of experience in France and with the 'Neddy' experiment in Britain, the potential usefulness of economic planning in raising the rate of growth. On the whole the conclusions reached here are hopeful, while those of Chapter 6 are less encouraging. No doubt some readers will feel that this strikes precisely the wrong balance between scepticism and credulity. Chapter 8 is concerned with the relationship between education and training and the rate of growth of productivity. It argues that the expansion of the education system that has already taken place has increased the growth potential and will continue to do, possibly at an accelerating rate. A number of conclusions are drawn about the kind of education and training policies which are likely to be most conducive to growth.

Finally, we include a chapter which has little relation to the main theme of the book, on the problems of world poverty and economic development in the poorer countries. One could argue that in principle there are two main connections between these problems and the rate of growth in Britain: first, the rate of growth might affect the extent to which we are prepared to help poor nations; and secondly, their accelerated development may improve our trading and investment opportunities and thus assist our own growth. But as to the first connection, it is clear that at present, for good reasons and bad, the amount of aid is determined by quite different considerations, in spite of the declared intention to devote one per cent of our national income to aid. As to the second connection, it is obviously true that rising prosperity in developing countries and international peace benefit Britain. But it is much less obvious that this can be the main justification for giving aid.

Another and more plausible connection between the two subjects is that the export earnings of underdeveloped countries are obviously dependent on the rate of growth of output in a world economy dominated by industrial nations such as Britain. However, our main justification for including such a chapter is to set Britain's problems into the world scene, a scene in which poverty, deprivation, illiteracy and disease are still provocations to violent and destructive upheavals.

In conclusion, three limitations of this book should be acknowledged. The first, over which we have no regrets, is that we have not provided a collective manifesto or a programme for growth. Such things are usually better done by one or two

24

people than by a committee. In any case our object was to analyse as much as to prescribe, though the relative emphasis varies as between different chapters. Although conclusions and recommendations emerge, both explicitly and by implication, these do not amount to anything more than individual expressions of view.

The second limitation, which is far more serious, is that we have failed to cover a number of factors which have – or can be thought to have – an important influence on the rate of economic growth. Thus we have no chapter or section on regional policies; restrictive practices, mergers and competition; the allocation of resources; the management of the public sector; or the problems of any particular industry or set of industries. Perhaps the most unfortunate omission is labour questions. We have nothing about the interrelations of trade union structure, collective bargaining procedures, and incomes policy; the effects of mobility on growth, and ways of increasing mobility (other than training, which comes into Chapter 8); and the ways in which changes in wage systems or other factors might help to reduce overmanning and the wasteful use of labour.

The third limitation is that the book does not set out to be topical. Except for this introduction, it was effectively completed by the end of 1964, and no attempt has been made to take into account very recent events or to revise the text in the light of them. For several of the contributions there would be no point in this – for example, the next two chapters, and the two concluding ones. Moreover, there are advantages in not trying to be up to the minute, since this carries with it the dangers of excessive preoccupation with current issues, and of projecting present conditions or trends too uncritically into the future. All the same, it could be argued that the developments of the past two years have underlined the seriousness of British economic problems; and that implicitly, by failing to take account of the most recent of these developments, we may have presented too favourable a picture. Further, 1965 has brought a number of changes and innovations in areas of policy with which some of our chapters are particularly concerned: in taxation, prices and incomes policy, planning, and the handling of the balance of payments. We have not been able to comment on these. But allowance for what has recently taken place would not significantly affect either the form of the argument presented, or the general conclusions reached; three of the four central chapters would have been virtually unchanged if they had been written several months later.

It is only the editor for whom the risk of obsolescence is a serious matter, since the chapter on planning (as also the present introduction) has been prepared before the publication of the first economic plan to be drawn up by a British government. Because of this misfortune, he may perhaps be allowed to add here a brief postscript to Chapter 7, which can also serve as a suitable conclusion to this introductory chapter.

In the course of Chapter 7, the unexceptionable (and unoriginal) argument is presented that short-term policies, to regulate the level of demand and the balance of payments, should be formulated in such a way as to conform with what is expected to be the longer-term growth in the output potential of the economy. Failure to do this may have had unfavourable effects on growth in the past. There is no reason to amend this statement in the light of recent events; but it is worth adding that the converse is also true. Longer-term plans will appear credible and relevant only if the objectives set can be shown to be consistent with short-term policies, and with the prospective growth of output over the period in which short-term policies are expected to determine what happens. Any plan that is thought to be inconsistent with decisions that are being currently taken will almost certainly be worthless from the start; and the result of failure to establish consistency might well be to discredit the whole idea of planning.

If this were to happen, it would be a further illustration of what some observers have felt to be a general and besetting weakness of British economic policy: the attempted pursuit of incompatible objectives.

SUGGESTIONS FOR FURTHER READING

Several of the publications listed and described at the end of Chapter 3 are equally relevant to the discussion in this introductory chapter. They are:

OECD, *Policies for Economic Growth* (Paris, November 1962).

United Nations Economic Commission, *Some Factors in Economic Growth in Europe during the 1950s* (Geneva, 1964).

Angus Maddison, *Economic Growth in the West* (Allen and Unwin, 1964).

A. Lamfalussy, *The United Kingdom and the Six* (Macmillan, 1963).

Odd Aukrust, 'Factors of Economic Development: A Review of Recent Research', *Weltwirtschaftliches Archiv*, 1964, Band 93, Heft 4.

W. Beckerman and Associates, *The British Economy in 1975* (NIESR and Cambridge University Press, 1965).

Additional recommendations are:

Edward F. Denison, *The Sources of Economic Growth in the United States* (US Committee for Economic Development, 1962). Both the assumptions used and the conclusions reached in this study have been disputed, but it is not necessary to agree with them in order to appreciate the quality of the work. The analysis is clear, candid and vigorous, and the statistical resourcefulness of the author extremely impressive.

R. R. Nelson, 'Aggregate Production Functions', *American Economic Review*, September 1964. A good critical survey of the content and implications of the (now extensive) literature analysing the relation between changes in labour and capital and the growth of output.

Colin Clark, *Growthmanship* (Hobart Papers No. 10, Institute of Economic Affairs, 2nd edition, 1962). This is a spirited attack on the argument that high investment is the main requirement for growth. Among other things, it is argued that Britain's economic difficulties have been much increased by too high a pressure of demand, and that planning is a waste of time.

J. R. Sargent, *Out of Stagnation* (Fabian Trust No. 343, Fabian Society, 1959). The main argument is that growth in Britain has been low because investment has not been of a sufficiently labour-saving character.

D. C. Paige and others, 'Economic Growth: The Last Hundred Years', National Institute *Economic Review*, July 1961. A basically statistical article, which sets out the record of past growth in different countries with a lucid commentary.

J. C. R. Dow, *The Management of the British Economy, 1945–60* (Cambridge University Press, 1964). Part IV of this excellent study contains the main conclusions, and draws out the lessons to be learned from past experience; and within it Chapter XVI is concerned with problems of growth and stability.

I. M. D. Little, 'Fiscal Policy', Chapter 8 of *The British Economy in the Nineteen-Fifties*, edited by G. D. N. Worswick and P. H. Ady (Oxford University Press, 1962). Like the study just referred to, this concludes that greater reliance on fiscal measures should make for steadier growth of output, and that this should lead to a higher average rate of growth over time. There is also a good short discussion of interrelated policy objectives in Part IV of the chapter.

Samuel Brittan, *The Treasury under the Tories, 1951–64* (Penguin Books, 1964) gives an interesting critical account of British economic policies in this period, and of the ways in which policy decisions have emerged from the government machine.

THE OBJECTIVES OF
ECONOMIC POLICY

Let us begin by stating certain widely accepted goals of economic policy:

1. Economic progress, that is to say, a high rate of economic growth.

2. A high current level of living, which comprises: high current consumption; leisure; decent working conditions.

3. Stability, which comprises: avoidance of unemployment; avoidance of inflation, i.e. avoidance of demand inflation and of cost inflation.

4. Greater equality of income and wealth.

5. Efficiency in production, including the preservation of economic incentives.

6. An adequate surplus in the balance of payments.

This list is neither exhaustive nor free from overlapping, nor do all the objectives have the same status. As we shall see, some are largely means to others, some are constraints on the achievement of others, some should, perhaps, be subdivided. But it will appear later why this particular list seems convenient for this discussion. A few brief comments on each of these objectives are in order.

Economic growth

A number of questions arise here, of which we shall ask four. First, growth of what? Second, why do we want a high or a faster rate of growth? Third, can government policy affect the rate of growth? Fourth, should government policy affect the rate of growth?

The four serious candidates for the answer to the question

'growth of what?' are: growth of (gross or net) total national income, irrespective of whether it results from more heads or from higher income per head; growth of (gross or net) national income per head; growth of aggregate consumption; and growth of consumption per head. Since material well-being depends on consumption, it is natural to use growth of consumption as the objective. Investment is merely a means of raising future consumption above what it would otherwise have been. A society which has a fantastically high rate of growth of income because it reinvests all resources above the subsistence minimum and never enjoys the fruits of this investment cannot be said to behave very sensibly. On the other hand, there are important uses of a growing national product besides present and future consumption. There are military objectives, foreign aid, space travel. Moreover, we also desire the growth of leisure. And it is conceivable, though not perhaps very likely, that we are getting better off by an accelerated growth of longer holidays, shorter working weeks and a shorter working life, while the rate of growth of measured consumption declines. This is not very likely, because people do not enjoy their leisure in pure contemplation, but want more time in order to consume more. The problem is further complicated by the fact that some leisure activity is non-measured investment – both physical investment in the form of do-it-yourself construction and improvement, and human investment in the form of education.

The question whether it is growth in total consumption or growth in consumption per head that matters is controversial. Most people would perhaps opt for consumption per head, subject to not cutting off heads to increase the ratio. If it were possible to draw a line, above which life is enjoyable and below which it is miserable, there might be a case for advocating a larger population enjoying a life above this line in preference to a smaller population at a still higher level of enjoyment. There is certainly a point beyond which we should not want to limit population, even if it meant a higher rate of growth of consumption for the remainder. Such questions were much debated in the nineteenth century and are still discussed. The fact that even very affluent societies do not encourage immigration and large families as part of their growth policies might suggest that aggregate growth is not their aim. But we cannot conclude from this that consumption per head is their objective, for neither are emigration and family limitation normally encouraged in rich countries in order to raise consumption per head. In under-developed countries the objective is much clearer. But in a country like Britain, does the absence of a conscious population policy mean that the government considers this is not a proper field in which to interfere, even though it aims at growth of consumption per head, or does it mean that the government is not clear about what it is that it wants to grow? If population policy is excluded, and if growth of consumption per head is the objective, we may have to abstain from consumption today in order to raise consumption per head after two generations simply because the population will be larger. Some people might object to making sacrifices now in order to satisfy the propensity to procreate of others.

In spite of these objections, growth of consumption per head seems more sensible than the other possibilities, as long as we remember to include the growth of leisure and of consumption goods and services provided by the government, subject to the proviso that some growth of non-consumption is wanted for other reasons than to increase consumption later.

We next turn to the question: why do we want a high rate of growth or a faster rate of growth than we have now? For under-developed countries with low incomes per head the answer is abundantly clear. But the case for growth beyond a decent level at which all our necessary wants can be satisfied is less obvious. It is true that, when people are asked what would make them just comfortable and remove their main worries, the answer is generally something like 20 per cent more – irrespective of what level of income they enjoy. This can be used both as an argument for growth – we should let people have what they want – and as an argument against growth – they still will not be satisfied when they have more. But even on the interpretation most favourable to growth it would constitute an argument for growth over one individual's life span only – not over generations.

Is there then a case for accelerating growth over periods long enough to span several generations? The general argument for a policy of accelerated growth is that the technical opportunities to increase consumption later are such that the rate of return on forgoing consumption now exceeds the rate at which we discount these later returns. If I consider £2 for my grandchild an adequate compensation for sacrificing £1 now, and if by refraining from consumption now I can get a return of £3 for my grandchild, there is a case for saving and investing more and accelerating the transformation of current into future consumption. The difficulties of formulating a growth policy are twofold: first, widely varying estimates are offered as to the technical opportunities of reaping returns from investing now; second, the valuations of future consumption compared with current vary widely from person to person, from time to time, and from a person acting as a gay spender to the same person acting as a responsible voter.

For what it is worth, the economic evidence suggests that the social returns to not consuming now are substantially in excess of what we are able to get as private savers. This is reflected in the fact that bond-holders receive around 5 per cent on their investment, whereas companies receive more than 10 per cent after allowance for depreciation, obsolescence and taxes. Some of this difference is ascribed to risks, but first it is not obvious that society should have the same risk aversion as private investors, and secondly, many private risks, such as uncertainty about rivals' behaviour, are not social risks. Moreover, risks alone do not account for the large difference between the returns to savers and the requirements of companies. Another explanation is the monopoly power of those companies, which prevents competitors from bringing down the high rates of return. Furthermore, many investments, particularly those essential for new products and new processes, yield benefits which accrue to others than those who incur the expenses. Men learn how to do things and acquire new skills which they can use when employed elsewhere. Although this is also true of production of consumption goods, it is probably more important for investment and constitutes an argument for carrying investment further than the private capital market would permit.

Even if it could be shown that the private and the social rates of return to saving were the same, we might wish to give a different expression to our social time preferences than we can do in the capital market. As responsible citizens, voting for a government that spends our money, we may attach greater weight to later generations – not only our own children and grandchildren – than we reveal in our private saving choices.

I am suggesting that both the social rate of time discount may be lower, and the social rate of return higher than are reflected in an individualistic, monopolistic private capital market.

There is also the strategic argument for growth: in a world in which potential enemies increase their armaments we must do the same. But a high rate of growth of output does not guarantee a high level of military preparedness, and a high level of armaments can be achieved without growth. In the past, general military power was much more closely related to industrial capacity; swords and ploughshares were much closer substitutes in production. But for a nuclear power it is a certain critical level that matters rather than the rate of growth of output. This critical level can be achieved without growth by a country which allocates enough resources to it, whereas a rapidly growing country may fail to achieve it. There are, indeed, reasons to believe that rich societies, accustomed to rising living standards, are handicapped in waging war. In so far as mobilization is possible shortly before the bugles summon us, there is a choice between reducing consumption later, when we face war, and reducing it now in order to have to reduce it less later. On the other hand, this choice is not open if the challenge is such that later mobilization would be too late.

Against such considerations, we should remember that the arms race is a race. Unilateral cessation may slow down others and reduce international tensions, while growth of armaments beyond a point may increase the threat of destruction. There are strategic arguments for growth, but they are both more complex than is often assumed, and less conclusive than past experience would suggest.

Historically, the present concern with growth has a number of causes. First, it is now generally realized that long-run growth depends upon the growth of output per unit of factor input. It was absurd to worry about this before the war when there was large-scale unemployment. Second, there has been something like a demonstration effect. Because we have seen others attaining high growth rates, we too wanted to boast one. It is a thing with which to impress uncommitted nations.

Perhaps we have too readily accepted the rules proposed by the Soviet Union, without sufficiently looking at the content of growth, its quality and composition, the kind of things we should wish to do with the growing production, the conditions in which growth occurs, and its non-economic costs.

Men like Mendès-France and Gunnar Myrdal have argued that growth makes people nicer: less xenophobic, less aggressive, more tolerant and, generally, more civilized. This is highly controversial and difficult to prove. It would be gratifying if we could establish causal links between high growth rates and the flowering of the arts. A superficial examination suggests that these do not coincide but that high levels of artistic creation, like the Renaissance, are often achieved some time *after* a period of rapid growth.

Perhaps the most persuasive argument for growth is that it makes the achievement of other objectives easier. Thus it is said that greater equality, or the elimination of structural unemployment, or aid to developing countries, is easier in a growing economy than in a stagnant one. This assumes, of course, that our attitudes to, and institutions for, equality, full employment and developing countries are not unfavourably affected by growth. It could be that competitive growth makes us more self-seeking, and although more is available for good causes, we become less willing to use it for them.

Even where growth does not make it easier to achieve other objectives, it may make it easier to bear their absence. Thus a certain amount of inefficiency, inequality, perhaps even unemployment, is easier to accept if all are getting richer fast. We may be able to tolerate more waste and the virtues that go with the gestures that do not count the cost. Thus growth either helps to solve other problems or makes it easier to live with the failure to solve them.

But, although growth may promote *some* of the other objectives or may make it easier to accept failure to promote them, it is clearly in conflict with *others*. Indeed, if growth did not conflict with other objectives, if it could be achieved without cost, it would hardly be worth discussing or even writing a book about. In so far as it requires a high ratio of saving and investment, it conflicts with high current living levels; in so far as growth means continual change, it conflicts with a quiet life.

The next question is what determines the rate of growth and how government policy can accelerate it – if the government wishes to do this. It must be confessed that in spite of a number of ingenious theories, economists do not really know how growth could be accelerated. Some believe that aggregate growth is a function of the ratio of investment to national income and that growth of income per head is a function of investment per worker (and of changes in the age distribution of the population). If a fairly fixed relationship between capital and output is assumed, say a ratio of 4 : 1, and the desired rate of growth of income is 5 per cent per annum, then, so the argument goes, we need a savings and investment ratio of 20 per cent. This view is subject to a number of qualifications.

(1) It must be remembered that, even if there is an association between high rates of capital formation and high rates of growth, it is also the latter which make the former possible.

(2) There is no proportional or even easily predictable relation. In some countries and at certain periods quite a small investment ratio can yield a given growth rate, while at other times and in other countries this ratio has to be much higher. The general view that nowadays less investment is required to yield a given growth rate than one hundred years ago can be used as an argument for *higher* investment now. If we can now double our standard of living, by investing a given amount annually, in twenty-five years, while it would have taken fifty or a hundred years a century ago, this can be an argument for, rather than against, stepping up investment now.

(3) Much depends upon the composition and quality of investment. It has been argued by Professor Barna that Germany's higher growth rate was due not so much to a higher ratio of investment per worker as to the proper direction of investment, particularly into engineering and export-orientated industries, whereas in Britain investment has been concentrated on clothing, textiles and food. Also, a good deal of investment here has been amenity investment, which makes no contribution to production.

(4) A lot depends on factors other than investment, which must accompany it to make it effective: education, research and development have been stressed recently, but there are also attitudes of mind, the quality of management, the growth of

skills, etc. If one bears these qualifications in mind, the rate of investment, either as a ratio of national product or per worker, can be used as a rough guide to the sources of growth, even though the precise relationship is uncertain.

According to another view, the ability to step up growth by raising the ratio of investment to national income is confined to a relatively short period. In the long run, this argument says, aggregate growth is limited by the growth of the labour force and the growth of productivity due to technical advance. In other words, the rate of growth of output per worker and (subject to qualifications about changes in the age distribution) of income per head is dictated by the rate of growth of technology. The investment ratio, according to this view, determines the height of the growth curve but the percentage growth rate will eventually always be the same.

The long run will, however, be quite long, and until we reach this long-term growth rate a higher investment ratio will accelerate growth. Moreover, this view assumes that technical progress is God-given and cannot itself be influenced by spending more on research and development, and instituting other reforms. But although it is very likely that this assumption is wrong, we do not know precisely how technical progress is related to expenditure on research and to these other measures.

We may conclude that, whatever theory about the determinants of growth is true, there is a good deal a government can do, if it wishes, to accelerate growth over a period of, say, five to ten years. This subject is pursued further in the following chapter.

The final question is whether the government should in fact do this. It is quite possible to argue that we should grow faster, that we can grow faster, but that the government either should not or cannot accelerate growth. Here we touch upon a fundamental difference between Conservative and Labour philosophy. There are some Conservatives, a minority, who would argue that, though growth is desirable, it is not a proper objective of government policy at all. They would let individuals express their time preferences freely in the market and thereby determine the rate at which current consumption is sacrificed for more future consumption. If we do not enjoy a sufficiently high rate of growth, this group would argue, it is because numerous imperfections, including the effects of the actions of government, prevent individuals from fully expressing their choice. By encouraging more competition we should narrow the gap between the high rates of return on investment earned by monopolies and the low rates enjoyed by individual savers. By keeping government interference to a minimum, we should liberate initiative and enterprise. But the majority of Conservatives would not object to a growth policy on the ground that only choices expressed in a competitive market are legitimate choices, while choices expressed through the ballot box and implemented by the government are wrong. They would, however, argue that the tax measures that would be necessary to generate more savings and investment 'distort' the economy, blunt incentives and impede growth. Government-promoted growth, on this view, is not so much wrong as ineffective.

We shall deal with this second view, and the question of the effectiveness of government policy, later when we discuss the effects of policies on incentives. At this stage, we shall indicate some of the reasons why we want the government to accelerate growth and why we cannot rely on private decisions to yield the optimum growth rate. (a) We may know that we are short-sighted in our market choices and may want the government to safeguard our long-term interests. (b) We may be incapable of giving expression to our saving choice except through collective action and therefore voluntarily agree to force all, including ourselves, to act in accordance with this choice. (c) The returns to society of accelerated growth exceed, as we have seen, the returns to ourselves of saving more, rendering private incentives a bad guide. This may be the result of monopoly in the capital market, where rates of return to firms greatly exceed the returns to those who provide capital; or it may be the result of a divergence of private and social risks leading to under-investment, or it may result from returns to investment which accrue to others than the investor. (d) We may want to offset policy measures which are desirable on other grounds but which reduce savings, such as inheritance taxes. These are desirable on the ground of increasing equality of opportunity, but they reduce the incentive to provide privately for future generations.

37

Other objectives

There is little to be said about *high current levels of living*. It is obviously sensible to sacrifice current consumption and leisure for a better future, certainly for oneself and, with certain qualifications, for later generations. If growth is measured in terms of national income per head, we have already said that to go on getting richer without ever enjoying the fruits is confusing ends and means. Only misers and masochists would want to maximise growth without regard to its enjoyment. But even if growth is defined as growth of consumption per head, there comes a point where we should not want to reduce our own consumption below what it could otherwise have been for the sake of raising the consumption per head of later generations, particularly if there are going to be many more heads.

We have already seen that current levels of living include, beside private consumption, leisure and collective consumption of goods and services. There has been a good deal of discussion about the proper combination of these three sources of satisfaction and about the biases which a free enterprise economy introduces. Professor Galbraith, in *The Affluent Society*, has argued that we suffer from an inadequate provision of public goods and services; that capitalism produces private affluence and public squalor. Professor Milton Friedman, on the other hand, warns us that socialism would lead to public affluence and private squalor. With regard to leisure, economists have argued that our methods of taxing income and goods discriminate in favour of current leisure and against both current consumption of goods and future consumption of goods and leisure. But we have also seen that the complementarity between goods and leisure on the one hand, and the difficulty of treating leisure wholly as consumption on the other, cast doubt on such generalization. The last point is relevant to consumption generally. With the growing importance of durable consumers' goods and consumers' inventories and the recognition of the contribution to growth of training and education, health, and other components of consumption, the dividing line between current enjoyment and increases in future enjoyment no longer coincides with that between consumption and investment as conventionally measured by economic statisticians. In particular, services like education may be both current consumption and (human) investment, yielding first current satisfaction, second a stream of future direct satisfactions derived from the 'stock of education', and third future indirect yield by raising future productivity.

Similarly, healthy and pleasant working conditions and a sense of participation are valued both in their own right and as ways of contributing to higher production. The task of a fuller analysis would be to separate the independent value from the instrumental value of these conditions and activities, to impute values of both kinds to the non-measured components, and to distinguish between their direct contribution to future satisfactions and their indirect contribution, via higher productivity.

Stability is more tricky. There are really two distinct goals which may come into conflict. Price stability may involve unemployment and full employment may only be attainable with some inflation. If this were an ultimate choice, many would accept a certain rate of price increase, if this were necessary to attain full employment and growth. Demand inflation can always be eliminated. If demand exceeds full employment supply at current prices, the excess can, in principle, always be cut off by fiscal and monetary policies. But cost inflation, income inflation, or sellers' inflation arise from contradictory claims of rival groups with market power. A reconciliation of such claims probably involves a change of institutions, such as trade union structure and industrial monopolies, whereas institutions can be assumed to remain what they are for the removal of demand inflation.

It is beyond argument that a civilised society should not tolerate prolonged unemployment. Indeed, some excess demand in the labour market, in spite of its inflationary dangers, is desirable because it widens the range of choice of workers, married women and old people by giving them the opportunity to work overtime and part-time if they wish. But it is not equally clear why inflation is bad. Bankers assure us that it is an evil, and the electorate seems to share their view. Much effort is spent on thinking out ways of reducing inflation and considerable sacrifices are accepted in attempts to avoid it. It is often true that particular groups, often the least productive but also

39

the weakest, lose by inflation. But this is not inevitable and they could be insured against price rises. There is no evidence that inflation must inevitably lead to hyper-inflation, that it reduces growth or that it on balance diminishes welfare. There may also be an optical illusion in the way we measure inflation, which does not fully allow for quality improvements and new products. It is true that a rate of inflation that exceeds that proceeding in other countries makes it more difficult to balance our international payments at a fixed exchange rate. Equilibrium in the balance of payments, as we shall see, is better regarded as a constraint than an objective; but excessive inflation relative to inflation abroad may make it necessary to impose measures which conflict with fundamental objectives of policy. But it is important to remember that it is this rate of inflation *compared with that in other countries* that matters. Preaching to foreigners to inflate more is in logic just as appropriate as preaching at home to inflate less.

But since public opinion and other authors in this book consider the avoidance of domestic inflation as an important objective, we shall accept this here.

Distributional goals are more specifically political. Socialism at one time was almost exclusively about equality, and equality still is an important part of it. It was once thought that Capitalism had solved the problems of production and it remained for Socialism to establish social justice. But the emphasis has shifted and many socialists now see the limits of further material improvement of the workers in productivity growth rather than in collective bargaining, social services and redistribution. At the same time, equality of income and wealth has remained an important objective even for those socialists who lay the strongest emphasis on growth. I myself would say that the emphasis of the earlier socialists is once again correct and that automation and the new industrial revolution in chemistry, energy and other sectors have, or will soon have, solved the problem of production in advanced industrial nations. The main problem is how to prevent the new dehumanisation and relative pauperisation of the large number of people whose skills will become obsolescent, whose productivity is sharply reduced and whose income-earning power in a capitalist society may vanish. Automation and cybernetics bestow new vast powers on ownership of property and the exercise of certain skills, and raise the problem of equality in an acute form. Excessive preoccupation with growth may make us neglect these problems of the rising productivity of machines and certain types of skills, the increasing returns to ownership and certain types of ability, and the obsolescence of other types of skills. These reflections are admittedly speculative, although evidence from the United States suggests that they are not unfounded. The prognosis depends upon the adaptability of human beings, and the incentive in a private enterprise system to carry out these adaptations, if they are possible.

The kind of equality we should aim at should be not only apparent, as registered in income tax returns, but should cover all sources of spending power. Many of these are at present concealed as capital, capital gains, business expenses, benefits in kind, trusts, covenants, and the rest of the tax avoidance devices which permit ever-increasing inequality behind an egalitarian façade. But measures for equality will have to go deeper than redistribution of income and wealth. They will have to embrace educational opportunities and equal opportunities of promotion, and the encouragement of activities that permit greater participation in industrial, social and cultural life.

Efficiency is really not an end but a means to achieving all the other objectives more effectively. However, it is convenient to separate it here for three reasons. First, although efficiency has instrumental value, it has also *some* independent value. Like courage, another virtue with instrumental value, we admire it for its own sake and we deplore its absence not merely because it makes the attainment of other objectives more difficult. Secondly, the attainment of greater measured efficiency has costs which are not measured. The efficient deployment of resources presupposes an attitude of mind and the existence of social institutions which are incompatible with other attitudes and institutions to which value is attached. The age of sophisters, economists and calculators cannot coexist with the age of chivalry. Thirdly, it is convenient for the purpose of the discussion to separate efficiency because the effects of certain policies, such as taxation, on incentives to work, manage, save, bear risks, or migrate, should be studied separately. We can collect these repercussions under the heading 'efficiency'.

Balance of payments equilibrium is not a goal but a constraint. Since it will always be achieved somehow, the problem is not how to achieve it, but how to achieve it with the minimum sacrifice of other objectives. On the other hand, a certain amount or proportion of annual lending and granting abroad can be regarded as a proper objective. We need a surplus in order to invest (profitably) abroad, in order to aid developing countries (and in particular Commonwealth countries) in their development efforts, in order to repay past debts, and in order to increase our liquid reserves. This objective is one of the reasons for wanting growth, which is either not at all or only indirectly related to consumption per head. One could argue that we can always render foreign aid by reducing our own level of consumption. The purpose of growth of income per head is then that we can render that same aid with a smaller reduction in our consumption than would otherwise have been necessary. But foreign aid, like defence, is an objective quite distinct from consumption.

The sources of disagreement

Although some of these six aims are necessarily conflicting, and although each may conceivably conflict with any other, there is much more compatibility than is often admitted. Occasionally, the regrets over some objective that would have to be – it is said – sacrificed for the sake of other objectives, are reminiscent of the sentiments of the Walrus for the oysters:

> 'I weep for you' the Walrus said:
> 'I deeply sympathize.'
> With sobs and tears he sorted out
> Those of the largest size,
> Holding his pocket-handkerchief
> Before his streaming eyes.

It is, as we shall see, possible to combine, for example, the following objectives:

1. any desired rate of capital accumulation and therefore, with some qualifications, any desired rate of growth of income per head;
2. full employment without demand inflation; and
3. greater equality of income and wealth.

Political differences arise partly because different people believe in different objectives and are either indifferent or opposed to the aims of other people; partly because, although they share the same aims, they give different weights to these aims where they conflict and where sacrificing something of one objective can achieve more of another; and partly because they differ with respect to their analysis as to which objectives are, and which are not, compatible. This last difference again may be due either to faulty reasoning or to the differences as to what policies are permissible, perhaps because different policies affect other values which have not been brought out explicitly. But the differences about facts and their relation are themselves related to the valuations: not, indeed, logically, but psychologically. Opinions and beliefs conform to valuations, so that, for instance, those who give much weight to price stability as an objective typically believe that wage and salary rates are highly sensitive to the pressure of demand; those who favour equality do not believe in the deterrent effects of taxation; and those who believe in the government's duty to accelerate growth by larger public savings do not believe that taxation would greatly reduce private saving. It is a psychological fact that our picture of reality is coloured by our system of values.

A difference of the first kind – over political objectives – is the Socialist belief in equality of income and wealth against some Conservatives' belief in privilege and inequality. An illustration of the second difference – over relative weights – would be the stronger emphasis on price stability, even at the cost of some unemployment and some growth, by many Conservatives, against the Socialist belief that some inflation would be acceptable if otherwise higher growth and full employment could not be achieved. Differences which rest on differences in analysis would arise if Conservatives were to say that 3 per cent unemployment would be sufficient to give price stability, whereas Socialists were to say that at least 6 per cent would be

43

necessary. It is interesting to note that some Conservatives and all Marxists believe that a reserve army of unemployed is needed to discipline workers and make free enterprise work.

But more subtle are those differences with regard to consistency and inconsistency which rest on differences about the permitted policies. Thus it may be acknowledged that full employment and price stability could be achieved only with an incomes policy or with certain price controls, but one group rules out such measures as interfering with personal freedom. A characteristic story is told by Sir Roy Harrod in his book on Lord Cherwell:

> We discovered that the time taken for the turn-round in our ports was abnormally great and not to be accounted for by the difficulties of the 'black-out' alone. We exerted pressure accordingly. I recall an interview with a senior official in the Ministry of Shipping. He explained to me that the different shipping companies had their own quays and that ships sometimes had to wait about accordingly. 'But must not all the quays be pooled,' I said, 'so that if there is any quay capable of accommodating the ship, it should go straight in, whatever the Company?' He explained that the different companies had different routines and that labour difficulties might arise. 'But surely all these difficulties can and must be adjusted.' I added a bromide. 'You know we have got this war on.' He turned to me with a very sad and wistful expression. 'When I hear you talking with indifference about scrapping all the old practices of the shipping companies for the sake of the war, I begin to wonder whether, when the war is over, we shall find anything left that has been worth fighting for.'

> (*The Prof.*, pp. 194–5)

Similarly, it may be agreed that the variation of the exchange rate of the pound, or the introduction of price controls or building licences, would achieve certain objectives; but these instruments are barred or deplored because negative value is attached to them. The fact that hardly any instruments of policy are entirely free from independent value, i.e. value distinct from their value as means for other objectives, is one of the reasons why a rational discussion of economic policies is so difficult.

Possible conflicts

If there is full employment, then high current living standards and accelerated growth conflict. It is not necessary that current living standards be reduced to achieve more investment, but their rate of increase must be less than it otherwise would be. There is a clear choice between jam today and more jam to-morrow. If there is unemployment, consumption and invest-ment can go up together, but we are then violating the aim to avoid unemployment.

We therefore have to strike a balance between accelerating growth and high current living. The extremes can be dismissed at once: nobody would want to maximise the growth of income per head and eat and rest only just enough to keep in good working order. Nor would anyone want to maximise the com-munity's current living standards if it meant eating up capital. But where precisely between these two extremes the right balance lies is a matter of choice. Here is a necessary conflict.

There are some aims which *may* conflict.

(a) Greater inequality may promote growth. In Victorian England the saving that went into capital accumulation was done by the rich. Even today we often hear the argument that, in order to have more for all in the future, we must now allow some to have much more than others. But this argument has been undermined, since the government can save on behalf of the community through the Budget surplus and through the surpluses of public enterprises. By raising more money in taxa-tion than it uses for current expenditure, the surplus can directly or indirectly finance investment. What is left over in the pockets of the people can be as equally distributed as we desire.

It may be objected that government savings are worse than private savings. A budget surplus implies that more investment will be financed through fixed interest borrowing, and this raises the risks of business. But the reply is that the government could provide risk-sharing capital through appropriate institu-tions to private industry. If the objection is raised against ex-ternal finance generally, we should remember (a) that even if all savings were private, there may still have to be increasing recourse to external finance, and (b) there is no reason why firms should finance expansion out of their own profits only.

45

It has also been argued that high redistributive taxes will blunt incentives, reduce ambition, encourage emigration, discourage saving and retard the rate of economic progress. These arguments are possibly valid at some level of taxation and we shall return to them later.

(b) Gentle inflation may stimulate growth by stimulating investment. There may be conflict between progress and price stability. But this depends either on the money rate of interest not fully reflecting inflation, so that the real rate of interest is too low, or on a peculiar form of inflation, in which prices rise faster than money wages. There are other ways of stimulating investment, which do not rely either on a low real interest rate or on such transfers to profits.

(c) Price stability may be attainable only at the cost of some unemployment. The precise percentage of unemployment has been a much-disputed topic amongst economists and econometricians, and this question is referred to in Chapter 5 of this book.

(d) Full employment may conflict with growth. A dynamic, progressive, innovating economy requires more frequent job-changing and this in turn may mean a higher rate of unemployment. If the length of unemployment were reduced to short periods, and if unemployment benefits, transfer grants and re-training facilities were much more generous than they are now, no great hardships would be imposed and a small increase in the unemployment percentage might facilitate mobility and change. Clearly, complete absence of redundancy has great attractions, but it may be attainable only at the cost of economic progress.

(e) The balance of payments target may require a cut in domestic investment and a consequential slowing down of growth. This has been the sad story of the last ten years, although investment cuts were not very effective in achieving external equilibrium.

Compatibilities

On the other hand, some aims can clearly be complementary with or indeed instrumental in achieving others.

(a) Getting rid of depressions and unemployment makes it

possible to have both higher current levels of consumption – in so far as the demand for consumption goods is raised – and accelerated growth – in so far as the investment ratio and expenditure on research and development are raised. There are, perhaps, some who would argue that depressions are healthy because they purge the economy of inefficient firms, but economic history is not on their side. Similarly, any other measure which increases efficiency without costs, such as the removal of taxes which reduce efficiency, enables us to raise either current living standards or the rate of growth, or both.

(b) A progressive tax structure which promotes equality also helps to stabilise the level of demand and employment. It generates budget surpluses in periods of demand inflation and budget deficits in periods of depression.

(c) A high rate of economic growth may reduce inflationary pressures by making it possible to accommodate a given rate of growth of money wages with less price inflation.

(d) An egalitarian tax structure may encourage greater wage restraint and either reduce cost inflation directly, or make an incomes policy more acceptable.

Where there is conflict, we have to choose. The economist is no better qualified to choose wisely than anyone else. But the economist can show the implications of certain choices. He can attempt to calculate the social costs of, say, a certain percentage of unemployment; and he can compare these with the social costs, resulting from loss of income and wealth of certain groups, through a certain rate of inflation. Alternatively, he can probe into the institutional assumptions and suggest that by changing some of these constants, what previously appeared incompatible may turn out to be compatible after all. Thus a reform of trade union structure or the general acceptance of an incomes policy may make full employment and price stability compatible; or, even although conflicting objectives may not be reconciled, it may be possible to eliminate or reduce the social losses resulting from the conflict. Thus, certain groups may be insured against inflation or generous unemployment benefits may be paid to the unemployed. In many cases we do not have to choose between apparently conflicting objectives because no conflict exists. Although economists are often accused of stressing the dismal aspects of choice, here is a field in which economic reasoning leads to more optimistic conclusions and cheerfulness keeps breaking in.

The crucial questions relate, of course, to the methods appropriate to promoting the various objectives. Only when we know the means can we know whether they conflict with other objectives. Thus, in so far as growth can be accelerated without having to compress current consumption, there is no conflict between growth and high current consumption, whereas in so far as saving and investment are necessary conditions of faster growth, there is conflict.

Progress and stability

Our first proposition is that we can have full employment and absence of demand inflation *and* whatever rate of growth of capital we want. It is often said that a high rate of investment carries with it inflation, and that stability can be bought only at the expense of growth: we are told to cut investment and thus reduce excess demand. Experience both in this country and in the United States seems to confirm this dilemma. Policy in the last fifteen years has fluctuated between, on the one hand, high investment combined with rapid inflation and, on the other, moderate price stability combined with stagnating production. The Republicans in America and the Conservatives here have written an honest currency on their banners, while the Democrats and Labour have given more weight to economic progress, thus contributing to a new kind of political trade cycle, as voters' choices swing between dislike of inflation and of stagnation. Yet there need be no dilemma between avoiding demand inflation and high investment.

If we wish to stimulate investment, we should pursue low-interest policies combined with generous capital allowances. If the total level of effective demand then is excessive, we should tax consumption. If this reduces investment, we have to increase further the investment stimuli.

It is therefore not correct to say that all elements of monetary and fiscal policy should always support one another. Certain monetary measures may well have to act in opposition to some fiscal measures and some other monetary measures, just as some taxes may have to act in opposition to others. The point is to stimulate investment while restricting consumption. For demand inflation is the result of the pressure of demand, rather than, as is sometimes thought, of the rate of growth of productive capacity.

Clearly, other things, and in particular buoyant expectations, besides easy credit and generous capital allowances, are needed to achieve productive investment. Capital formation between 1961 and 1963 was stagnant, and manufacturing investment (in constant prices) falling, in spite of liberal capital allowances, although there was a recovery in 1964. On the other hand, as we have seen, other things besides investment are needed to achieve growth. Indeed, we defined growth as rising output per unit of factor input – both labour and capital. But although investment in productive equipment is not a sufficient condition for growth, it is essential for a wide range of improvements and innovations and only limited progress is possible without a high rate of gross investment.

Progress, stability and justice

So far we have seen that any desired rate of capital accumulation is compatible with absence of demand inflation. But someone may reply: 'All right: I grant you that, but you have to sacrifice equality if you want progress and stability. For if you intend to reduce consumption to release resources for investment, you have to tax the high-spending classes – and that means the lower income groups. If you tax the rich, they'll only cut their savings and you won't get price stability.' But this is wrong. We can have full employment and absence of demand inflation, *plus* the rate of capital accumulation we want, *plus* any degree of income redistribution we desire.

Assume we want to step up the rate of growth, but also redistribute income to the poor. (The argument is equally valid if we want to slow down growth but maintain inequality, but such aims do not interest us here.) Our expansionary monetary policy and the initial and investment allowances will stimulate investment. Since the poor have too much to spend consistent with stability and the desired investment, we must raise taxation on their incomes. Since we want progressive taxation, this means raising even more the taxes on the rich. Since their taxes fall largely on savings, we have to increase the budget surplus. Having decided upon the ratio of investment to consumption at full employment, whatever consumption there is can be divided in any politically desired way between rich and poor.

We may summarise by saying that by fiscal and monetary measures we can determine:

(a) the relationship between aggregate demand and aggregate supply;

(b) the division of aggregate demand between investment and consumption; and

(c) the division of consumption between the (pre-tax) rich and the poor.

This means that we can eliminate demand inflation and unemployment by (a), can produce growth by (b), can secure equality by (c) and get rid of cost inflation through an incomes policy made possible by (b) and (c).

Incentives

But, the pessimists might now say, you may attempt to combine progress, stability and justice, but you may have to impose such high taxes that you will widen the gap between social and private returns to saving and capital accumulation and reduce incentives not only to save and invest, but also to work and bear risks. In the process of pursuing the objectives of full employment and stability, you kill the goose that lays the eggs of progress.

In fact, we do not know at what level, if any, incentives are blunted. Satisfactory rewards for managerial and professional people are largely a matter of convention. Power, status and the satisfaction derived from work are important inducements. These effects are even more difficult to assess for unearned incomes.

In principle, there is an optimistic answer even where incentives can be shown to be blunted. Ideally, it is possible to devise taxes that combine the previous three objectives without harmful effects on incentives. In practice it is only possible to approximate this ideal.

We have already seen that the preservation of the *incentive to invest* is compatible with justice and stability. If investment depends upon income, the interest rate, and investment allowances and initial allowances, a tax on consumption depresses the incentive to invest by depressing income, but lower interest rates and more liberal allowances stimulate investment. This means that we have to take indirect repercussions into account in our investment policy.

There remain the *incentives to work, take risks* and *manage*. It can be argued that, just as the industrial worker has been the main concern of Socialists in the last hundred years, so the new technical and managerial classes will set the problems of the future. Their recruitment, their education, their vigour and also their frustration will be crucial to the type of society we shall have. What kind of status and what material rewards they enjoy will determine the quality and composition, as well as the rate, of growth that we shall have.

It is, in principle, possible to impose taxes on potential rather than actual performance, so that extra effort is liberally rewarded, but any shortfall severely penalized. In practice an estimate of potentialities is impossible, but we could have more justice and more powerful incentive if we introduced more scope for tax provisions which discriminate more subtly between high incomes which are temporary and those which are permanent, and which avoid hitting extra effort particularly hard. Assessing income tax on average income over a number of years, permitting losses to be more liberally offset against gains and assessing tax on, say, last year's earnings would meet this point to some extent. But there will remain an ultimate choice, which will depend upon the sort of society we want, between high financial rewards to certain economically valuable groups and economic equality.

Balance of payments surplus

A persistent dilemma that has plagued us in the whole post-war period has been that between growth and external equilibrium. The problem is complicated because the short-term effect of speeding up growth has tended to worsen the balance of payments, while the long-term effects may be favourable. The manner in which the short-term deterioration is met depends partly on political preferences and partly on permitted measures. Thus, if the investment decided upon leads to excessive imports, the solution lies in cutting off imports or increasing exports rather than in slowing down growth. This may be done in a number of ways, discussed by Mr Scott in Chapter 4. A reduction in imports or an increase in exports will divert demand to the home market and create inflationary pressures. These will have to be reduced by higher taxes on consumption. But there is no need to slow down the growth rate by a dear money policy and credit restrictions.

As in the case of internal equilibrium, it is the pressure of demand rather than investment which interferes also with external equilibrium. A given level of aggregate demand with a high proportion of investment is not necessarily more detrimental to a current balance of payments surplus than one with a relatively high proportion of consumption. This does not mean that there may not be a number of ways in which a high rate of growth may affect and may be affected by both the level of demand and the balance of payments. But these are separate problems.

Objections

In many respects the argument has had to be simplified and over-simplified. We still know very little of the causes of growth and the appropriate policies to accelerate it, or of the incidence of redistributive taxation. We do know how to maintain effective demand and to avoid mass unemployment, but this is no longer an important issue. Perhaps the most serious objection is the failure of the above discussion to deal effectively with cost inflation. It may be granted that excess demand can always be taxed away, but if certain groups then take steps to recapture the ground lost, incompatible claims are made on available resources. It may be granted that demand inflation and high investment need not go together, but does not the dilemma between income inflation and progress remain, particularly in an open economy?

In so far as specific measures – such as redistributive taxation, a high rate of growth of consumers' goods, etc. – reduce pressure for higher money wages, they can be fitted into the optimistic prognosis. Otherwise the question arises of how an incomes policy can be made acceptable to the mutually contradictory claimants. If the general tone has been optimistic, this is not to suggest that there are no important problems to be solved. To accelerate economic growth of the right kind within a framework of personal freedom; to reconcile workers and their representatives to negotiate for real shares of the national product rather than money incomes; to induce business to cut real costs rather than raise prices to maintain profits; to reconcile the need for economic incentives with the spirit of co-operation and fellowship; to eliminate restrictive practices and improve social motivations; to anticipate the effects of the new industrial revolution on the demand for human skills and to avoid the emergence of a new proletariat; all these remain important and unsolved problems.

SUGGESTIONS FOR FURTHER READING

In Chapters 17 and 18 of the sixth edition of his *Economics: An Introductory Analysis*, Paul A. Samuelson shows how a judicious combination of monetary and fiscal policies can achieve a number of economic objectives. He explores this line of thought more fully in a chapter called 'Full Employment versus Progress and Other Economic Goals' in *Income Stabilisation for a Developing Democracy*, edited by Max Millikan (Yale University Press, 1953). James Tobin in 'Economic Growth as an Objective of Government Policy' in the *American Economic Review*, Vol. LIV, No. 3, May 1964, talks to economists about the costs of growth and its relation to other policy goals.

The composition and direction of British and German investment have been analysed by T. Barna, in 'Industrial Investment in Britain and Germany', *The Banker*, January 1958, pp. 12–13. This paper is referred to on page 35. Objectives of economic policies and how to reach them are also discussed in J. K. Galbraith's *The Affluent Society* (Hamish Hamilton, 1958), and Gunnar Myrdal's *Beyond the Welfare State* (Duckworth, 1958) and *Challenge to Affluence* (Gollancz, 1963).

3

THE DETERMINANTS OF
ECONOMIC GROWTH

Introduction

A strategy for accelerating the rate of economic growth must depend on three main classes of consideration. First, it will depend on one's view as to what are the most important determinants of growth, for example, how far is economic growth a function of the level of investment, the rate of technical progress, the skill and education of the labour force, the volume of scientific research, the competitiveness of a country's exports, and so on.

Secondly, even among economists who may agree as to the technicalities of economic growth, differences of opinion as to the strategy to be adopted could still emerge as a result of different value judgements concerning the price they are prepared to pay in order to obtain faster growth by one means rather than another, or different views as to the objectives being pursued. For example, it might be argued that faster growth would be achieved by running the economy at a rather lower level of employment, or by arranging the pattern of national expenditure in such a way as to have more investment, and so on. But opinions could still differ widely as to which strategy should be adopted on account of different value judgements concerning how far we are willing to sacrifice the welfare of the extra unemployed in the interests of faster growth or to sacrifice present consumption for future consumption.

Thirdly, the growth strategy adopted will be influenced by assumptions as to the type of society and political environment in which we are operating. For example, agreement that greater restriction on the power of trade unions or of monopolies would facilitate faster growth does not necessarily lead to agreement that such restrictions should be imposed, since this will be partly a matter of one's political and social preferences. Unfortunately economics being the subject that it is, differences of opinion as to social and political objectives and assumptions frequently intrude into the discussion of the economic technicalities of growth. Even in the natural sciences it is now generally accepted that observations are sometimes influenced by the observer. In economics the reverse is the case: the observer is sometimes influenced by his observations.

Of the three classes of consideration that should shape the strategy for growth – the view as to the determinants of growth, the particular objectives one has in mind, and the type of society one prefers – the present chapter is concerned almost exclusively with the first. The objectives of growth and the value judgements that have to be made in selecting alternative policies are discussed in Chapter 2. However, it will be impossible to avoid some reference in this chapter to the third class of consideration, namely, those relating to the type of society in which we are operating.

Unfortunately, the fact that, in this chapter, we are not concerned with value judgements does not make it possible to present a simple, clear-cut and generally accepted view of the more technical aspects of the growth mechanism. For there is not yet any very full understanding among economists of the process of economic growth; and we are still some way from having reached a satisfactory theory of growth that is both (i) operational, in the sense that it provides a sufficiently articulated framework for the derivation of a practical strategy for growth, and (ii) readily verifiable, in practice, by empirical tests. This chapter does not, therefore, aim at summarising an established body of economic doctrine about the causes of economic growth. It is much more a personal view about the main causes of economic growth in more or less developed Western economies. At the same time an attempt is also made to suggest a general analytical framework in order to set the ground for policy analysis, though the latter objective is incidental to the main body of the chapter.

The absence of any generally accepted explanation of the growth process is not the result of any lack of attention to the problem of economic growth. On the contrary, the causes of economic growth have been a central preoccupation of economists from Adam Smith to today. The gap in our knowledge is largely the result of special difficulties that are encountered in this particular field of inquiry.

One of these difficulties is that almost any conceivable cause of economic growth could equally well be an effect. For example, higher investment might be a cause of faster growth. But it requires no great stretch of imagination and no violence to logic to suppose that higher investment might be an effect of higher growth, since the more buoyant prospects for future sales that faster growth will generally engender will tend to stimulate investment. Again, it is often maintained that faster growth, even in terms of output per employed person, is facilitated by a faster growth in the active labour force (on the grounds that this will permit economies of scale, or lead to greater mobility of labour from low-productivity to high-productivity industries or firms). But it is equally reasonable to expect that faster growth will, other things being equal, cause a faster growth of the labour force by enlarging the attractiveness of employment to wider sections of the population (particularly married women), or by facilitating changes in the distribution of population between, say, rural and urban areas, or by attracting immigrants.

In a situation where almost any conceivable cause of growth could equally well be an effect it is not easy to verify alternative hypotheses by simple statistical correlations. A high correlation between investment ratios and growth rates can tell us nothing about which causes which. Whilst this may not matter in some respects it does matter very much if we are concerned with growth strategy and are obliged to take a view as to whether measures to raise investment will necessarily *cause* an increase in the rate of growth of national product. Of course, the problem of the direction of causality arises in many other fields of economics. But the process of economic growth embraces such a wide and complex area of activity that the scope for interactions between the relevant variables is exceptionally great. Consequently, in moving from theories of growth to prescriptions for policy one is tempted to adopt the rather agnostic attitude that the present state of understanding precludes an analytical formulation of policy alternatives even as between, for example, the relative importance of policies that operate mainly on demand and those that operate mainly on supply, so that all that one can say is that one should try all policies that are conceivably favourable to growth and are not socially unacceptable or economically very costly.

One of the objects of this chapter is to set out a view of the growth process which provides some rational framework for this eclectic approach to growth policy. This is done by arguing that the important variables in growth vary according to

(a) how far we are concerned with the growth of a unit – such as a firm, or an industry, or a country – that is competing with other units and that must, therefore, depend on its competitive strength, and

(b) how far we are concerned with short-run as distinct from long-run determinants.

As, for practical purposes, there is no sharp distinction between competing and non-competing units, nor between the short-run and the long-run, there is little scope for exclusive reliance on some particular types of growth policy.

Growth of the firm, the industry and of the whole economy

Ideally, a model, or explanation, of the process of economic growth should find a place for growth at different levels of the economy. That is, it should explain not only why some economies grow faster than others but also why some firms grow faster than others, and why some industries grow faster than others, and ideally, it should also explain how to change the growth rate of all economies taken together. In principle, that is, the theory of the growth of the firm, or of the industry, or the national economy, or some region, or the world economy, should each be a special case in a sort of 'unified' growth theory. A failure to distinguish between the theory at one level and the theory relevant to another level could lead to quite misplaced and futile studies of possible measures to accelerate growth.

A simple instance of this is the study of the growth of the firm. It is conceivable that the most important means by which firms grow is by taking over other firms. This does not necessarily have any effect at all on total national output; the expansion of the former could conceivably be offset by the disappearance of the latter. Only if this process leads to a more efficient organisation of resources or to a greater input of total resources does the total output of the economy as a whole rise. Thus a theory of the growth of the firm need not tell us anything at all about growth at some higher level of aggregation even though a theory of the growth of output per head in the economy is, roughly speaking, a theory about the growth of output per head of the *average* firm in it. A theory of the growth of the firm is not likely to concentrate on the same variables as a theory of growth for the whole economy or the whole industry, for the conditions which must be taken as given and the factors which can be varied will differ from one level of aggregation to another. At the level of the individual firm total demand for the product must be taken as more or less given and it will be concerned mainly with obtaining an increasing share in that demand. At the level of the whole industry, total incomes, educational systems, tax policies and many other popular ingredients of theories about national economic growth must be taken as given. At the level of the whole economy certain variables which may be important at the level of the firm, such as the relative innate energy and ambition of managers and entrepreneurs, must be taken as given. Thus, because a theory of growth pertaining to one level of aggregation has to select those variables which are important at that level, it may have little bearing on the variables important at another level.

For example, Professor Edith Penrose's view that it is relative managerial talent which largely explains the relative growth performance of individual firms, to which Professor Barna's researches have contributed valuable support, is often supposed, quite wrongly, to imply that the slow growth of the British economy compared with, say, the French or German economies, must also be explained by slack management. Yet although an explanation of why some firms grow faster than others might throw light on why the average firm in a country grows faster than the average firm in another country, it does not necessarily do so. The important variable determining inter-firm differences in growth could be one that is invariant as between whole countries.

The desirability of fitting the different levels of aggregation systematically into a comprehensive explanation of the growth process inevitably further complicates the task of empirical verification. Meanwhile action is required and policies have to be formulated and applied. Hence, scanty and inconclusive as the evidence may be, it has to be exploited to the full in order to extract a view as to what are probably some, if not all, of the vital determinants of growth at the level at which policy operates.

What kind of evidence is available? As every first-year student of economics knows, economists are limited in their evidence by their inability to carry out controlled experiments. The economist's substitute for the controlled experiment of the natural scientist is the comparison between situations at different points of time or in different countries. Inter-country comparisons are particularly valuable since they can be restricted to a fairly recent period, say the post-war period, when the availability of statistical data has been much greater than in the historical past and when certain political and social factors – particularly those leading to full employment policies and freedom of collective bargaining – that are common to most countries are essential ingredients in any growth strategy appropriate to modern conditions.

In the succeeding sections of this chapter, therefore, we will first consider what generalisations about national economic growth can be drawn from international comparisons. We will then try to see how such generalisations would have to be modified in order to fit an analytical framework that is applicable to growth of firms or industries or other economic units, and what generalisations remain that apply to any economic unit. Finally, we will consider very briefly what such an analytical framework implies for growth policy.

The lessons of the post-war international experience

What conclusions can be drawn from an international comparison of the economic growth experience of more or less advanced countries? Many of them are negative and some are positive. The most important negative conclusions seem to be as follows:

(a) There is no general law that countries which emerged badly from the war had persistently high growth thereafter, or vice versa. It is true that Germany, on the one hand, and the USA on the other, appeared to fit such a law but taking a large number of countries no significant correlation can be found. And even Germany and the USA do not fit the law all that well: the USA continued to grow rapidly up to about 1956, and Germany's growth has persisted for about ten years after regaining pre-war levels of output per head. Of course, the testing of the 'catching-up' hypothesis must allow for alternative interpretations of what this hypothesis is really about. For example, it might be argued that countries will have an advantage in growth until they have caught up with their pre-war trend line. And this introduces a further difficulty since there are many ways of measuring what the pre-war trend rate of growth happened to be: this is not an objective statistical matter. However, alternative measures of such trends still fail to produce any correlation between post-war growth rates and the extent to which countries deviated, at the end of the war, from their longer-run trend lines.

But not only is there no satisfactory empirical evidence for the 'catching-up' hypothesis, it is also difficult to establish any *prima facie* case for such a hypothesis. The hypothesis would appear to rest on the view that long-run rates of growth are somehow divinely determined and beyond the wit of man to influence. Temporary aberrations are allowed for but in the longer run some hidden hand will force countries back to their normal position in the hierarchy of poor or wealthy countries. Such a view of the economic process, in which human phenomena are reduced to the determinism of some parts of the physical world, has little to recommend it.

(b) It is not true that, in general, countries with fast-rising labour forces achieve faster increases in output per head. The French labour force increased very slowly whilst that of the United States and Canada rose rapidly, yet French productivity growth in the period 1955 to 1963 was much faster than that of the North American countries. In particular, during the 1950s, the British labour force grew at the same rate as the average of the Western countries, though our productivity growth rate was one of the lowest. Of course, it is possible to think of theoretical reasons why a fast-growing labour force should accelerate the rate of growth of productivity. For example, it might facilitate economies of scale or the mobility of the labour force. But on the other hand, there are theoretical reasons to the contrary. For example, a given rate of investment would leave less for raising capital per head if the labour force is expanding faster. Again, a slowly growing labour force might, in the appropriate circumstances, stimulate management to introduce labour-saving equipment or raise productivity, in order to meet prospective demand. But in any case, whatever the balance of the theoretical arguments, the facts show that there is no relationship between rates of growth of the labour force and productivity. During the last few years even Germany has become an example of continued fast increase in productivity with relatively modest rates of growth in the labour force.

(c) It is not true that countries with continuous low pressures of demand had systematically faster rates of growth of output per head than countries with continuous high pressures of demand. France, Switzerland and the Netherlands are examples of fast growth with high pressure of demand (also Germany since about 1959); whereas Belgium, the USA and Canada are examples of low pressure of demand and slow growth. And again, there is no clear theoretical reason why low pressures of demand should lead to high rates of productivity increase. If anything, the balance of the theoretical considerations is in the opposite direction. As with the argument concerning the rate of increase in the labour force, it is difficult to see how the existence of spare capacity (fixed capital or manpower) can fail to inhibit the rate of investment.

(d) It is not true that shifts in the distribution of the labour force from, say, agriculture into industry explain a significant part of the inter-country differences in rates of growth of productivity. Statistical measures of the contribution of such shifts, made by the United Nations Economic Commission for Europe, demonstrate this decisively. This is one of those hypotheses which had too long been left to qualitative appraisal. Everybody knows that much labour has moved from relatively low-productivity sectors (particularly agriculture) in, say, France or Italy. But too little attention has been paid to the precise quantitative significance of such shifts. The United Nations estimates now confirm that, in the fast-growing economies, the rates of productivity growth within individual sectors have generally been so much above that of the same sectors in the slow-growing economies that the contribution to the overall rate of growth of productivity made by inter-sectoral shifts has been relatively unimportant.

(e) It is not true that statistical incomparabilities invalidate international comparisons of growth rates or that the view that Britain's growth performance has been a poor one depends on the selection of some particularly unrepresentative portion of the post-war era. This too has been decisively demonstrated by the studies made at the OECD. These show, amongst other things, that large-scale revisions of national accounting methods in some countries, including revisions of estimates for previous years, have not significantly altered their growth rates. Nor are these significantly changed by changes in the years used for weighting the various indices. Nor, even, are relative growth rates significantly affected by large changes in underlying concepts, such as the use of Soviet concepts (which involves excluding the output of most services – the sector in which measurement is most arbitrary and uncertain).

There are other hypotheses about growth that are probably equally suspect but which cannot be tested very easily. For example, the hypothesis that it is the laziness of British workers or the ignorance, inertia, apathy and general amateurishness of British managers that explains our growth performance is difficult to verify empirically. But there are reasons for having doubts such as the fact that, until only a few years ago, Britain did have the highest output per head of any country in Europe (though this was no doubt partly the result of factors such as capital per head); or that British workers transplanted to the United States seem to have the same average output per head as the indigenous population; or that similar accusations were levelled at the French about ten years ago whereas they are now regarded as shining examples of economic dynamism.

The fact that these quasi-sociological explanations of the growth process cannot be readily tested does not, of course, mean that they are untrue. In fact, it would be surprising if social attitudes and traditions did not affect economic performance in some way. But the nature of the connections is probably very complex and we do not yet know how far the weight of tradition and custom may retard the spirit of economic innovation and how far propitious economic circumstances can sweep aside the restraints imposed by certain traditions or, in some cases (notably Japan, for example), exploit favourable traditions for the purposes of rapid economic growth.

Are there any positive conclusions that may be drawn from the international comparisons? If we are very bold we may say that there are five.

First, as is widely recognised, faster growth rates seem to be associated with higher investment ratios (i.e. the share of national output devoted to capital formation). As already indicated, this tells us nothing about which is the cause of which.

Secondly, what is less widely recognised is that the international differences in growth rates are not *proportional* to the differences in investment ratios. That is to say, on the whole, a doubling of the growth rate does not seem to require a doubling of the investment ratio – far from it. Thus a large part of the differences in growth rates is still found to be explained by differences in the rates of return (in terms of additional output) per unit of additional capital. In other words, faster growth appears to be closely correlated with low requirements of new investment per unit of additional output – i.e. lower 'marginal capital-output ratios'.

This analysis is, of course, complicated by the need to allow for (a) depreciation, and (b) social capital of a more or less overhead character which is not likely to lead to faster economic growth anyway. Thus, if two countries invest 10 per cent and 20 per cent respectively of their national products, and if in both countries the amount to be set aside for replacing worn-out equipment and for building schools, houses and so on amounts to, say, 8 per cent of their national products, then the amounts devoted to net productive investment are 2 per cent and 12 per cent of national product respectively, i.e. it is six times as large in one country as in the other, not merely twice as large as the crude comparisons of total gross capital formation might suggest. However, in so far as one can make allowance for these factors it still appears that the rate of return on net productive investment has been higher in the fast-growing countries.

Thirdly, fast growth seems to be closely associated with fast rates of increase in exports, at least in countries heavily dependent on foreign trade. This, too, does not by itself tell one whether it is the fast-rising exports which lead to fast growth or the other way round. One interpretation, for example, might be that it is fast growth that leads to fast-rising exports since (a) more exports will be required to match the faster rise in imports, and (b) faster growth will provide the capacity to increase exports faster. However, this interpretation fails to explain what precise mechanism will ensure that the exports to match the imports are, in fact, forthcoming and sold abroad, since it is not the business of any individual importer to ensure that total exports match imports.

Fourthly, fast growth of exports appears to owe little to the precise commodity or regional pattern of exports of the countries concerned and has been achieved mainly through obtaining a greater share of trade in individual commodity markets in individual countries or regions.

Fifthly, these gains (or losses) of shares in world trade are highly correlated with changes in competitiveness (i.e. in export prices) which, in turn, are closely correlated with domestic changes in wage costs per unit of output. And the latter is simply the arithmetical resultant of two forces: the rate at which money wages rise and the rate at which output per head increases.

From these observations, and other information (such as the detailed history of 'stop-go' measures in Britain and their impact on investment; or of statistical and econometric work on the determinants of investment; or the factors affecting the labour markets in various countries) the following explanation of the growth process at the level of the whole economy appears to emerge.

Economic growth is very much dependent on expectations concerning the future growth of demand. If entrepreneurs expect demand for their products to expand rapidly they will expand capacity more rapidly. In the course of doing so they will also generally achieve a faster rate of increase in productivity per unit of new capacity than if they were expanding capacity slowly. This may be partly the result of a deliberate and purposeful increase in entrepreneurial ingenuity and energy responding to the challenge to produce more in the face of the wider market opportunities. And it may be partly the automatic effect of economies of scale, both internal (to the firm) and external, or of the greater 'embodied' technical progress accompanying a higher rate of gross capital formation. But we do not yet have enough data for evaluating the likely relative importance of these possible alternative mechanisms by which confident expectations are transposed into a faster growth of productivity per unit of additional input of capital (and labour).

The second step in the growth process concerns the relationship between confident expectations and foreign trade. This is that, in an economy heavily dependent on foreign trade, confident demand expectations require a reasonably fast rate of increase in exports. Again, the precise mechanism involved is not clear and various alternatives suggest themselves. It may simply be that, in the absence of the necessary increase in exports, entrepreneurs in general become accustomed to the fact that attempts by the authorities to allow demand to rise rapidly are never sustained because they lead to balance of payments crises. This would inhibit the growth rate in any sector of the economy, not just those directly concerned with exports. However, it may be that, in most industrialised countries, exports have a large direct impact on the demand for manufactured goods. Or it may be that a strong export position relieves certain entrepreneurs from preoccupation with awkward problems – such as what to do about laying off workers, or short-time work, or accumulating stocks – whenever domestic demand seems to flag. Or it may be that competitive exports is a means of maintaining high profits in the corresponding industries and hence of encouraging investment. In fact, the actual situation is likely to be a mixture of all these and other ingredients and it is not necessary for this particular 'model' to adopt any exclusive interpretation of exactly how a rapid increase in exports tends to affect expectations and entrepreneurial behaviour.

The third main step in the hypothesis being advanced here is that the above process leads to a strong virtuous – or vicious –

circle situation. For in so far as fast-rising exports is obtained through competitiveness and in so far as it then leads to a faster growth of productivity it is more likely, other things being equal (notably the rate of increase in money wages), that any initial competitive advantage will be maintained, or even improved. This further strengthens the export position and so further consolidates the growth expectations and so on.

Of course it cannot be claimed that the evidence for this view of the basic determinants of growth does more than fit the hypothesis – i.e. it is purely circumstantial evidence. However, it is a hypothesis which seems to be able to accommodate a considerable amount of circumstantial evidence. For example, though the rapid growth of France *without rapidly rising exports* up to 1958 is an exception to the rule that exports are of vital importance, it establishes the more basic rule, namely that the overriding factor is demand expectations. For, as domestic demand in France was not restrained, demand expectations were not hampered by the failure to preserve balance of payments equilibrium. On the contrary, by meeting the foreign deficits largely through import controls in the mid-1950s domestic demand expectations were presumably strengthened. But this situation could not persist indefinitely, even for France, and in December 1958 a substantial devaluation of the franc was carried out. France, as pointed out above, is also a striking example of the way that entrepreneurial attitudes can be changed by a sustained period of buoyant demand expectations.

As well as fitting the facts remarkably well, this view of the growth process seems also to have been more or less accepted by a cross-section of expert opinion in different countries represented on an OECD working party; and certain features of it – particularly the role of exports – are now fairly widely accepted in Britain. At the same time it does rather go against the grain of certain deeply entrenched areas of economic doctrine. This becomes apparent in discussions of what are feasible growth prospects in the long-run future, where there is a tendency to pore over the entrails of past growth statistics in order to identify the 'norm'. Again, in many discussions of planning models, or of planning policies in some countries, it is frequently assumed that the major constraint on long-run growth is the balance of payments equilibrium and that even in the longer run faster growth means a less favourable balance of payments.

As for the former conflict, this arises largely because of the central role in economic theory taken by the concept of 'equilibrium' – i.e. the concept of a balance between conflicting forces being established at some equilibrium point. Growth theory, too, has its moving equilibria, embodied in the concept of equilibrium rates of growth. And, it must be admitted, the idea of virtuous and vicious circles that enable growth rates to diverge indefinitely is somewhat abhorrent to a profession that has been weaned on the beautiful concept of 'equilibrium'. As Professor Joan Robinson says, 'There is an irresistible attraction about the concept of equilibrium – the almost silent hum of a perfectly running machine; the apparent stillness of the exact balance of counteracting pressures; the automatic smooth recovery from a chance disturbance. Is there perhaps something Freudian about it? Does it connect with a longing to return to the womb?'

As for the tendency to assume that, even in the longer run, the balance of payments is a major limitation on growth, this is a fairly natural misapplication of the now generally accepted Keynesian theory of income determination. This theory is concerned with short-run changes in effective demand with capacity taken as more or less fixed. A rise in national product therefore is only important in its role as providing a rise in incomes, and hence in demand. Changes in capacity are a matter for longer-run adjustment, and though the original Keynesian theory has implications for longer-run growth theory (notably as developed by Professor Joan Robinson and Sir Roy Harrod) it was not primarily concerned with it since the short-run problem of avoiding wasted resources (of men as well as machinery) was, at the time, the most urgent problem. With capacity given, the growth of national product will tend to have an adverse effect on the balance of payments. From this it is very easy to slip into the unconscious assumption that in the longer run too faster growth makes it more difficult to achieve balance of payments equilibrium. But once it is recognised that (a) growth of national product in the longer run refers to growth of capacity as well as of demands and (b), in so far as faster growth tends to lead to faster growth of productivity, it

68

will tend to increase competitiveness and hence create the additional foreign demand for our exports to accompany the rise in our capacity, fast growth and balance of payments equilibrium become complementary rather than conflicting objectives.

Another respect in which the above view of the growth process departs somewhat from a frequently accepted view of the limitations on growth is that it does not emphasise the investment effort required to get faster growth. It is true that some rise in investment ratios seems to be associated with faster growth, but as already indicated, the rise is moderated by the apparent greater productivity of new investment in conditions of faster growth. Thus this widely assumed obstacle or limitation to faster growth, whilst more real than the balance of payments obstacle, is not necessarily a major obstacle. Furthermore, in so far as faster growth and higher investment increases the excess of depreciation allowances over scrapping the finance of investment is facilitated from the point of view of the firm.

Growth as a competitive process

What then *are* the limiting factors on longer-run rates of growth? If balance of payments equilibrium and the propensity to save (determining the investment limit) are not, after all, important limitations, we have to look much harder elsewhere. The theme of this chapter is that growth, at least over a very wide range, depends on expectations and is therefore limited largely by what people expect it to be. But this does not take us very far. We would still like to know what determines what people expect it to be.

We have argued above, on page 66, that, at the national level, expectations are largely determined by the behaviour of exports, at least in countries heavily dependent on foreign trade. This view is not only consistent with the evidence but is also one which lends itself naturally and easily to a more comprehensive model of some aspects of the growth process that satisfies the requirement, set out earlier in this chapter, of presenting the growth process at different levels of aggregation as special cases of a more general process. The way this could be done is as follows.

We start with the central proposition that the limit to the demand expectations that may be legitimately entertained by any one unit among a number of units (such as firms) all of which compete in a given market is, subject to its being sufficiently competitive *vis-à-vis* the other groups, much greater than that for the group of units combined together. For example, a highly competitive firm can hope to benefit not only from a rise over time in the total sales of the industry of which it is a member, but also by raising its own share in the total. Now if, in addition, faster growth brings economies and hence maintains or increases competitiveness by the sort of virtuous-vicious circle process outlined above, an initial competitive advantage by one competing unit will tend to be perpetuated or increased, so that it will tend to absorb a greater and greater share of the total. But in so far as its expectations to exceed the average must diminish, since it will itself form an increasing part of the average, its growth rate would eventually slacken off. The consequences for its growth of productivity would vary according to the particular technical production relationships involved.

However, these two limitations on growth, namely (i) the scope for increasing market shares, and (ii) the technical relationships of production, will vary from one level of aggregation to another. This can be seen if we now look more closely at each level to see how far the proposed type of model would apply.

(a) *The national level* – We have already outlined the variables which would apply at this level, given the above view of the growth process, namely the role of exports in determining expectations in an open economy and the way that faster growth consolidates or accentuates any initial competitive advantage in world trade. The salient differences between this and the other levels of aggregation are best seen by passing directly to these other levels.

(b) *The industry level* – At the level of the industry higher demand expectations will also probably lead to a faster growth of capacity and economies of scale, but the parallel stops there – i.e. it lacks two essential features of the national growth process. First, in the absence of corresponding changes in the economy as a whole, an increase in the capacity of one industry is unlikely to create the corresponding increase in demand for its products and is therefore unlikely to lead into a virtuous circle of fast growth. For overall national full employment policies, which aim at ensuring that increases in capacity are fully exploited thereby providing the demand to match total national capacity, will not apply to individual industries (though there are some, notorious, cases where the creation of capacity is used as a lever for ensuring that it is utilised). But more important, in the context of the model advanced here, there is relatively little scope for the faster growth of capacity in a given industry, resulting from a rise in its demand expectations, to lead to an increase in its share of the market at the expense of the products of another industry. Even accepting one of the central postulates of the model, namely that faster growth of output tends to facilitate faster growth of productivity and hence to restrain or reduce costs per unit of output, price competition against other industries is a process which is confined within much narrower limits than price competition between countries engaged in international trade in more or less the same types of product.

Precisely how restricted is price competition between industries depends on how the industries are defined, but in general it must be true that industries cannot expand very far at the expense of other industries through the same sort of virtuous circle process that appears to apply to large industrialised trading nations taken as a whole. Of course, a given industry within one country can operate the virtuous circle process to its benefit in overseas markets, where it is at the expense of the sales of the corresponding industry of some other country. But even here the process may be limited because a failure of other domestic industries to be equally successful abroad, in so far as it leads to balance of payments difficulties and to domestic demand restraint, will still threaten the buoyancy of the given industry's total demand.

Another important difference between the industry and the whole economy is that, on the whole, money wages rise at about the same rate in different industries within an economy whereas money wages can, and do, rise at very different rates in different countries. This means that an individual industry cannot launch itself into a virtuous circle at the expense of the sales of other industries (or even of the corresponding industries in other countries) by operating on the rate of increase in its money wages (or, for that matter, by changing its exchange rate).

Finally, the price mechanism is such that the forces of competition will tend to keep rates of profit on capital more or less equal, in the long run, in different industries within a country. Hence investment cannot be indefinitely encouraged in one industry as compared with another simply because of a persistently higher rate of profit in the former. Different rates of investment must therefore depend largely on different rates of expected growth of demand (as well as different techniques of production). But, as between countries, the forces of price competition and the movements of capital are much less able rapidly to force rates of profit to equality. Hence, strong foreign trade competitiveness, which necessarily means relatively high profits (since it signifies a high ratio of the internationally determined price in world markets to domestic costs and thus a high residual element, profit) can persistently encourage higher investment. In the world markets for exports the country with the competitive advantage is in the position of the particularly profitable firm in a given industry. That is, the rate of profit in the industry as a whole will be continuously adjusted towards the normal rate for the whole economy in which it is operating, but the rate of profit in some firms in the industry (the intra-marginal firms) will be well above normal and may remain so. The rate of profit in a whole economy, in so far as it is affected by its foreign trade position, may, like that of the firm, equally stay well above that of the average normal rate for the competing countries taken as a whole.

(c) *The firm* – The growth of the economy resembles that of the firm rather than the industry in other ways too. In particular, the possibilities for whole economies, or at least that part of them engaged in international trade, to expand at the expense of competing economies, if not open to industries in the same manner are certainly open to firms. And it is not difficult to see a type of virtuous and vicious circle mechanism at the firm level. For example, an initial competitive advantage, by raising profits, will facilitate the expansion which will tend, up to a point, to consolidate or increase the competitive advantage. Mrs Penrose's very interesting concept of the 'economies of growth' as distinct from the conventional 'economies of scale', at the level of the firm, would obviously fit into such a mechanism. 'As a firm grows in size, therefore, it will reorganise its resources to take advantage of the more obvious opportunities for specialisation. . . . This has been called the "virtuous circle" in which "specialisation leads to higher common multiples, higher common multiples to greater specialisation".' (*The Theory of the Growth of the Firm*, pp. 72–3.) A similar form of competitive process has been admirably analysed by the late Jack Downie.

There is, however, one important respect in which the growth process of the firm would resemble that of the industry rather than of the economy. This is that the firm, like the industry, will have little freedom as regards the money wages which it pays or the rate at which these increase. Also, the firm does not generally sell an important part of its own sales to its competitor firms, whereas a whole economy is not only competing with other economies in some lines but is also selling its exports of other lines to them. Thus, to the firm, the complete disintegration of a rival firm may have only advantages, but to an economy, part of what it gains from a competitive advantage *vis-à-vis* another country is lost in so far as the import capacity of the other country is diminished. The precise net outcome of such interdependence obviously depends, in a rather complex way, on the whole pattern of trade.

But although there are these and other important differences it is still true that the position of the firm *vis-à-vis* other firms resembles that of the whole economy *vis-à-vis* other economies in that (a) it can effectively compete on price to a far greater degree than can an industry, (b) it can continuously maintain above-average rates of profit, and (c) it has available to it more or less the same technical conditions of production as other firms.

And at the level of the firm the importance of expectations in determining growth, which we have stressed at the national level, can be rather easily identified and comprehended. It is certainly well established in statistical studies (such as by Stigler, Meyer and Kuh, or Eisner) of the relationship between sales and investment. This suggests that, if the average expectations of all firms in an economy can be raised, the growth rate can be raised. In other words, it is necessary to act on those elements in expectations which are external to the firm. As Mrs Penrose has put it, 'Many changes in the external world are appropriately treated as environmental changes affecting the rate of growth of firms through their effect on entrepreneurial expectations about productive possibilities.' What is required, therefore, in a growth policy is to influence these 'environmental' factors common to the expectations of all firms.

(d) *The region* – The characteristic feature of a region is its particular location in space. Hence, any theory of the growth of the region must make special provision for the implications of space, notably in reducing the mobility of the factors of production therein and in imposing costs of transport both on those factors or local resources which are not completely immobile (such as labour) and on transactions between regions. In most respects the growth prospects of a region must be identified in terms of the prospects for the particular firms and industries therein. The same limitations apply in respect of inability to vary the exchange rate and, within limits, the money wages prevailing, limitations which do not apply with much force to whole economies (certain practical considerations apart). In other respects, however, regions are similar to whole economies, for example, in that their growth rate will be influenced by the extent to which they 'import' from other regions.

But in general, given the basic spatial character of regional analysis, changes in the pattern of demands for final goods and services, in the derived demands for the factors of production needed to produce them, and in transport facilities and costs, will have far-reaching effects on the growth of any region. In a sense, therefore, regions are much more at the mercy of outside developments than are other economic units. Though they share, with whole economies, the relative immobility of factors and their sensitivity to transport costs and links with other regions, they will be handicapped, as compared with whole economies, by virtue of (a) being, in general, less diversified than a whole economy, and (b) being unable to restore a lost competitive position arising out of adverse changes in the patterns of demand or technology by varying their exchange rates or the rate of increase in their money wages.

(e) *The closed economy* – It may seem curious to bother about the growth problems of a closed economy, since there are no important instances of closed economies in the world. However, it is instructive to consider briefly what are the determinants of growth for an economic unit in a situation where it does not compete with other units – such as a closed economy or, for that matter, the world as a whole. They would appear to fall into three categories:

First, in the absence of any scope for wide variations in expectations, the main ingredients of more traditional growth models, such as capital-output ratios, technical progress, savings propensities, rates of change of population and so on, should become much more important. Apart from our emphasis on economies of scale and the dependence of efforts to raise capacity and productivity on expectations, we have not attempted to evaluate the practical applications of this type of basic growth theory. The British economy is still very much a competing unit in world trade and the ingredients of basic growth theory are more relevant to the limiting cases where the unit concerned is less sensitive to changes in market shares.

Secondly, however, even in these limiting cases, such as the world economy as a whole, the role of expectations does not necessarily disappear. There is no reason why in, say, a closed economy, total expectations cannot vary or be made to vary. If, among competing units, differences in competitiveness and hence market shares and hence demand expectations do seem to lead to differences in growth rates, it follows that as long as the expectations can be raised growth rates can be raised. The competitive process engendering the expectations among competing groups is by no means an essential feature of the formation of expectations in a non-competitive situation. But the converse to this also has to be accepted. If, in the limiting cases, supply factors are accepted as being important, then there is no reason why they should not be applied in the competitive case. We shall return to this point below when discussing policy implications.

Thirdly, as the response of supply to demand expectations will presumably vary from one unit to another, depending perhaps on supply factors such as capital, management skill and so on, and as, in world trade, countries are not only competitors but are also markets for the products of other countries, the aggregate growth rate of the world as a whole, at any period of time, will depend on the particular pattern of competitiveness and world trade flows.

(f) *Growth theory and oligopoly* – In considering how far the features of the growth mechanism among non-competing units differ from those among competing units, however, it must be emphasised that there is no sharp division between the two cases. The non-competing unit is simply the limiting case in a series of situations of gradually diminishing degrees of competition. At one extreme, where competition is active and important, the range of demand expectations can vary so much around the average expectations for the units taken as a whole that differences in expectations may be by far the dominant variable. But at the other extreme, even though demand expectations may be confined within narrow limits, they are not completely inflexible.

The limits to the growth of a unit in a strong competitive position are, of course, a topic to which considerable attention has been given in the analysis of the behaviour of firms. The emphasis has usually been placed on the diseconomies of scale that are reached after a point or on the growing oligopolistic character of the market (i.e. the tendency for the market for a given product to be in the hands of a few large producers). But, if the above theory is accepted, it is not necessary to appeal to diseconomies of scale to explain the limits to growth. For as the competitive unit benefits from the postulated virtuous circle process and continuously increases its share of the market it will become increasingly difficult for it to maintain the same *proportionate* rate of increase in sales unless it could progressively increase its competitive advantage. In so far as it is unable to do this indefinitely, the *proportionate* rate of increase in its sales will fall off and the virtuous-vicious circle process will then go into reverse. On the other hand, the growing oligopolistic character of the market remains relevant. As it becomes large, any unit will have to take account of the effect of its own actions on the market as a whole and on the behaviour of its competitors. Growth theory then becomes part of the theory of 'oligopoly' (or vice versa). For example, the devaluation issue in Britain is complicated because, amongst other things, an attempt by Britain to raise its share in world trade by devaluation might be self-defeating if it merely forced other countries to follow suit.

The short run and the long run

Superimposed on the distinctions elaborated above between different types of economic unit and hence on the different key variables in their growth prospects it is also important, for policy purposes, to distinguish, again at the cost of apparent over-simplification, between short-run and longer-run determinants of growth. We are not referring here to cyclical fluctuations and to the special scope for expanding output from situations of less than full capacity utilisation. We are referring simply to the fact that, even from the point of view of raising the growth of capacity, not output, there are some measures that can be taken quickly and others that take a long time to introduce. Also, some measures have rapid consequences and others only reap rewards in the more distant future.

There is consequently a tendency to select measures that can be rapidly introduced and that may be expected to show early results. But this may often result in neglecting areas of economic policy where by far the most fruitful contributions to our long-run growth prospects may exist. For example, in formulating growth policies one tends to take as given:

(a) social attitudes, including those that shape society's aspirations and objectives and those that fashion the degree to which society in general, and management and labour in particular, are receptive to economic change and innovation;

(b) techniques of production – other than major current changes, and

(c) administrative machineries and other institutions.

However, it is quite likely that, in the very long run, much more can be done to raise the limits on growth rates by operating on these factors. If we knew, for example, the sociological reasons why a very large proportion of businessmen here (and abroad) used such crude and archaic methods for evaluating when to replace old equipment, or why the attitudes of certain sections of the British labour force did not facilitate change and technical innovation, it is likely that in the very long run a considerable increase in the pace of technological innovation could be obtained. People's attitudes to changing their jobs or their houses, to the division of their time between work and leisure, to the type of material possessions they want as against other elements in modes of life, to the type of environment in which they wish to live, all play a part in shaping society's will to raise its standard of living and to adapt traditions when these prove an obstacle to faster growth.

Such sociological factors are, as argued above, not necessarily more important in Britain than in most other countries. But not very much attempt is made to investigate their impact on growth potential. This is chiefly because they do not have any rapid 'pay-off'. It is also because of an unjustified suspicion that such considerations are somehow less 'scientific' than the hard quantifiable facts that economists like to think they are dealing with. But in fact, as far as growth is concerned, economists are not in a position to claim that their science has been all that decisive.

As for techniques of production, there has, of course, been growing awareness of the role that a national strategy with respect to scientific and technological research can play. But again, the benefits of such a strategy are likely to be too far in the future to arouse the enthusiasm of the average policy maker. The same applies to institutional change. It would be a great coincidence if the present pattern of our administrative machinery and institutions were perfectly adapted to the needs of a dynamic and growing economy. But again, it is not immediately obvious how one should set about changing it nor how quickly the benefits would be reaped.

Determinants of growth and growth policy

In the central sections of this chapter we have argued that what determines the growth possibilities of any economic unit depends very much on the particular relationship between that unit and other comparable units. Of these relationships the most important is that of continued competitiveness. The possibilities of continued competitiveness vary according to the type of unit in question – i.e. the firm, the industry, the region or the whole economy. The relevant technical factors will also vary according to the type of unit under discussion. Hence, in formulating growth policy with respect to any particular unit one should, apparently, single out those characteristics of the overall theory that apply to that particular unit. But there is no clear dividing line between a unit that is competing with others and a unit that is not, particularly when that unit is a large economy, much of which will have only indirect links with other economies.

Secondly, we have also emphasised, in the last section, the difference between measures that act in the short run and measures which may only bear fruit after a considerable lapse of time. Hence, which policies one would adopt must depend on the political objectives and on society's scale of valuations as affecting the relative weights attached to the short-run and the long-run future.

Thirdly, it must be acknowledged that there is not even any clear-cut distinction between 'growth policies' and other areas of economic policy. Measures aimed, for example, at dealing with a short-run balance of payments disequilibrium will have consequences for the longer-run rate of growth of the economy, and there will often be a choice between measures that have the least unfavourable impact on longer-run growth and measures which deal more effectively with the short-run problems.

For these three reasons it would be obviously absurd to insist on any one simple type of measure to accelerate economic growth, or to pretend that there is any single determinant of economic growth.

In such a situation it might appear that policy should simply operate on all the factors that can contribute to growth in one way or another. One should try through, say, exchange rate adjustments or incomes policy to raise British competitiveness by means that do not necessarily involve acting directly on the supply side (e.g. on technical efficiency). And one should also act on these supply factors, by seeking, for example, to improve workers' on-the-job training facilities, or by adjusting the tax system in the direction required to stimulate the level of investment, faster replacement and innovation, or to improve the distribution of investment; or by better methods of training and selecting managers, by stimulating, subsidising and protecting scientific research, and by raising the mobility of labour, and so on.

Such a policy of adopting all measures that are likely to promote growth in one way or another is obviously desirable if all possible policies are costless (and do not conflict with other means, or even with some of the basic social objectives of the growth policy). But some of the ways of promoting growth may be very costly. Hence, there is some case for concentrating on those growth factors which satisfy two criteria, namely, (a) their effect is fairly conclusively demonstrated, and (b) the costs involved, in terms of real resources or other objectives, are not necessarily very heavy. On these grounds measures operating directly on the supply side do not rank very high.

In the first place, Britain as a whole is, *par excellence*, an example of a competing unit in world trade. And among such units competitiveness is, almost by definition, the most effective means of growing. Secondly, in so far as we give much weight to the short run and to minimising the real costs of the measures adopted, competitiveness can be raised faster, and probably at less real cost and effort, through changes in exchange rates or in rates of change in money incomes than through measures aimed at improving the longer-run rate of change in real costs. Thirdly, as argued above, a short-run improvement in our competitive situation will tend, by itself, to stimulate some longer-run increase in the rate of growth of productivity as the reward for having entered a virtuous circle.

Furthermore, as has been stated in an earlier section, there is little or no evidence for the view that international differences in growth can be related to differences in, for example, the skill of labour or management, or differences in mobility of labour. International differences in incentives to invest also appear to play little part in explaining differences in investment rates – though this is partly because on the whole, with notable exceptions, countries which took measures to stimulate investment were those which needed to do so because their investment was low and vice versa.

This illustrates how difficult it is to assess which growth policies pursued in other countries have been effective and hence which ones should be adopted here. For the effect of any one policy will depend both on the general environment and on the other policies being adopted. Policies are not additive in a simple way. Consequently, it is very difficult to identify which of the various policies pursued in fast-growing countries abroad have made significant independent contributions to their growth rates. And even if one could do so, one would still need to weigh up the costs of, say, much greater scientific research, large-scale workers' retraining and resettlement schemes, and the like.

By contrast, as argued above, there is both strong evidence from international comparisons, and compelling theoretical reasons, for the view that some of the needed response on the supply side in the way of greater investment, more dynamic management, more adaptable labour, faster technical innovation, etc., would be almost automatically forthcoming given an initial rise in competitiveness. This points to concentration on measures such as those in the field of exchange rate adjustment, or in the field of incomes policy, which operate on competitiveness via relative prices rather than via relative real costs in the first instance. These policies are discussed in the two following chapters.

At the same time, as one cannot be sure how great a supply response would follow automatically from an improvement in British foreign trade competitiveness, particularly after so long a period of very slow growth, there would still be a case for investigating, as is done in some of the other chapters in this book, policies which are designed to operate directly on the supply side, the benefits of which can be shown to be substantial relative to the likely costs. Such policies would also deserve increasing emphasis as soon as Britain can afford to be less preoccupied with the immediate short-run position of the economy. This is partly because, in the very long run, the returns to measures designed to transform the sociological determinants of growth might be remarkably high. But more important in the very long run is the fact that international growth should not be allowed to remain a competitive process. That it may be so today does determine the emphasis in British growth policies. But a more rational organisation of the world economy would involve a shift in emphasis towards the supply factors.

SUGGESTIONS FOR FURTHER READING

Edith Penrose, *The Theory of the Growth of the Firm* (Basil Blackwell, Oxford, 1959), for analysis of factors determining growth of individual firms. It constructs a theoretical framework on the basis of extensive empirical observation. (Quoted on pages 72 and 73.)

Joan Robinson, *Economic Philosophy* (Watts and Co., London, 1962), includes an explanation of use of the concept of equilibrium as well as general description of the evolution of problems with which economists are concerned. (Quoted on page 68.)

Joan Robinson, *Essays in the Theory of Economic Growth* (Macmillan, 1962). This contains a survey and analysis of certain theoretical growth models.

OECD, *Policies for Economic Growth* (Paris, November 1962), for very brief survey of growth record of Western countries during the 1950s and implications for policy.

United Nations Economic Commission for Europe, *Some Factors in Economic Growth in Europe during the 1950s* (Geneva, 1964). This contains a more detailed analysis of many of the possible causes of growth discussed in Section 3.

Angus Maddison, *Economic Growth in the West* (Allen and Unwin, 1964). In addition to some analysis of the role of capital and labour, this emphasises the impact of different growth policies in the various countries covered.

Jack Downie, *The Competitive Process* (Duckworth, London, 1958); a theoretical and statistical analysis of the process of relative growth of firms within an industry.

Tibor Barna, *Investment and Growth Policies in British Industrial Firms* (National Institute of Economic and Social Research, 1962). This study is particularly relevant to the discussion of the role of management attitudes in determining the growth of firms.

Thomas Wilson, *Planning and Growth* (Macmillan, 1964), contains essays on the role of value judgements in selecting growth policies and on certain international generalisations concerning the growth process and its relation to planning.

A. Lamfalussy, *The United Kingdom and the Six* (Macmillan, 1963). This presents a view of the growth process very similar to that given here, and illustrated by the comparative growth record of Britain and the Common Market countries.

Odd Aukrust, 'Factors of Economic Development: a Review of Recent Research', *Weltwirtschaftliches Archiv*, 1964, Band 93, Heft 4. This contains a concise survey of much of the work published in the UN and OECD studies referred to above or of working documents prepared for these studies.

J. McGibbon, 'The Statistical Comparability of Rates of Growth of Gross National Product', *Productivity Measurement Review*, February 1964 (OECD, Paris), describes work done at the OECD on the extent to which differences in growth rates can be ascribed to statistical quirks.

W. Beckerman and Associates, *The British Economy in 1975* (NIESR and Cambridge University Press, 1965). Chapters 1 and 2 contain an analysis of the comparative growth record of Britain in the 1950s with implications for the future growth prospects.

T. P. Hill, 'Growth and Investment According to International Comparisons', *The Economic Journal*, June 1964. This examines in detail the relationship between investment ratios and growth rates in different countries.

4

THE BALANCE OF PAYMENTS

The balance of payments and economic growth

At various times in the past decade it has seemed that our
balance of payments has set an upper limit to our rate of
economic growth. In the three years following the crisis of 1955
the rate of growth of total output in the economy was a mere
1 per cent per annum, and it was roughly the same in the
year following the crisis of 1961. These slow rates of growth were
partly attributable to restrictive measures taken by the government, and the measures were taken largely because of the weak
balance of payments situation.

The restrictive measures helped the balance of payments in
three main ways:

(a) By reducing total demand they also reduced the demand
for imports.

(b) By reducing the pressure of demand in the economy (thus
increasing unemployment and creating excess capacity) they
slowed down the rate of increase of prices. After some time, this
tended to stimulate exports and reduce imports. Some also
believe that, by reducing order books and making the home
market less attractive, the lower pressure of demand increased
exports directly (i.e. apart from its effects through lowering
prices). Empirical evidence in support of this contention is hard
to find, and there are those who would argue that the reverse
is true.

(c) Most immediately, by convincing everyone that the
government intended to improve the balance of payments by
means of (a) and (b), and not by devaluing the pound, they
improved the capital account of the balance of payments. In
1961 it was not only speculators who had to be convinced that
measures were being taken which would improve the balance

of payments, but also the authorities controlling foreign central banks and the International Monetary Fund, who lent us money to tide us over the crisis.

The years of slow growth were followed by years of exceptionally rapid growth, and it might be argued that the crises had no *permanent* effect on our rate of growth. True, we lost output in the years 1956–58 and in 1962, but the level of output in 1960–1961 or in 1964, say, could not have been appreciably higher than it was even if there had been no crises and no measures. On this view the long-term growth of the economy is set by various factors which determine what might be called the growth of the supply potential. In years such as 1955, and possibly 1960 or 1961, we produced almost the maximum we could. In between, we produced less, largely because of balance of payments difficulties, but the growth of the supply potential was not much affected by this. The balance of payments did not, therefore, limit the rate of growth of the economy. It did force us to reduce demand at various times, and it therefore limited the degree to which we could approach the full supply potential on average over the whole period. We had to maintain enough slack in the economy, on average, for the rate of increase in prices to be moderated sufficiently to keep the balance of payments in equilibrium taking one year with another. In principle, this could have been done without the need for 'stop' and 'go'. We could have had a smooth rate of growth, always keeping the pressure of demand low enough to maintain a satisfactory balance of payments on *average*. Some years would have been worse than others, but, with the average satisfactory, and with sufficient reserves, this would not have mattered. In practice, this smooth development was not achieved, partly because the reserves were not big enough (so that we could not 'ride out' the bad years), partly because the technical difficulties of keeping the economy on a smooth and steady course have not yet been overcome, and partly because the government wanted to maintain a higher average pressure of demand than we could really afford on balance of payments grounds. Hence it tended to inflate the economy until forced to reverse engines by a balance of payments crisis.

If the above analysis were accepted, it would seem that

specific measures to improve the balance of payments, other than the restriction of demand, while they would not enable the long-term rate of growth to be raised, would at least allow the economy to be run at a higher average pressure of demand. Hence, at any given time, output would be higher and unemployment lower, even though the average *rate of growth* of output might not be increased.

However, this probably understates the case for specific measures to improve the balance of payments. The preceding chapter has argued that there is a connection between the rate of growth of the supply potential and the behaviour of demand. An appreciably faster increase in the former could be achieved if businessmen could be convinced that a continuous rapid growth in demand was going to be maintained. The National Economic Development Council's Report on 'Conditions Favourable to Faster Growth' concluded that a low pressure of demand might well result in a slower rate of growth of the productive capacity of the economy. If, then, specific measures could be taken to improve the balance of payments, they might not only permit the average level of output to be higher and unemployment lower, they might also enable the rate of growth of output to be increased.

After 1962 the government's strategy in regard to the balance of payments contained the following elements:

(a) General measures to stimulate efficiency and growth (e.g. investment allowances, measures to increase labour mobility, better training and education, etc.). These could be expected to stimulate the growth of exports as well.

(b) An incomes policy to slow down the rate of increase of prices.

(c) Increases in international liquidity, which would lessen the need to take restrictive measures to deal with purely temporary balance of payments difficulties, and would give time for (a) and (b) to take effect.

On several occasions the Chancellor emphasised that he was prepared to see a temporary worsening in the balance of payments as stocks were built up and imports rose when the growth of the economy speeded up. This temporary worsening could, if necessary, be financed by borrowing from the IMF or by using the reserves. If, however, the first two measures and, in particular, the incomes policy, were not successful, then it seemed that demand would once again have to be restricted and growth slowed down.

In the autumn of 1964 confidence in the pound weakened. The measures adopted by the new government to deal with the crisis included a 15 per cent surcharge on virtually all imports of manufactured goods, a scheme to remit certain indirect taxes which enter into the costs of exports, the remission being estimated at about £80 million a year, or rather less than 2 per cent of the value of exports, an increase in Bank Rate from 5 to 7 per cent, a drawing of £357 millions from the IMF, and an arrangement to borrow up to £1,070 millions from foreign central banks. It was emphasised that the import surcharge was a temporary measure which would be reduced or removed as soon as the balance of payments situation permitted. The surcharge and the borrowing from the IMF and the foreign central banks were designed to give time for other measures to take effect, these other measures being essentially (a) and (b) above.

Hence the new government's long-term strategy to deal with the balance of payments seems very similar to its predecessor's. Its elements are not controversial. General measures to stimulate efficiency are desirable for more important reasons than their effects on exports. An incomes policy would be desirable as a means of slowing down the rise in prices even if the balance of payments was strong. The desirability of these measures is therefore not in question, but their adequacy is.

We return to this question at the end of the chapter. It is sufficient here to remark that there is a risk, which cannot be dismissed, that they will not be adequate. In that case, if we wish to avoid the restrictions of demand to which we have resorted in the past, we must use other measures to improve the balance of payments.

In what follows, we consider possible measures one by one. Before doing so there are two misconceptions about the British balance of payments problem that must be dealt with: first, that it is all a matter of restraint, or living within one's means, and, second, that it is all a matter of insufficient reserves of gold or foreign currencies or of means of supplementing them by short-term borrowing from abroad.

The nature of the balance of payments problem

What is the nature of Britain's balance of payments problem? Put simply, it is the problem of selling sufficient to other countries to pay for what we want to buy from them, given that we also want to lend and give aid to them. The analogy with the similar problem which confronts almost all of us can be misleading as well as helpful. If the individual overspends his income, he will find his bank balance dwindling or, possibly, his overdraft increasing. In the same way, Britain's reserves of gold and foreign currencies may be drawn down or her borrowing from the International Monetary Fund or from the central banks of other countries increase in a balance of payments crisis. But whereas it makes sense to advise the spendthrift to curtail his expenditure on most things, it may not be equally sensible to pursue a national policy of retrenchment. The maxim 'cut your coat according to your cloth' is an inadequate guide here. The problem is how to redirect resources so that a little more will be exported and a little less imported, and possibly also a little less lent or given away abroad. In relation to our total national income the adjustments required are small. An improvement averaging £300 millions a year in our past balance of payments accounts would have made a big difference to them. Our reserves fluctuate around £1,000 millions. But our national income is more than £25,000 millions a year, so only a small part of this needs to be diverted from its existing use and somehow transformed into exports or substitutes for imports. Hence the problem is *not* primarily one of tightening our belts and making do with less, nor even of working a lot harder to produce more. It is rather a problem of producing or consuming according to a slightly different pattern from our present one, and of selling to or buying from a slightly different pattern of markets.

This is not to say that the need for restraint is negligible. In 1964 our deficit was unusually large so that, if one starts from that as a base period, the change required appears quite substantial. But (as in other crisis years) the rate of stock building was unusually high in 1964, so that reversion to a more normal rate would itself release many millions of pounds of resources. The further amounts required are probably less than are provided by one year's normal growth of the economy, and, if the adjustments are spread over a couple of years, will not require restraints on the increase in consumption of a different order from those imposed in some budgets since the last war. In short, this part of the problem is one which can be dealt with by fiscal and monetary measures which have handled problems of similar magnitude in the past. What these measures do not do is to ensure that the resources which are released flow into the right channels: that they become exports or substitutes for imports, rather than merely run to waste.

At first blush it seems puzzling that there should be any great difficulty about this. Why, one may ask, is it difficult to effect this slight rearrangement of our resources when so many tremendous changes in their use are occurring all the time? It is not as if we had an ossified industrial or social structure like the Incas. Nor are we dependent on the sales of one or a few commodities so that a slump in their price faces us with the need to make a sudden large cut in our consumption or to switch over to producing an entirely new range of goods for export. These and other difficult problems are faced by some less fortunate countries. But our problem seems a much easier one.

On going through the possible remedies one by one, the difficulties become apparent. They are very real, but there is a danger of losing one's sense of perspective. To an outsider, the attention given in our newspapers to the monthly figures of exports, imports and changes in our reserves may seem obsessional. Rightly regarded, our problem is not a severe one. What is needed is a determination to overcome it by some means or other and not to let it dominate much more important issues which must be faced.

The need for reserves and short-term borrowing facilities

A balance of payments crisis occurs because our immediate means of paying other countries, our reserves of gold or foreign currencies, are in danger of running out. An obvious remedy is to borrow, and so to avoid the need to draw on the reserves. The borrowing may be arranged officially (e.g. from the International Monetary Fund or foreign central banks) or it may be induced by raising Bank Rate and so attracting an inflow of funds from abroad. It is clear that this cannot continue in-definitely, but if the deficit in our balance of payments is due to some temporary factor (such as, for example, a surge of stock building in this country which temporarily increases imports) borrowing may enable us to ride out the crisis. There are some who would argue that lack of reserves or borrowing facilities has been the cause of our post-war balance of pay-ments difficulties. Each crisis passed away, and if our reserves had been larger we could have avoided the unpleasant measures which were sometimes taken. In fact, some of the crises might not have occurred, since they arose only because speculators thought that with low reserves we would be forced to devalue the pound, hence they took their money out of the country, thus bringing on the crisis.

It is true that larger reserves or borrowing facilities would have helped us in every crisis and might have eliminated some. Nevertheless, the fundamental balance of payments problem (already described) would have remained. The unpleasant measures which were taken were not without effect. If we had done nothing, our present balance of payments would probably have been a good deal worse than it is. With much larger reserves we could have tolerated this for a while, but eventually the need for adjustment would have arisen.

Not only are larger reserves or borrowing facilities an in-adequate solution to our balance of payments problem, they may also be an unnecessary one. If we can find some way of increasing exports or reducing imports or cutting our flow of investment or aid abroad, so that our annual average balance improves by a few hundred millions of pounds, our present reserves and borrowing facilities may prove adequate. It would admittedly help us to have larger reserves, and it would also help us if other countries had larger reserves. They would then be more likely to pursue expansionary policies and be readier to reduce restrictions on trade, all of which would help our exports. Hence we should undoubtedly continue to press for measures to increase international liquidity by reform of the International Monetary Fund or in other ways. But we do not have to wait until these reforms are made, and even if they were made now our fundamental problem could still remain.

Measures to improve the balance of payments

Our balance of payments problem is not, therefore, primarily a matter of the restraint of demand, of securing less consumption out of a given income. Nor is it primarily a matter of increasing our foreign exchange reserves or borrowing facilities. These aspects of the problem have their importance, but the most difficult, and so important, aspects are those concerned with the redirection of patterns of expenditure and sales. What measures could effect this redirection? Why have they been, hitherto, unacceptable as elements in a *permanent* strategy to deal with the balance of payments problem?

Restrictions on imports – Restrictions on imports are a direct method of tackling the problem which we and other countries have used. We have never regarded them as providing more than a temporary solution to it, however. Two methods which we have used have been quantitative restrictions (q.r.) and tariffs (the import surcharge is essentially a tariff). A third method used in some other countries is to require importers to make prior deposits with the banking system in respect of orders placed abroad. This might be less effective in this country, where there is a well-developed capital market and where many large firms claim that they are seldom short of finance. In what follows, we confine our attention to q.r. and tariffs.

The General Agreement on Tariffs and Trade allows countries which are party to it to impose q.r. to safeguard their balance of payments in an emergency. There is no similar provision for the emergency imposition of tariffs, and under a series of negotiations we have bound our tariff rates over a wide range of goods. Hence, whereas we could, without breaking our agreements or being released from them, impose q.r., we have broken several agreements by imposing the import surcharge. On this account we should prefer the use of q.r. to tariffs.

The main additional point that might be said to favour q.r. as opposed to tariffs is the greater certainty of the former. Once the quotas were decided, a known ceiling would have been placed on the imports affected. This advantage can, however, be overstated. There would be an appreciable lag between the imposition of q.r. and their effects on imports, so that it would not be easy to estimate what imports would be in a future period. In any case, since one cannot predict the other elements in the balance of payments with any accuracy, one cannot tell exactly how big a cut in imports is required. What is wanted is the assurance that a large cut will be achieved, and the use of either q.r. or tariffs can give that assurance.

Tariffs would avoid some of the administrative headaches which would accompany import licensing. The machinery for allocating quotas sensibly and fairly no longer exists and would have to be set up. The lucky receivers of import licences might make substantial profits from selling scarce imports at higher prices, which would seem unfair. If the licences were auctioned as has sometimes been suggested, this might secure the profits for the state, but would introduce other difficulties.

Tariffs can be used to induce import saving at the margin over a very wide field which it would not be practicable to cover by a system of import licensing. The latter might have to take the form of fairly drastic cuts of 'inessentials'. The same total saving could better be secured by smaller reductions more evenly spread. Each commodity has inessential as well as essential uses, and a tariff would discourage the former in a way which would be difficult to reproduce by administrative control.

Both tariffs and q.r. are open to the objection that they would lead to speculative buying of imports from time to time if they became part of our normal strategy for tackling the balance of payments. Whenever the balance looked weak, importers would try to 'beat the gun', thus weakening the balance still more.

It is sometimes said that import restrictions may be ineffective in a fully employed economy since the demand diverted from one group of imports may spill over to another, or may be satisfied at the expense of exports. There is some truth in this, but total demand can be restricted, if need be, by, for example, fiscal measures, thus preventing any net increase in demand for other products.

Any improvement in the current balance of payments will require *some* cut in domestic demand, if total home production cannot be increased. The argument in favour of import restrictions is that they do not require an unnecessarily large cut in domestic demand and they enable one to maintain full employment. Because the cut is concentrated on imports by the q.r., one only need reduce domestic demand (ideally) by the size of the required improvement in the current balance of payments, say 1 or 2 per cent of total domestic demand. If, however, one were simply to curb total demand without doing anything to switch it away from imports one might need to cut it by, perhaps, five times as much, and full employment would have to be abandoned. If, among any five soldiers, one is a potential mutineer, and if the time has come when at least one potential mutineer must be shot, one can either take out five soldiers and shoot the lot or else choose the one who is a potential mutineer and shoot him. Someone is going to be shot anyway, but the latter method keeps it to the minimum necessary. Import restrictions are therefore better than a general cut in demand, even though they may need to be accompanied by measures which reduce demand a little. Tariffs are rather better than import licensing (unless the licences are auctioned) in that the extra revenue accruing to the government itself tends to reduce demand and to that extent reduces the need for other deflationary measures.

An objection sometimes raised against both import restrictions and tariffs is that they shelter inefficient domestic industries. By lessening competitive pressures at home they reduce efficiency and hence total national output. There may be something in this argument, but its proponents would probably be unwilling to accept its full implications. An incomes policy which lowered the general level of money costs and prices in this country relative to those abroad would also shelter domestic industries, just like a tariff. The difference is that it would also stimulate exports. However, a uniform tariff of, say, 5 per cent, accompanied by a uniform export subsidy of 5 per cent, would have the same effect as a 5 per cent reduction in the general level of costs and prices in this country relative to those abroad. If the competitive and efficiency effects of the 5 per cent tariff were thought to be bad, while those of the export subsidy were thought to be good, then presumably one should (at least on this account) prefer a policy of export subsidies to an incomes policy as a means of improving the balance of payments. But perhaps it is quota restrictions rather than tariffs which are thought to be particularly damaging to competition and efficiency. A low-cost foreign competitor may surmount a tariff, whereas he may be excluded altogether by a quota. If this is true, it is an additional argument for tariffs as opposed to q.r.

One form of import restriction which may have damaging effects on efficiency is that which requires government departments or public enterprises to discriminate in favour of home products and against imports. The requirement may be stated formally (as in the United States, for example, under the 'Buy American' Act) or it may be informal. The effects of the latter on efficiency may be worse than the former, since it leaves the way open for lobbying which could lead to a very high effective degree of protection in particular fields. Furthermore, those who are compelled to buy more costly or inefficient home substitutes may be tempted to adopt a cynical attitude to requests from higher authorities to keep down costs. On the other hand, *some* degree of discrimination in favour of home products can be justified in a situation in which most imports are restricted in one way or another, or in which deflation would otherwise be necessary to keep the balance of payments in balance. Informal discrimination has the advantage that it is widely practised and provokes less of an outcry from one's trading partners than would a straight increase in tariffs. In most other respects, however, the latter is preferable.

It seems, then, that most of the arguments tell in favour of tariffs as compared to q.r. (or informal discrimination), but that international agreements and conventions favour the latter – an odd state of affairs which we, as a leading trading nation, could attempt to change. This does not mean that we should abandon our general aim of reducing tariffs through the GATT, but that we should seek international recognition for their temporary use in balance of payments difficulties, in preference to q.r.

The word 'temporary' needs to be stressed. Were we to raise our tariffs permanently or revert to q.r. as a permanent policy, we would run the risk of breaking up the GATT and the EFTA and of inviting retaliation in kind against our exports. Our experience with the import surcharge shows that this risk is far from negligible. Hence a policy of *permanently* higher tariffs or of q.r. might not, in the end, improve our balance of payments at all, could conceivably worsen it, and could lower our total trade and efficiency.

95

If the restrictions are to be very short-lived, tariffs may be less effective than q.r. For home producers may be unwilling to undertake production of substitutes for imports if their tariff protection is going to be removed in a short time, and foreign exporters may lower their prices in order to retain their markets. With q.r. the volume of imports must fall regardless of whether home substitutes are produced or not, and however much foreign exporters cut their prices. It is true that a reduction in the prices paid to foreign exporters will help the balance of payments (and an incomes policy) and there is *some* tariff rate sufficient to produce the required cut in the *value* of imports. However, a very high rate, even for a very short time, would be unacceptable to our overseas suppliers.

There is one last difficulty which should be mentioned. The q.r. which were in force after the last war discriminated between different sources of supply, as well as between different commodities. There were virtually no restrictions on imports from countries in the sterling area, and the most severe restrictions were on imports from the dollar area (i.e. North America and certain countries in Central and South America). The GATT requires that all restrictions shall be non-discriminatory as between countries, though discrimination between commodities on grounds of essentiality is permitted. By skilful choice of commodities we might avoid restricting imports from sterling area countries to any great extent, but there would have to be *some* restrictions, and the more severely we wanted to cut imports the more numerous would these restrictions have to be. One might want to restrict tourist expenditure abroad on grounds of inessentiality, as was done after the war, but non-discriminatory restrictions would mean that expenditure in the Republic of Ireland would have to be restricted as severely as expenditure in Europe or the United States. The import surcharge, introduced in October 1964, applied to imports from all countries, and led to strong protests from those countries with which we have preferential trade agreements, such as the members of the EFTA.

Import substitution – A more indirect method of curbing imports is to subsidise in one way or another the output of goods which are close substitutes for imports. During and after the war we followed a policy of stimulating home agricultural production, largely for this reason. In recent years, subsidies to agriculture and food have amounted to some £300–£350 millions a year, or about 20 per cent of the gross output of the industry. Cynics may say that the main reason for the continuation of this large subsidy is the rural vote, but one could argue that if the subsidy were reduced there would be a fall in home food output and a rise in imports of food. It is true that these imports would come in part from countries like Australia and New Zealand which would, in consequence, import appreciably more from us, but it seems probable that there would be a net deterioration in our balance of payments. Hence those who want to reduce or abolish the subsidies should show how this deterioration is to be dealt with. Deflation would almost certainly be a more costly remedy, and while tariffs or import restrictions, if practicable, would be better than deflation, they might be no better than the subsidy. Many manufactures in this country already receive protection by a tariff of the order of 20 per cent, or even more, so that it is hard to see why further protection for these, at least, would lead to a better use of resources than does a 20 per cent subsidy for agriculture. A case could be made for lowering the subsidy to agriculture and increasing the protection given (whether by tariff or subsidy) to manufactures which are now protected by a smaller tariff than 20 per cent. An advantage of agricultural protection, however, is that it is almost universally practised and already in existence. Hence any move of the kind described would probably worsen our commercial relations with other countries. It is probably easier to get away with continued agricultural protection than with higher tariffs on imported manufactures even if accompanied by smaller subsidies to agriculture. A further argument for the agricultural subsidies is that they help to keep down world prices of temperate foodstuffs, since they reduce our demand for wheat, meat, butter, eggs, etc., on the world market. This may harm the Australians and New Zealanders, regrettably, but it may benefit poorer nations such as India which are net importers of at least some of these foodstuffs. In a hungry world there is something to be said for special inducements to maintain or increase food output. (See also Chapter 9, page 270.)

One might accept these (and other) arguments for agricultural subsidies and *in addition* seek to subsidise other home-produced substitutes for imports. One might select products least likely to provoke a hostile foreign reaction, but there would certainly be *some* reaction if the subsidies were effective, and especially if they were intended to be permanent. Temporary subsidies would be less effective in influencing home production. It would not be easy to find other criteria by which to allocate them. Almost every commodity produced is a substitute, directly or indirectly, for some import. It would be difficult to judge how closely substitutable a particular candidate for subsidy was, how responsive its output would be to a given subsidy, and what the resources used to produce it would otherwise have produced; yet all these factors seem relevant.

A final objection to subsidies which should be mentioned is that they necessitate higher taxes (or else economies in some other item of government expenditure), and that these are almost certain to have some adverse effects on output or efficiency.

Export promotion – 'The balance of payments has been the constant concern of successive governments for many years. It is not surprising to find, therefore, that measures to improve it which are free from serious disadvantage are likely to bring only small benefits.' Thus the NEDC's report on 'Conditions Favourable to Faster Growth'. Amongst the measures 'free from serious disadvantages' are the numerous devices to help exporters by free advice, market research, special credit and insurance facilities, trade fairs, etc., and to spur them on by ministerial speeches, honours for leading exporters and publicity campaigns with slogans such as 'export or die'. These efforts are worth making and perhaps intensifying. Conversation with businessmen sometimes leaves one with the impression that the questions of whether they export and of how much are not decided by considerations of profitability but by a feeling that it is patriotic, or by the fact that they have always, in that business, exported x per cent of their turnover. If any of the above measures can induce businessmen to regard $x+y$ per cent as a more desirable normal percentage, it will have performed a very useful function.

All the same, the scepticism expressed in the quotation is probably justified. If exports are to be increased substantially, something more is needed, and it seems probable that an export subsidy would have more chance of success than an increase in publicity, slogans or speeches. There is evidence that financial considerations do influence exports (see also page 107). In what follows, we review the advantages and disadvantages of export subsidies on the assumption that they are effective.

A general export subsidy is rather like a general tariff – a measure for improving the balance of payments which has much to commend it, but which is not internationally respectable. In its favour one can argue that it expands rather than contracts trade, which is usually thought to be helpful to international relations, and which may (as we saw earlier) be thought to sharpen competition. It spreads the burden of adjustment in the pattern of resources more widely than would the internationally respectable quantitative import restrictions. It would be administratively easier to give a small subsidy over a wide range of products than to make small cuts in a wide range of imports. Furthermore, it is probably better that some of the adjustment should take the form of increased exports and some of reduced imports, rather than that the whole adjustment should fall on imports. If one is looking for measures to deal with difficulties for a few years in the hope that faster growth and an incomes policy will then be able to 'take over', a general export subsidy has the advantage of anticipating the effects of these ultimate cures. They will stimulate exports, and their task will be eased if the pattern of resources can be altered in the right direction as soon as possible. Otherwise, if reliance is placed on import restriction alone, one may be left with pockets of unemployment and excess capacity when the restrictions are removed.

Despite these advantages, there has been a drive in recent years, in which this country has taken a leading part, to eliminate all 'artificial' aids to exporters. Along with other countries, we have undertaken through the GATT not to give such aid. The EFTA also outlaws all forms of financial assistance to exports by member countries. It is probably right that export aids should be outlawed in the normal course of trade, as should tariffs. There may, however, be special situations in which they should be allowed. Depending on the circumstances, they may be as good, or better, at dealing with temporary balance of payments difficulties as quantitative import restrictions. From an international point of view they have the advantage (among others) that they tend to worsen the terms of trade of the country using them, since they cheapen its exports to other countries. The latter may complain of disruption to their export or domestic industries, but at least they are getting their imports more cheaply. Quantitative import restrictions would create as much disruption, it might be thought, and would, generally speaking, improve the terms of trade of the country using them (since that country could then probably buy its imports more cheaply). It seems paradoxical to permit q.r. but not export subsidies.

From the domestic point of view, export subsidies have the disadvantage just mentioned of worsening the terms of trade and also the disadvantage mentioned in the preceding section of necessitating higher taxes to pay for them. There would be administrative problems. If the subsidies were stated to be temporary, in an effort to placate other countries, and to avoid the risk of retaliation, they would be less effective in encouraging producers to export. One would have to convince producers that when the subsidies were terminated something else would take their place – presumably an incomes policy or an exchange rate adjustment. The former might not sound convincing, and the latter suggestion would scarcely be mentionable.

Changes in the tax system – The proposal which is considered here is to substitute a tax on value added (profits plus wages) for a tax on profits. We shall not consider remissions of profits or income tax linked to export performance, as these are similar to direct export subsidies, and suffer from the same disadvantage of being outlawed by international agreements. The value added tax, which is also imposed on imports and remitted on exports, is allowed by the rules of the GATT and the EFTA, which makes it a much more attractive proposition. The proposal to substitute this tax for profits tax was examined by the Richardson Committee, which reported in 1964, and recommended that this substitution should *not* be made. Since the arguments and evidence are set out fully in that report, and since the writer does not disagree with the conclusion, it is only necessary to give a very brief summary of the argument here.

The substitution would benefit the balance of payments if domestic prices rose by less than the tax. Suppose, for the sake of argument, that the value added tax was levied at a rate of

2 per cent on the value added in the production of all goods and services, and that the revenue raised in this way compensated for the elimination of profits tax. Then if, on average, firms offset one tax against the other, internal prices would not rise. Manufacturers would then buy their materials at the same price as before but would be able to claim a rebate of 2 per cent on the *total* selling value of any exports. Exporting would thus be more profitable than before, and exports would be encouraged. Likewise, imports would be discouraged since purchasers would have to pay a 2 per cent tax on them. The net result would thus be rather similar to a 2 per cent devaluation of the pound.

If, however, businesses passed on the whole of the value added tax, and offset none of it against the elimination of profits tax, internal prices would rise by 2 per cent. If this were the end of the matter, it would at least not *worsen* the balance of payments, but, in fact, the rise in internal prices, combined with the elimination of profits tax, would certainly increase wage demands and make it more difficult to get agreement to an incomes policy. The resulting further rise in internal prices would worsen the balance of payments, since the remission of taxes on exports would still leave their costs higher than before, and the tax on imports would still leave them cheaper than home goods.

The evidence submitted to the Richardson Committee suggested that the outcome was more likely to be that described in the last paragraph than that described in the one preceding it. The Committee has been criticised for accepting too readily businessmen's accounts of how they would behave. Businessmen may say one thing and do another. While this is true, it is difficult to see the case for putting in hand a massive reorganisation of the tax system whose outcome is uncertain and which, most businessmen apparently believe, will have the opposite effects from those intended. One may not altogether believe the businessmen, but one wants some *other* empirical evidence in favour of the proposal before accepting it, and that evidence is lacking at present.

Cutting private investment abroad, foreign aid or other governmental expenditure abroad – In the early 1950s the government stated that a satisfactory average surplus on the current account of the balance of payments would be £300 to £350 millions a year. For the 1960s, the Treasury at one time put the figure at £450 millions a year. The NEDC took a figure of £300 millions for 1966, later revised to £225 millions. These were all meant to be the averages over a number of years, or figures for representative years. In fact, in the last ten years we have only once achieved a recorded current surplus of £300 millions or more (in 1958). Our average for the ten years 1955 to 1964 inclusive was only about £30 millions.

This record of pious aspiration and failure has convinced some that we should set our sights lower. We have, after all, achieved a current surplus, albeit a smaller one than we aimed at. We should recognise our own limitations and ensure that in future a current surplus of this size will be adequate. Since the current surplus is largely used to finance private or public long-term capital expenditure abroad, it is suggested that we should cut either or both of them.

We shall discuss private and public capital expenditure abroad in turn, and we shall also discuss, with the latter, the case for cutting public grants to underdeveloped countries and other public current expenditure abroad (e.g. for military or diplomatic purposes). These last two items come in the current account of the balance of payments, so that the argument stated above does not, strictly speaking, apply to them. Nevertheless, the basic issue is the same – should we cut these expenditures, whether current or capital, to strengthen our balance of payments?

(a) *Private investment abroad* – One sometimes hears it said that £100 of investment abroad adds less to the national income than £100 of investment at home because the former only adds the profits on the investment whereas the latter adds both the profits and the wages of the labour which is employed on the extra capital. This argument is fallacious. If there is full employment at home, the labour employed on the extra capital must have come from some other employment, and the output lost there may roughly balance the value of the extra output attributable to labour in its new employment. Hence, in this case, the gain to the national income is (approximately) the extra profits, whether the investment is made at home or abroad. If there is not full employment, there is no need to cut investment abroad in order to provide the resources to increase investment at home. The latter can be increased by using unemployed resources.

There are other reasons, however, for believing that investment abroad may add less to the national income than the same amount of investment at home. The existence of double tax agreements means that, if the private return net of tax is the same on both types of investment, the return including tax accruing to the British Government will generally be less on investment abroad. Investment abroad may also worsen our terms of trade by stimulating the output of manufactures competing with our exports, and it may, through competition with investments previously made, reduce the profits on them. Sometimes the opposite might happen, however. The investments might develop primary products which we import, thus improving our terms of trade, or they might be complementary to and so increase the profits on investments we had previously made. It would thus be very difficult to tell what the probable total effects on the national income would be of any particular investment abroad. Nor would it be easy to discover the total effects of the alternative investments at home – supposing they could be identified. There are no simple criteria by which investment abroad could be controlled with a view to maximising the national income.

Furthermore, in so far as there are benefits which accrue to other countries rather than our own, it is by no means evident that we should ignore them. It is national policy to aid underdeveloped (or poor) countries, and nearly a half of the net outflow of private long-term investment has gone to them in the last few years. The question of whether we should cut this investment is therefore best considered in the general context of aid below (page 104). Much of the remaining investment goes to countries such as Australia and New Zealand with which we have close political and social ties. So far as they are concerned, it is rather as if the citizens of London should complain that investment of their money in the north of England benefits them less than the same amount of money invested in London, ignoring the benefits which accrue to the north.

From the point of view of improving the balance of payments it is also doubtful whether there is much to be gained by cutting investment in the richer countries of the sterling area. Against the immediate saving of funds must be set the following possible losses. Since these countries tend to import heavily from us, and since they would probably have to take measures to curb their imports as a result of the reduced inflow of funds, our exports to them might suffer. They might even cut our exports to them more than proportionately in retaliation. They hold the bulk of their reserves in sterling at present, but might be less willing to continue to do so if we cut off the supply of capital to them. This is, after all, one of the more tangible advantages for them of membership of the sterling area. In the longer run we would, of course, lose the dividends and interest on the investment, and we might lose commercial contacts which are helpful to our exports. Hence, if there was some immediate balance of payments benefit to be derived from cutting the flow of investment to these countries, it would be nothing like as big as the cut made, and in the longer run there might well be a net loss.

There remains the category of private long-term investment in the richer non-sterling countries, principally Western Europe and North America. This is already controlled, and much of it is only permitted if it is expected to bring a gain to the balance of payments within a short period of time. Some, however, does not have to satisfy this criterion. If the foreign currency is obtained by selling existing investments in non-sterling countries, then reinvestment of that foreign currency in, say, a factory overseas is freely permitted. On the face of it, this puts no strain on the reserves and seems harmless from the point of view of the balance of payments. In fact, however, it may mean exchanging a more for a less liquid foreign asset. Since we are short of liquid foreign assets, there is something to be said for preventing this kind of investment and, indeed, for converting some of our existing portfolio investments abroad into more liquid forms, the very reverse of the above process.

(b) *Public current and capital expenditure abroad* – Much the greater part of public current and capital expenditure abroad consists of either aid (gifts or loans) to underdeveloped countries or military or diplomatic expenditure. Aid is discussed in Chapter 9. Here we may content ourselves with remarking that one of the reasons why we want to grow faster is to be able to give more aid, and that it is absurd that the limiting factor on our aid should be its effects on our balance of payments. There may be limits to the absorptive capacity of the receiving countries which prevent any rapid increase in aid. Perhaps the aid going to some countries is largely wasted, and would be better used elsewhere. But to say (as we do) that our own balance of payments is a serious limitation to what we can give is to provide yet another argument for specific measures to strengthen that balance.

Although different considerations apply to military and diplomatic expenditure abroad, the same argument holds. Issues of war and peace should be too important to be dominated by balance of payments considerations. Our total resources limit what we can afford to spend on defence, but if, in addition, we have to skimp our defence expenditure abroad because of a weak balance of payments, then this is one more reason why we should eliminate that weakness.

It is true, nevertheless, that if we are in what may be called a 'disequilibrium situation' in which we are deflating or restricting imports, or subsidising exports, for balance of payments reasons, then a pound spent abroad costs us more in real resources than a pound spent at home. In this situation (which has been endemic since the war), we need to take particular care to get value for money spent abroad. But although this justifies the careful scrutiny of such expenditure, it does not justify the subordination of major decisions of foreign policy to the dictates of the balance of payments.

Use of the exchange rate – We have left to the last the measure which is at once probably the most effective, the simplest to administer and the most conducive to an efficient use of resources, is explicitly permitted, at least in one form, in the Articles of Agreement of the International Monetary Fund, and yet, if one is to believe their spokesmen, is never never going to be used by any of the leading trading nations of the world. Why is the use of the exchange rate so firmly rejected? In part, no doubt, its rejection is merely a pious hope which has to be expressed in firmer language in order to discourage speculation. But there is more to it than that. It is not only the politicians in their public speeches, but also the officials, bankers, economists and others in their more private conversations who conclude, with very little dissent, that the exchange rate is not a suitable weapon with which to attack the balance of payments problem. Hence the weight of advice which is given to the politicians confirms their own instinctive preferences.

The reasons for rejecting it which we shall consider are:

(a) that it would not solve our 'fundamental' problem;

(b) that it would be ineffective;

(c) that it would lead to inflation;

(d) that it would substantially worsen our terms of trade;

(e) that it would be impracticable for a country with an international currency, such as sterling;

(f) that it would gravely damage the international financial system; and

(g) that it would be morally wrong, and damaging to the nation's prestige.

There are at least three different ways in which the exchange rate could be changed, and the above objections apply with different force to each of them. We shall consider, first, how they apply to what is known as the 'adjustable peg' system. Under this system, which is the only one permitted in the Articles of Agreement of the IMF, countries generally maintain rates of exchange which are fixed within narrow limits, but in appropriate circumstances (when there is a 'fundamental disequilibrium' in their balances of payments) they can change the rate. They remove the peg, as it were, and replace it in a new hole where it is intended to be kept for as long as possible. The other two systems which we shall consider are freely fluctuating rates and controlled gradually moving rates, but further description of these is postponed until the adjustable peg system has been dealt with.

The contention that a devaluation of the pound would not solve our fundamental problem could mean several different things. It could mean that devaluation would not, even temporarily, improve the balance of payments; or that any gain would be only temporary because it would be wiped out by devaluations in other countries or by subsequent increases in the internal price level due to the devaluation itself. These points are considered below. What is sometimes meant by this assertion, however, is that Britain's balance of payments problem could be solved if (for example) technical progress in our industries could be speeded up, if managerial drive and efficiency could be improved, if harmful restrictive practices both by management and labour could be eliminated, and if the rate of increase of money incomes could be slowed down so as to match the rate of increase of real output, so that the general level of prices remained stable; if all this could be done, there would be no need to devalue, and, if it is not done, we may need to devalue again and again.

Even if this assertion is accepted *in toto*, it does not dispose of the issue. We have already seen that the present and previous governments have attempted to improve economic efficiency, speed up the rate of growth of output and slow down the rate of growth of prices by a variety of means. These are generally accepted aims of policy quite apart from balance of payments considerations. But although they are *aims*, they are not *variables* under the control of the government. There are, alas, no levers which will regulate the rate of growth of productivity or of prices so that the government can be sure of maintaining equilibrium in the balance of payments by these means. Despite all that can in practice be achieved, we may still run a deficit in our external accounts which must be dealt with by some *other* means. One of these other means is devaluation, and the fact that it may have to be repeated does not automatically rule it out of court. We might still prefer it to, for example, a continued deflation. At all events, the case for and against merits examination.

There are two different sorts of reason for believing that a devaluation of the pound would not in fact improve the current account of our balance of payments (the capital account is considered below). First, one could argue that, even if it was successful in securing a change in relative prices, the latter would not bring about an improvement in the current balance. Secondly, one could argue that a devaluation would not succeed in changing relative prices, either because other countries would retaliate by devaluing their currencies, or because inflation would be speeded up in this country by enough to cancel out the effects of the devaluation.

There is evidence that relative price changes can bring about substantial shifts in trade such as would be needed if devaluation was to improve the current balance of payments. On several occasions large changes in tariffs or exchange rates have been quickly followed by large changes in imports or exports. Such occasions provide the most convincing evidence of these effects, but statistical studies which have attempted to disentangle the effects of relative price changes over a number of years from other influences bearing on the volume of trade, although sometimes inconclusive, have frequently shown a significant and substantial price effect, especially for trade in manufactured goods between industrialised countries.

It is not, on the whole, disbelief in the efficacy of relative price changes which has convinced so many experts that exchange rate adjustments are undesirable. On the contrary, the attention which is paid to tariff changes and the efforts made to slow down the increase in incomes and prices all show that relative price changes (even the rather small ones resulting from different rates of increase in prices in different countries) are thought to exert a substantial effect on the balance of payments. It is true that businessmen are fond of asserting that non-price factors such as the quality of the product, selling techniques, after-sales service, etc., are more important than price in obtaining customers. Even if this were true, price could be important as well. Furthermore, some of these other factors depend upon price. If exports can be sold at a good profit, then it is worthwhile to make great efforts to sell them; but if export prices do not allow the exporter much profit he will probably not bother to push sales very hard. Few businessmen would assert that their sales would scarcely have been affected in the long run had they charged prices 5 or 10 per cent higher than they did. Any that do assert this must explain why they have neglected an easy way of multiplying their profits from exports.

If the pound were devalued, what other countries would follow suit? No categorical answer can be given, since it would depend on the circumstances in which the devaluation occurred. In 1949, when most of the world outside the Americas was suffering from dollar shortage, almost all sterling area countries and much of Western Europe devalued with us, though some countries (notably France, Germany and Italy) devalued by less than we did. The situation now is very different. The Continental European countries are not, for the most part, in balance of payments difficulties as they were in 1949, and the

United States' balance of payments is no longer so immensely strong as it was then. The sterling area countries, or at least some of them, might want to retain the link with the pound, but this is not the key factor in determining whether devaluation can secure the relative price changes needed to improve our balance of payments. What matters is the relation of our costs to those of the other main manufacturing countries, since this determines our competitive power *vis-à-vis* their exports in third markets, *vis-à-vis* their producers in their own markets, and *vis-à-vis* their exports of manufactures to this country. Hence it is the reaction of the Continental Europeans, the United States, Canada and Japan which would be crucial.

If the United States did not devalue, it seems unlikely that any of the others would, unless there was one which happened to be in severe balance of payments difficulties at the time. We are no longer in the 1930s and inflation rather than deflation seems the more immediate danger. The reasons which make us reluctant to devalue would operate to prevent others imitating our example.

It seems unlikely that a small devaluation of the pound would be followed by the dollar. It might provoke large movements of hot money, as did the 5 per cent up valuation of the Deutschmark in 1961, but these could and almost certainly would be countered by lending between Central Banks, as in 1961. A large devaluation of the pound, of the same order as the 30 per cent devaluation in 1949, might be followed by a devaluation of the dollar, though even this seems unlikely. Speculators might attempt to buy gold in case the dollar was devalued, and Central Banks might find it difficult to satisfy demand for gold at current prices. Stricter controls on the buying of gold might be imposed, and black markets in gold might appear. Provided Central Bank co-operation was maintained, it seems unlikely that the dollar, or any other major currency, would be forced to devalue purely because of speculative pressures against it. Even if, in the end, the dollar was devalued, and if some other major currencies followed it down, there might still be scope for a readjustment of the exchange rate between the pound and other currencies, and there would be an increase in the value of gold stocks and gold output which would provide a welcome increase in international liquidity.

But there would also be a very unwelcome period of uncertainty, some dislocation of international finance and trade, and some danger that countries would reimpose strict controls which would undo the progress achieved since the war in the direction of freeing trade and payments. This last chain of events seems unlikely, however, unless co-operation between central banks were to break down altogether. It seems fair to conclude (despite current alarmist opinion to the contrary) that a small devaluation of the pound, or one that was no more than necessary to provide us with a satisfactory current balance of payments, would almost certainly not be offset by devaluation of the currencies of our major competitors. A larger devaluation might be followed, and this is a disadvantage which must be counted against it; but it would probably still leave room for a moderate readjustment of exchange relationships.

A more serious danger is that devaluation would be rendered ineffective by a rise in internal prices. If, for example, a devaluation of 10 per cent led to a rise in import prices, expressed in sterling, of 10 per cent, this might directly increase the cost of living by something like 2 per cent. This, in turn, might lead to wages increasing by an extra 2 per cent which would have further repercussions on prices and the cost of living. If wage-earners insisted on full compensation for any increase in the cost of living, and if producers kept their percentage profit margins constant, passing on any increase in costs, then one can show that the initial 10 per cent rise in import prices would lead approximately to a 10 per cent rise in the general price level, so that the devaluation would have been ineffective.

It is unlikely, however, that such a large increase in the general level of prices would occur. In the first place, our import prices would probably not rise by as much as the devaluation. Since we are a large market for some primary products, their prices in dollars might be forced down a bit. Secondly, statistical studies suggest that a rise of 1 per cent in the cost of living does not lead to a subsequent *extra* rise in wage rates of as much as 1 per cent – the likely figure is more like one half of 1 per cent (this does not mean that wage rates rise more slowly than the cost of living, only that the *difference* made to the rate of increase of wage rates by an *extra* 1 per cent on the cost of living is about one half of 1 per cent).

Thirdly, profits and wages are not the only elements which determine prices. Those whose incomes were fixed in money terms would tend to receive a smaller share of the national income, and this would damp down the rate of increase of prices.

A different reason for thinking that devaluation might have a serious effect on the rate of increase of prices is that it might make it much more difficult to secure agreement to an incomes policy. If, for example, the trade union leaders thought that full employment could always be ensured by devaluation, they might not be willing to accept wage restraint. It is only, perhaps, if they or their followers can be convinced that large wage increases are likely to deprive them of jobs that they will be prepared to reduce their wage demands. The government, too, is less likely to pursue such a thankless task with vigour if there is an easy escape route through devaluation. On this analysis, it is the threat of deflation and unemployment which induces the various parties concerned to seek ways of restraining the rate of growth of money incomes and prices.

Whether devaluation really would seriously jeopardise the chances of securing an incomes policy must depend partly on the circumstances of the time. A large devaluation, like that in 1949, might well have this consequence (the 1949 devaluation may have been partly responsible for the ending of Cripps's wage freeze in 1950). But a small devaluation, or a series of very small devaluations on the lines described below, might not. It also depends on how seriously the trade union leaders take the possibility of continued deflation and unemployment. They may believe that, in the last resort, the government will devalue rather than deflate for any length of time, and to convince them otherwise might require further prolonged deflation, which would be very costly and unpleasant. It might not even secure their co-operation in an incomes policy. There is a fable which tells how the wind and the sun vied with each other to make a traveller remove his cloak. The wind blew hard, but the traveller clutched his cloak more firmly about him. Then the sun came out, and its warmth soon made the traveller throw off his cloak. The cold wind of unemployment might make the unions cling all the harder to their well-tried methods of independent collective bargaining. It may require the warmth of economic prosperity, plus the discomforts of rising prices, to make them discard or modify them. Rising prices are un-popular, and may provide the most effective sanction to induce all concerned to co-operate in an incomes policy.

Even if we accept the proposition that devaluation would seriously reduce the chance of working out an incomes policy, that does not mean that devaluation would be ineffective. So long as it is true (as argued above) that an x per cent devalua-tion would not, by itself, and apart from any effects on an incomes policy, cause internal prices to rise by nearly as much as x per cent, then loss of competitiveness due to a failure to achieve an incomes policy could always be compensated by a bigger devaluation. This would, however, cause the internal price level to rise faster, and constitutes one of the important reasons why so many are opposed to devaluation.

It is often said that devaluation would seriously worsen our terms of trade, and that this would result in a substantial loss of real income for this country. Some worsening in the terms of trade is, indeed, likely, but this does not constitute an important argument against devaluation. In the first place, the worsening would probably be appreciably less than the devaluation itself. Devaluation works, essentially, by lowering the prices of home-traded goods compared to the prices of internationally traded goods. Prices of *both* imports *and* exports in sterling would rise relatively to internal prices. It is not essential for there to be a *greater* rise in import than in export prices, although there probably would be. Secondly, even if the worsening in the terms of trade equalled the devaluation, its effects on real income would be relatively small. For example, a 10 per cent devaluation would then lead to a loss in real income of the order of 2 per cent. This loss would soon be offset if devaluation permitted a higher level of output and a faster rate of growth. Thirdly, there is no reason to suppose that devaluation would worsen the terms of trade by more than would a successful incomes policy. Both work in essentially the same way – by lowering internal relative to external prices – and their effects on relative import and export prices would be roughly the same. Hence this disadvantage of devaluation is shared by other policies as well (export subsidies would worsen the terms of trade more, though import restrictions might improve the terms of trade).

We have argued so far that devaluation is an effective way of improving the current account of the balance of payments. What of its effects on the capital account and what of sterling's special position as an international currency? It is not always clear what the relevance or meaning of this 'special position' is. In this context it seems to matter for two reasons, first, because large sterling balances are held by non-residents and, second, because the management of these balances and other financial operations provide an important source of income for this country. It is feared that devaluation, and *a fortiori* a series of devaluations, would make non-residents very reluctant to hold sterling balances. Any large-scale attempt to convert them into other currencies or gold would put us in a very awkward position, since they amount to several times our reserves of gold and convertible currencies. Furthermore, London's position as a financial centre might be undermined if there was a lack of confidence in the stability of the exchange rate for the pound. This might lead to a loss of income from the financial operations already mentioned. One may also take a wider view of the matter. Sterling provides an important source of international liquidity, and (it could be argued) we have a moral duty to preserve its use. We have also a moral duty not to swindle our creditors.

It must be admitted that the possible loss of income and the moral obligations mentioned above do constitute a special feature of sterling which distinguishes it from most other currencies; but the danger of speculative capital movements is not peculiar to sterling. Residents as well as non-residents can and do speculate, and it is impracticable to prevent them altogether by means of controls. There are many examples of speculative attacks on currencies which are certainly not 'international' in the way that sterling is. Hence, so far as speculation is concerned, our position is little different from that of other countries. When our balance of payments looks weak, speculators naturally want to hold foreign currencies rather than sterling, and, by selling pounds and buying foreign currencies, aggravate the drain on our reserves. Because of the sudden and large change in the rate which may occur at such a time, they can hope to make a large profit (or avoid a large loss) in a short space of time. If they are wrong, and the pound is not devalued, they can bring their money back at roughly the same exchange rate as they took it out, so that their loss from mistaken speculation (though not always negligible by any means) is much smaller than their profit if the pound were to be devalued.

In these circumstances, it is understandable that the government should be extremely reluctant ever to change the exchange rate at all. For if they can convince everyone that they will move heaven and earth rather than alter the rate, the speculators will cease taking fright every time the balance of payments weakens. It will then be possible to right the situation without having one's hand forced by a very large drain on the reserves. Furthermore, exchange stability is respectable, and respectable countries can borrow large sums from others and then snap their fingers at the speculators. The unfortunate aspect of the matter is, however, that the process of avoiding devaluation may (as in the past) involve deflation, a sizeable sacrifice of income and an increase of unemployment. More recently, there has been the import surcharge, which has strained our relations with our trading partners. There may be cuts in aid and defence expenditure abroad. If things go wrong, there is likely to be a long-drawn-out period of agony while one measure after another is tried, and debts pile up, before we are finally driven to devaluation, which may have to be a large one, accompanied by all the disadvantages and risks described above. The adjustable peg system can hardly be described as one that is conducive to smooth changes and steady growth. On the contrary, unless we are fortunate it is likely to involve us in a succession of nasty jolts.

An alternative method which has been suggested is that of a freely floating exchange rate. The danger here is that the fluctuations might be exaggerated by speculators who would take a fall in the rate as a sign that a further fall was to come. These expectations could be self-justifying, since in the short run devaluation is unlikely to improve the current balance of payments very much and may even worsen it. Time is needed for trade to respond to changes in relative prices. Consequently the exchange rate would be largely determined by the actions of the speculators in the short run, and its movements could be large and erratic. The experience of France after the first world war supports this conclusion. Large movements in the rate would disrupt trade and might conceivably lead to a runaway inflation in which import prices, wage rates, internal prices and the price of foreign currency chased each other up an ever-faster-turning spiral.

If the exchange rate is to be changed it should be in a manner which avoids both the need for sharp jolts and the danger of large fluctuations. This could be done if the authorities were to control the rate so that it gradually changed in whatever direction seemed necessary. The rate would *not* be used as a method for securing equilibrium in the balance of payments in the short run. On the contrary, the government would be committed to preventing the rate changing by more than a few per cent per annum by using its gold reserves and by any other means at its disposal. Whether a particular figure for the maximum permissible rate of change should be announced, or form part of an international agreement, is a matter that would need careful consideration. Whatever was decided, the permitted changes in the rate would *not* take place once a year (for example), as that would lead to a build-up of speculative pressure around that time. Instead, the rate would be gradually shifted each day, probably irregularly (so as to cope with seasonal factors) and probably by no more than, say, one-tenth of 1 per cent in any normal day. Since these changes could all be in the same direction (though they need not be), it would be possible to secure quite substantial alterations in the exchange rate over a few years.

There would be technical difficulties to be overcome in operating such a rate, but they would not be insuperable. After all, we managed a flexible exchange rate for the pound from 1919 to 1925 and again from 1931 to 1939. Canada had a flexible exchange rate from 1950 to 1962. Other difficulties and objections are more important.

In the first place, would small relative price changes have any appreciable effect on trade at all? It might be argued that, although the evidence that large price changes have large effects is convincing, there is no evidence that small price changes would have proportionate effects. Traders would in all probability ignore them altogether. It is admittedly difficult to obtain evidence of the effect of small price changes, since other things are always changing as well, and the effects of the price changes are usually swamped. Nevertheless, it would be rather extraordinary if they did not have at least approximately proportionate effects. It is possible that a trader will ignore relative price differentials smaller than, say, 5 per cent. But if five successive changes of 1 per cent occur in the same direction, he will presumably then take notice. Since we are concerned with the behaviour of large aggregates of trade, the discontinuities introduced by such behaviour will be smoothed out, the crucial point at which each trader takes notice occurring at different times for different traders and commodities. It is likely, then, that small changes in relative prices *would* exert appreciable effects on trade, at least after some time. Indeed, unless this is true, it is difficult to see what hope there can be of righting the balance of payments by means of an incomes policy.

There would be less danger that a gradual depreciation of the pound would provoke a retaliatory series of devaluations in other countries than that a sudden large devaluation of the pound would have this effect. Other countries would not be faced with a sudden crisis, to which a quick response was necessary. There would be time to see how affairs developed and, provided the United Kingdom did not attempt to secure and maintain an unduly large balance of payments surplus, there would be no need to retaliate.

It is possible that some other countries might decide to adopt the same system themselves. In that case there would need to be close and frequent international consultation about the management of the rates. The discussion of the problems which might arise would take us too far afield, but in the writer's opinion a world of managed flexible rates might have much to commend it.

A slow depreciation of the pound would certainly make prices in this country rise faster than if the exchange rate were kept fixed by means of deflation. But, for the reasons already given, it is unlikely that the effects would be sufficient to cancel out the gain in external competitiveness from depreciation. The probable effects on an incomes policy are difficult to determine, and the main considerations have already been given.

What would be the effects of a slow depreciation of the pound on capital movements and, in particular, on overseas holders of sterling? Would there not inevitably be a massive withdrawal of such funds? If a steady depreciation was confidently expected, who would want to hold sterling? It is probably because they return unfavourable answers to these questions that many, in so far as they accept the need for any exchange adjustments at all, prefer the adjustable peg system.

Let us ignore, for the moment, the problems raised by introducing a system of managed flexible rates. Let us assume that they have been overcome somehow, and that the system has been in operation for a few years. In this situation, the crucial necessity, if speculation is to be deterred, is to convince everyone that, at worst, only a *slow* depreciation of the rate is going to occur, and to offset the expected rate of depreciation by a sufficiently high interest differential. If, for example, a rate of depreciation of the pound of 3 per cent a year relative to the dollar were expected, then, ignoring considerations of taxation and forward cover, it would still pay better to hold pounds rather than dollars provided interest rates were more than 3 per cent per annum higher in this country than in the United States. With the adjustable peg system, since a sudden large change in the rate can take place in one day, interest rate considerations are of less importance; but with the slowly moving rate they would be highly relevant, *provided that* no one feared that the rate might be suddenly devalued by a large amount.

There would be less reason for anyone to fear this than at present. In the first place, it should be possible by reasonably skilful management of the rate to increase the current surplus on our balance of payments until it reached the average which we have aimed at for so long. With an average surplus of this size, a substantial devaluation of the pound would appear unnecessary and unlikely. Secondly, even if a surplus of this size were not achieved for a year or two because of an adverse turn in the world environment, or because the required change in the rate had been misjudged, there would be a line of retreat open, through slow depreciation, which is at present not available. Hence, again, the need for a sudden large devaluation would be lessened.

In these circumstances there would be less financial incentive to speculate against the pound than there is from time to time under the present system. But even so, some monetary authorities of countries in the sterling area which at present hold a large proportion of their international currency reserves in the form of sterling might not wish to continue to do so, despite the fact that higher interest rates compensated for any fall in capital value. To meet their wishes, and to prevent the undesirable consequences of their attempting to convert their pounds into other currencies or gold, the United Kingdom might offer them a security denominated in some other currency than sterling. If, for example, a country preferred its reserves to maintain a value fixed in terms of dollars, the United Kingdom's debt to that country's central monetary authority could be denominated in dollars. Any depreciation (or appreciation) of the pound would then leave the dollar value of that debt unchanged. Withdrawals would be calculated in terms of dollars, as would interest payments. The appropriate interest rate would be that available on dollar securities of a similar category, which would probably be appreciably lower than that available on sterling securities. Hence there might be little difference in financial advantage between holding a dollar-denominated security or a sterling security – and, likewise, little difference in the cost to the United Kingdom. Nevertheless, some countries might prefer to hold a security of this kind and, indeed, might prefer it to their current position.

At present, overseas monetary authorities which hold their reserves largely in sterling are not covered against the risk of a devaluation of the pound, nor are they altogether free to convert their reserves into gold or other currencies, since such action, if widespread, would either force the United Kingdom to devalue or to declare a moratorium. Furthermore, if the pound were to be devalued, the United Kingdom would be open to the charge of having, in a sense, swindled its creditors. The situation is rather different as regards private overseas holders of sterling since they are quite free to convert their pounds into other currencies if they so wish (or to hedge on the forward market). Even here, however, there would be some natural resentment if the pound were devalued, since many assurances have been given that this will not be done. Under the present system it would be possible to offer an exchange guarantee to overseas holders of sterling, but to do so might cast doubts on the government's intention to maintain the exchange rate. Hence there is something of an impasse. Our freedom to devalue is impaired, yet some important holders of sterling must uneasily wonder whether we might not be driven to it, without being able to safeguard themselves against such an eventuality.

Under the system proposed here, there would effectively be an exchange guarantee for those monetary authorities who wanted it (and were prepared to sacrifice interest for it), and this would seem to be a real advantage, not only from the moral point of view, but also because it would discourage withdrawals which would put a strain on our reserves. Whether the 'guarantee' should be extended to private overseas holders of sterling, and in terms of what currencies the 'guarantee' should be offered, are questions which there is insufficient space to discuss here. Nor can we discuss the various proposals which have been made to 'internationalise' our sterling liabilities (and possibly the United States' dollar liabilities), and which might, if satisfactory terms could be negotiated, provide the best solution to this problem.

The controlled flexible rate system might, as we have seen, require interest rates in this country to be appreciably higher than in some other countries. This would be necessary so long as the pound was expected to depreciate slowly in terms of the other main currencies. This is a disadvantage of the system, but not a serious one. In the first place, it is pessimistic to assume that depreciation would be inevitable and perpetual. There might be long periods of approximate stability or even appreciation, when lower interest rates would be appropriate. Secondly, the position would not be very much different in this respect from the present one, when high interest rates are required whenever our balance of payments situation weakens. Thirdly, the periods of high interest rates would normally coincide with periods of rather more rapid price increases or of high pressure of demand in this country. In such periods the *real* as distinct from the *money* rate of interest might not be unduly high, and might in any case be deemed appropriate to the internal situation. Fourthly, it is questionable how far investment or savings decisions are influenced by interest rates, so the internal effects of high interest rates on investment or growth might be small. Finally, there are means open to the government to counteract these effects, by cheap loans to local authorities, or to building societies, or by higher capital allowances to business.

It is not possible to say whether the income we at present earn from financial operations of one kind or another would suffer seriously under the proposed system. There is no obvious reason why it should. The growth of the Euro-dollar market in London suggests that it is possible to conduct profitable business in debts denominated in dollars or in other currencies, and this practice might increase. Even if we did lose some income, it would be swamped, from the point of view of the balance of payments, by the gains through extra exports or lower imports.

So much for the working of a controlled flexible rate which has been in existence for some years. The above discussion is necessarily incomplete, but is sufficient, it is hoped, to show that the system would be practicable and would provide a means of keeping the balance of payments in equilibrium over a period of years. It would not deal with short-term fluctuations but, if the long-term average surplus was satisfactory, these could be managed with existing reserves and borrowing facilities. It would not deal with all conceivable long-term stresses and strains, such as a world slump, or a runaway inflation in this country. In short, it is not a panacea, but it could cope with a wider range of possibilities, without running into severe difficulties, than could the present system.

The long-term advantages of the system have been stressed because it is only they which would merit the immediate disadvantages and risks attendant on introducing it. Ideally, one should introduce it at a time when the balance of payments was very strong so that the most likely movement of the rate was upwards (this is what happened in Canada in 1950). At any other time, the mere announcement of our intention to depart from the present parity, however slowly, might touch off a wave of speculation. If large foreign loans could be arranged, this need not deter us. There is no reason to suppose that the speculation would be on a more massive scale than we have experienced in recent times. Our requests for assistance would, however, meet with a chilly reception from our trading partners. They would fear that there would be a dislocation of trade and of capital movements. Such fears would be unreasonable. On the contrary, a slowly moving rate would provide a smoother mechanism of adjustment than the present series of jolts to which we subject our overseas payments. The United States would fear that a gradual depreciation of the pound would threaten the dollar. Since we would be infringing the Articles of Agreement of the IMF we would not have a right to its assistance. Canada made no drawing while it had a floating rate (on the other hand, the Fund has permitted some countries with multiple and variable exchange rates to draw from it). Hence we could not count on getting the generous assistance we have had in previous crises.

There would, all the same, be some trumps in our hand. The alternative to assistance might be a sharp devaluation, followed by the same flexible rate system, and this might appear even more unpleasant to all concerned. A slow depreciation would enable us gradually to remove the import surcharge. There would be less danger of our having to cut overseas aid or military expenditure. Given determination on our part, and faith in the final outcome, we could push it through. Nor should our prestige suffer. On the contrary, if the above reasoning is accepted, our prestige should be considerably enhanced by a solution to our perennial difficulties which did not slow down our economic growth, drive us ever deeper into debt or compel us to impose restrictions on imports or other forms of overseas expenditure.

Conclusion

We have attempted to pick out the main considerations relevant to a choice of weapons to deal with our balance of payments problem. Many important details have not been discussed. The main conclusion is that there *are* ways of improving the balance of payments which, despite their limitations and disadvantages, are preferable to the weapon to which we have resorted in the past – deflation. Several of them conflict with present international conventions, but it is to be hoped that this will not deter us from leading the way in changing these conventions if we are convinced that the international economic system can thereby be improved.

The immediate choices before us (apart from deflation) may therefore be summarised.

(a) We can continue as at present, hoping that a successful incomes policy will emerge, that the rate of growth of productivity can be increased, that incomes and prices in other manufacturing countries will increase fairly rapidly, and that as a result of these favourable developments we shall be able to remove the import surcharge and our balance of payments will not seriously trouble us again.

(b) We can pay export subsidies, cut military expenditure, aid or investment abroad, encourage greater discrimination in favour of domestic products on the part of government purchasing departments or public corporations, and spend more money on export promotion. These measures should strengthen the balance of payments or enable us to reduce the import surcharge. They should therefore give more time for an incomes policy and any other possible long-term factors working in our favour to take effect.

(c) We can devalue the pound.

(d) We can replace our fixed rate of exchange by a slowly moving one.

The chief attraction of (a) is that it avoids the unpleasant measures, such as those listed in (b), (c) and (d), until they are clearly seen to be necessary. They may never be. It is impossible to predict the future course of the balance of payments with any accuracy, and it is possible that a favourable change in the wind and tide will float us off the rocks on to which we have drifted. If things go wrong, we shall have to take some of the other measures, but is there anything to be lost by waiting and seeing if they are really necessary?

Unfortunately there is. There are at least three dangers in delay:

(a) We may, in the end, find ourselves in a position in which only very drastic action will suffice. For example, we may exhaust our ability to borrow abroad, we may exhaust the willingness of other countries to tolerate the measures we take without retaliation against our exports, and our underlying payments deficit may grow to such large proportions that only a large devaluation (or deflation) will suffice to extricate us. We have already seen that the risks and disadvantages of a large devaluation are much worse than those of a small one.

(b) With this uncertain prospect before them, it may prove difficult to convince businessmen that a long period of uninterrupted growth is in sight. They may fear, reasonably enough, that the government will be forced to take strong deflationary action, whatever it may say to the contrary. Hence, if the argument in the previous chapter is accepted, one of the most important factors tending to speed up the rate of growth may be checked.

(c) During the period preceding devaluation (or whatever drastic cure is adopted in the end), not merely may the total of investment be checked, but its pattern may be distorted. If, for example, we persist with heavy import restrictions of one kind or another for some years, and then devalue by a large amount, the investment which takes place prior to devaluation may be designed chiefly to save imports rather than to expand exports. After the devaluation, a different pattern of output, with larger imports and exports, will be appropriate. Some of the import-saving investment will then be useless (or, at any rate, low-yielding), and the investment required to expand exports will not have been made.

These are serious disadvantages. In assessing them, it is worth reflecting on the course of events over the past few years. In 1958 our current balance was unusually strong. Had we adopted a slowly moving rate of exchange then, and allowed it to depreciate by a few per cent per annum, our present position might have been very favourable indeed, and we might have been under no necessity to depreciate still further. The course of events has not improved our position. On the contrary it seems to be worse than ever. Is there any reason to suppose that we shall do better in the future? Progress has been made in working out an incomes policy. What can one realistically expect from that? If it were to reduce the rate of increase of prices by 1 or 2 per cent a year, that would be a remarkable and very worthwhile achievement. But, in the past, our prices have tended to rise faster than those of our main competitors, who are also pursuing price stability. Can we hope to do much more than to stop any further deterioration in our competitive position? Even if we can lower our manufactured goods prices on average by 1 per cent per annum relatively to theirs, how many years may it take before this restores equilibrium in our balance of payments?

The measures listed under (b) (page 122) would increase our chances of avoiding devaluation or deflation *if* the long-term factors influencing our balance of payments were favourable. But they may be unfavourable, or so slowly favourable that we are forced to take other action before enough time has passed.

Should we then devalue? It is worth quoting the views of the Radcliffe Report on this. After stating that, in a situation in which the United Kingdom's competitive position has been deteriorating, 'everything possible should be done to bring the rise in domestic costs and prices under control and to put an end to the strain on the reserves by lagging behind the movement abroad instead of outstripping it', the Report goes on, 'But experience has revealed no other instrument as powerful as devaluation that can be used to restore competitive power; in conditions in which the failure of exports to make headway is plainly restricting the level of domestic activity and other countries are not experiencing similar difficulties, it offers a way of escape that cannot be excluded.'

While agreeing with this conclusion, the writer (unlike the authors of the Report) prefers the fourth alternative of a slowly moving exchange rate. It would be less disruptive than devaluation and it would provide a permanent means of keeping the balance of payments in balance in the long run. It would not solve the problem in every conceivable situation, but it would greatly increase our chances of ensuring that balance of payments difficulties did not hinder growth. Its main serious disadvantage is that it would probably make prices rise faster in this country than would a policy of deflation. The measures which might be taken to counteract this, or to ameliorate its bad effects, are discussed in the next chapter.

The Report of the Committee on the Working of the Monetary System (the Radcliffe Report, Cmnd. 827, 1959) contains, in Chapter 8, an excellent succinct description of the sterling area system and of the course of events since the war. It also discusses the alternative measures which might be taken to improve the balance of payments. Several of the *Memoranda* submitted to the Committee are worth studying as well. J. C. R. Dow's *The Management of the British Economy 1945–60* (Cambridge University Press, 1964), while mainly concerned with the internal economic situation, has an interesting analysis of short-term fluctuations in the UK balance of payments in Chapter XV, and something to say about policy in Chapter XVI. *The British Economy in the Nineteen-Fifties* (Oxford University Press, 1962) has chapters dealing with events and with policies. *Conditions Favourable to Faster Growth* (HMSO, 1963), NEDC, deals only with policies, with the notable omission of exchange-rate policy. The latter, and, in particular, the proposal for a slowly moving exchange rate, is lucidly discussed by Professor Meade in the September 1964 issue of *The Three Banks Review*, in an article on 'The International Monetary Mechanism'. This proposal was also described in an article by the writer entitled 'What should be done about the Sterling Area?' in a symposium on the future of the sterling area in the *Bulletin of the Oxford University Institute of Statistics*, November 1959. Arguments against the use of the exchange rate are to be found in the Radcliffe Report, in Sir Donald MacDougall's 'Flexible Exchange Rates', *The Westminster Bank Review*, August 1954, and in C. W. McMahon's *Sterling in the Sixties* (Oxford University Press, 1964), which also provides a highly readable description of the United Kingdom's balance of payments problem, of which a more optimistic view is taken than that given here. Mr McMahon also gives a most useful account of our current exchange control. *The Report of the Committee on Turnover Taxation* (Cmnd. 2300, HMSO, 1964) should be read by enthusiasts for tax reform as a solution to our balance of payments problem. For an authoritative account of the changing scene, see the *Bank of England Quarterly Bulletin*, which also contains articles on more technical aspects of the balance of payments. The international liquidity problem has stimulated a vast amount of writing and numerous proposals for reform. Many of the most important are to be found in *World Monetary Reform*, edited by H. G. Grubel (Oxford University Press, 1964).

5

INFLATION

Recent interest in the economics of inflation can be said to derive first from the catastrophic experiences of some of the defeated countries in Europe after the first world war. Prices rose to such astronomic heights in such a short space of time – as every schoolboy stamp-collector knows – that societies were overwhelmed, economic and social classes ruined, and the way paved for totalitarian regimes to take over the enfeebled economies of the inter-war years.

This gave rise to much literature and theorising in the 1920s, but the problems of the 1930s seemed to be remote from the hyper-inflation of the early twenties, which could after all be attributed mainly to the shock of defeat and the difficulties of balancing budgets in countries where tax revenues were difficult to collect and expenditures pressing.

Interest in the problem of inflation flickered into life with the publication of Keynes's *General Theory* in 1936, which, although it was mainly devoted to the problems of under-employment and deficient demand, contained fascinating sidelights on the opposite problem of excess demand.

This latter problem was faced by every belligerent country either at the outset of war (in the case of Nazi Germany three years before this), or soon after. But it can be said that theoretical interest in the problems of inflation grew much more slowly than the problem itself – a common fate of theoretical economics. It was only the experience of the late forties and fifties which impressed economic theorists and practitioners alike and suggested that here was a new phenomenon.

The experience of the United Kingdom

In the United Kingdom prices have risen steadily and without a break, but of course at varying rates, since 1934. This is an entirely new experience in the memory of any living Englishman. For some years after the war it could be held that we were still suffering from the excess demand of the war years and its aftermath. Economic behaviour is full of time lags of varying and sometimes considerable length. It was therefore possible that prices were still rising as late as 1948 as a result of the excess demand of the war years. In other words, a special circumstance which would soon pass.

The year 1949 produced another special circumstance – the devaluation of sterling followed by that of the majority of other currencies. Traditional economic theory could easily accommodate the rise in domestic prices which resulted from this readjustment of exchange rates. There was nothing new here. Then 1950 saw the outbreak of the Korean War and with it a new round of inflationary pressures. 1951 and 1952 saw the collapse of this small, wartime boomlet. By 1952 therefore, most people could feel that the inflation of the war years was now really at an end. We were all back to normal. This impression was reinforced for a short period thereafter as world prices of primary products slumped downwards from their Korean heights. The speed with which they had climbed and the altitude they reached at the peak of the Korean crisis were followed by a collapse of similar severity and then a slow but continuing downward drift.

This tragedy, as it was, for the selling countries, most of whom were poor or underdeveloped, or both, was a great boon to the industrial countries which imported such materials or foodstuffs. The collapse in prices was a considerable benefit in cutting their import bill (although typically, in the British case, we suffered at the same time because our main markets at that stage for our exports were precisely these primary-producing countries). At the same time, the fall in food prices and raw material prices helped to stabilise, if not reduce, pressures for higher wages, and to keep down industrial costs. Thus the collapse in the world commodity markets for a short period greatly assisted the fight being waged by the industrial countries to stabilise their own price levels.

But around the mid-fifties all Europe boomed at the same time. Commodity prices began to steady, if not to strengthen,

INFLATION

while internal pressures in the European economy began to push up prices and costs.

Basically, this was the start of a decade of peace-time creeping inflation. It was not caused by war; it was therefore quite abnormal in the general economic history of the world. All industrial countries were afflicted, although to varying degrees. It seemed as though the new norm was not steady prices but steadily rising prices. Inflation seemed here to stay. As Tables 1, 2 and 3 all show, the steady rise in price levels was universal, both throughout the British economy and in a very wide variety of countries.

Table 1 shows the steady rise of prices over the last decade in each of the main sectors of the British economy. Consumer goods prices rose by some 30 per cent over these ten years, those of all fixed assets by some 27 per cent, and those of all goods and services sold on the home market by 34 per cent. The rise in export prices, mainly no doubt resulting from the impact of severe international competition, was restrained to a mere 16 per cent, so that the price level of total final output rose by just over 30 per cent over the ten years, or by more than $2\frac{1}{2}$ per cent per annum.

A contrasting feature of the table is the movement in the prices of imported goods and services shown in Table 2. These moved fairly irregularly, rising in the first four years of the period by 5 per cent, then falling back to remain stable for five years. At the end of the period, import prices were only some 8 per cent above those at the beginning, mainly due to the fairly violent early fluctuations in imported oil prices, and to the continuing instability of food and raw material prices.

The British experience of rising prices has been duplicated by that of almost all other countries of which we have statistics. The countries in Table 3 show enormous variety from almost every point of view. They include the richest in the world and one of the poorest, some of the fastest-growing and some of the slowest. But one thing they share is a continuous rise in prices, albeit at widely divergent rates. The slowest price rises are to be found in Belgium, Canada and the United States, where prices barely drifted upwards over this period. Then there is a middle band of countries, which includes the United Kingdom, where prices rose by about 2 per cent per annum, and then at

TABLE I. UNITED KINGDOM: PRICE INDICES*

(1958 = 100)

	1954	1955	1956	1957	1958	1959	1960	1961	1962	1963	1964
Consumer goods and services	87	90	94	97	100	101	101	104	108	110	113
Fixed assets	86	90	94	97	100	99	100	102	105	107	109
All goods and services sold on the home market	85	89	94	97	100	101	102	105	109	111	114
Exports of goods and services	91	93	99	101	100	100	101	102	103	104	106
Total final output	86	90	94	98	100	101	102	105	108	110	113
Imports of goods and services	99	102	103	105	100	100	101	101	101	104	107

* The index number for any year, shown in this table, is based on weights of that year, and provides a direct measure of the change in costs or prices between that year and 1958. Comparisons other than with 1958 may be affected by differences in the weights which are generally more important over longer than over shorter periods.

Source: U.K. National Income and Expenditure (HMSO, London).

TABLE 2. UNITED KINGDOM: IMPORT PRICES

(1961 = 100)

	Total	Food, Beverages and Tobacco	Basic Materials	Fuels	Manufactured Goods
1954	104	108	104	110	98
1955	108	109	108	112	106
1956	110	109	111	119	107
1957	111	109	115	138	100
1958	103	104	100	120	96
1959	102	105	98	111	98
1960	102	104	101	104	101
1961	100	100	100	100	100
1962	99	102	96	98	99
1963	103	111	97	97	101
1964	107	115	103	95	105

TABLE 3. CONSUMER PRICE INDICES

(1958 = 100)

	Belgium	Canada	France	Germany	India	Indo-nesia	Italy	Japan	Nether-lands	Switzer-land	United Kingdom	USA
1958	100	100	100	100	100	100	100	100	100	100	100	100
1959	101	101	106	101	104	126	102	101	101	99	101	101
1960	102	102	110	102	106	169	102	105	103	101	101	102
1961	103	103	114	105	108	209	104	111	104	103	104	103
1962	104	104	119	108	112	582	109	118	106	107	109	105
1963	106	106	125	112	116	1,610	117	127	110	111	112	106
1964	111	108	130	114	130	2,520 (Sept.)	124	132	116	114	115	107

Source: International Monetary Fund: International Financial Statistics.

the top is Indonesia, where prices in the years 1961 to 1964 more than doubled in each year. This universal peacetime inflation is unique in economic history, although it was of course equally general during the war and early post-war years.

It has been argued by some that the rate of price rise in some countries, and this certainly includes the United States and Canada, where the rate has been fairly slow, and possibly also the UK, is a statistical delusion. It measures no more than the steady rise in the quality of the goods being sold. This argument can be decided introspectively by asking oneself what discount would one require on today's price of, say, a television set or a motor-car, in order to take a brand-new model of, say, a 1958 version of the good concerned. If the discount were more than, say, 10 per cent, then one might conclude that quality has so improved over the following years that the higher price does no more than match the 'better' commodity being sold.

This argument is hardly conclusive, since one of the reasons for preferring today's version over earlier versions has nothing to do with quality as such, but is partly a function of changing tastes and of tastes manipulated by advertisers. Further, consumer expenditure covers a very wide range of goods in which quality does not quickly alter and here the argument cannot apply.

Nonetheless, there may be something in the argument that consumer price indices, almost all of which are base-weighted, and hence take no account of consumers switching expenditure towards relatively cheaper substitutes overstate the genuine rise in the cost of living.

What is inflation?

So far, we have not in fact defined the term inflation. In ordinary speech, inflation can be defined as a process of generally rising prices – not just a few prices but many, and not just an occasional rise but steadily and cumulatively. This is the definition that the man in the street would recognise, and for our purposes it will do as the starting point.

In much discussion, however, especially that which took place in the 1920s and 1930s, a phrase, 'inflation of the money supply', was also current. This derives from the perennial fascination exerted by the quantity theory of money. This theory asserts that a given proportional increase in the quantity of money will lead to an equivalent increase in the general level of prices. It is based on rather restrictive assumptions, but not impossible ones. In particular, it assumes that all prices are flexible, that the volume of transactions to be financed does not change quickly, and thirdly, that the velocity of circulation of the money supply (i.e. crudely the speed with which money changes hands in order to finance that volume of transactions) is fairly constant. When the quantity theory reigned supreme, which it did for most economists until the *General Theory* was published, and still does for some, it could be argued that inflations were caused by increases in the money supply. And more importantly that inflations could be prevented or cured by proper control of the money supply.

The Keynesian revolution demoted the quantity theory and with it the independent role of money in determining changes in the price level. We might argue that the role of money was turned upside down. It could now more plausibly be held that the price level determines the quantity of money rather than the other way round.

How then could we explain a steady and general rise in the price level, i.e. an inflationary process? If one were to ask why any given single price rose, one would naturally say it was because, with a given supply, demand had increased, or that in the face of a given demand, the supply curve had shifted upwards. This is as true of the *general* price level, except that one now has to widen the concepts of demand and supply to those of the general levels of demand and supply throughout the economy.

Demand inflation

Let us look at the 'demand' side first. Suppose we take an economy with full employment of its resources so that total current output is given in the short period. Stocks cannot be run down without limit. If demand grows, one or a combination of four results will follow. First, imports will be sucked in to add to domestic output in order to expand supply to meet the extra demand.

It is also possible, secondly, that some of home output which earlier was sold abroad in the form of exports, is diverted to the now more insistent home market, thus adding to the supplies available domestically. Or thirdly, prices will be adjusted upwards as manufacturers and sellers generally charge what the market will bear. Or fourthly, some or all of the increased demand may simply remain unsatisfied. Finally, and most probably, these results could emerge in combination with each other.

But suppose that there is no external sector of any importance in the economy, or that for the moment exports and imports are closely controlled. Then prices will rise, if they are flexible enough. More importantly, the rise will be cumulative. This follows because prices are also incomes or costs. The price of labour is clearly the income of labour, just as the price of, e.g., machine tools generates the income of the machine tool industry. So that when prices rise, so too do the aggregate incomes of the sellers by exactly the same amount.

At the same time, some prices are costs. If good A is a raw material or a semi-manufactured good, a component for industries B, C, D, etc., then a rise in A's price will raise the costs of industries B, C and D. They will clearly be faced with the need to raise their own prices if they are to avoid a squeeze on their profits. But if industries B, C and D raise their prices, then the burden is simply passed further along. More industries will be faced with rising costs and the need to consider raising their own prices.

The market will be able to bear these higher prices because of course money incomes have risen by the same process. It is not certain that expenditures will have risen because that will depend upon the distribution of the additional money incomes, and it is possible that much of the extra income ends up in the hands of high-income groups, or firms who intend to save a great deal of their extra receipts. But firms save partly in order to spend in the fairly near future, and thus pass on in greater demand the extra receipts they acquire from raising their own prices. And this adds further fuel to the flames.

This sort of inflation is, naturally enough, called 'demand inflation'. The causal factor which initiates the whole process is an increase in demand which cannot be met by increasing current output. Output can grow only at the rate at which capacity is itself growing – there is no slack to be taken up.

This poses government with a dilemma. It must be a prime aim of any democratic government to employ its labour force to the full for a number of totally admirable reasons. But this means there is the danger that any rapid increase in demand cannot be accommodated before it exerts inflationary pressures – unless the rate of growth of capacity itself is perceptibly accelerated by the very pressure of demand.

If working near the ceiling itself pushes the ceiling higher, we are indeed in the best of all worlds. But the evidence on this in Britain can hardly be said to be conclusive, since we have not pushed the economy to the ceiling and held it there for very long. There have been, of course, short periods of full-capacity working, but they have been usually ended by balance of payments difficulties and hence contractionary policy.

Nonetheless, all we need to admit here is that an economy is likely to have more elbow-room if it can use up idle resources as well as the normal rate of growth of capacity, than if it must rely solely on the growth, even if slightly accelerated, of capacity itself.

It is conceivable that excess demand might emerge, not from a sudden increase in demand with a given supply, but from a fall in supply in the face of a given demand. The most likely causes of such a fall would be from a reduction in imports which might be brought about by deliberate policy, or from a crop failure in an economy heavily dependent upon its own food and raw material production. Most industrialised countries have by definition moved away from this latter position, while the possession of international reserves enables them to postpone, if not entirely to avoid, the need for frequent drastic cuts in imports with the consequent danger of excess demand at home. Thus we ought in the main to concentrate on the possibility of demand growing too fast rather than supply falling as the likely cause of a potentially inflationary situation.

The sources of demand in any given economy can be categorised as consumer expenditure, government expenditure on goods and services, investment expenditure, and exports. Any one of these can quite easily increase rapidly and by a large absolute amount, certainly enough in itself to generate excess demand when the economy is already operating at high levels of activity.

But more important is the fact that an increase in any one of these is likely to cause the others to increase. Excess demand in one sector of the economy may produce excess demand in another, and these sectors may go on reinforcing each other for a long time. Thus an increase in exports or investment or government expenditure will raise the incomes of those working in these sectors. This will induce an increase in consumption expenditure, by what is commonly known as the 'multiplier process'.

But an increase in consumer expenditure may in itself reflect back on investment by increasing the need for stocks and for adequate capital equipment. Equally, a rise in expenditure in the private sectors of the economy may generate demands for an increase in complementary government expenditures. Thus one could argue that the level of expenditure in the economy may be inherently unstable. A small increase in one sector will produce increases in other sectors, perhaps adding up to a large and cumulative increase in total. Hence a fully employed economy is bound to be inflation-prone.

This is a gloomy picture. It suggests that our desire to achieve full employment and maintain it, a desire which all men of goodwill must share, carries with it the inherent and grave danger of frequent cumulative excesses of demand. Full employment carries within itself the seeds of inflation – and some would argue, of its own destruction.

Some economic stabilisers

This would indeed be gloomy if one thought that there were no natural stabilisers at work in a private enterprise economy which would restrain the cumulative force of excess demand, or perhaps eliminate it entirely, or if one thought that policy was impotent to deal with what excess demand does emerge. There are in fact a number of natural stabilisers on which some weight, unfortunately sometimes very little, can be placed.

The first one is the inevitable, if slight, elasticity of supply which exists, even in a fully employed economy. Even when all the work force is employed the number of hours worked can remain flexible. And the actual number of people in the work force is itself fairly flexible. Housewives join the industrial work force, elderly persons decide not to retire, students work during vacations, and so on.

Thus there is some short-term flexibility in total output. But this helps, of course, only to the extent that total demand rises less than total supply, thereby reducing the pressure of demand. Whether this happens depends on the size of the multiplier and accelerator coefficients, and on this one cannot pontificate.

A second stabiliser might be the money supply. It is argued that demand cannot become increasingly excessive if the money supply is held constant. If it is so held, then the increasing demand for money to finance a growing volume of transactions at a rising price level will drain funds from idle balances, and thereby raise the velocity of circulation of the given money supply. This, it is argued, will raise rates of interest throughout the economy, as those who wish to borrow funds have to compete more vigorously with each other and with the need for spending balances.

Since some forms of expenditure are possibly sensitive to the rates of interest which must be paid on borrowed funds, an increase in general interest rates may cut back on some demand, thus eliminating the excess demand. In that case the rate of interest takes over the role of a governor of the price level.

But the effectiveness of this stabiliser clearly depends upon three things. First, the money supply must be fixed, or at least rise more slowly than the money value of the volume of transactions. That in itself may be quite difficult to achieve in certain monetary systems.

Secondly, it depends upon the effectiveness of a constant money supply in causing an increase in the rates of interest. If idle balances are large and widely spread throughout the economy, it may be possible for a great increase in demand for balances to be met simply by draining these idle balances into transactions balances with a very small rise in interest rates. Thus the elasticity of the effective money supply may be well-nigh perfect, even though the total money supply is rigidly controlled by the Central Bank.

And finally, the volume of expenditure in the economy which is sensitive to interest rate changes may turn out to be disappointingly small, at least in the short run, which is what is important, and given the likely changes in the levels of interest rates. We are talking here of changes of the order of from 5 per cent to 6 per cent, not from 5 per cent to 10 per cent. Almost all investigations of the effects of interest rates have been very discouraging. Government expenditure is clearly likely to be fixed so far ahead by other considerations that it is quite inflexible in the short run and certainly impervious to small changes in interest rates. Consumer expenditure, the largest by far of all the categories, is overwhelmingly determined by the level of personal disposable incomes, and only expenditure on consumer durables, much of which is financed by short-term borrowing, is at all likely to be sensitive to interest-rate changes. But this form of expenditure, although growing, and clearly of great importance to a narrow range of industries, is nonetheless not yet very large. And in any case, it is arguable that it is more sensitive to changes in the terms of borrowing than to changes in interest rates alone.

Export receipts are largely determined by demand conditions overseas, which can scarcely be greatly influenced by interest rates here. And in any case, our overwhelming need is to increase the level of exports receipts, and we would in fact hope that exports are completely insulated from any increase in British interest rates.

Finally, private investment expenditure in fixed capital equipment and in stocks might just be sensitive to changes in interest rates, if these changes are large enough, and announced with enough trumpeting. But the effect, at least on fixed capital, is long delayed and uncertain in amount, and in any case undesirable. It would be dangerous to rely on this effect, and even central banks have now come to realise this.

Thus the chain of argument from 'a constant money supply' to 'stabilising the level of expenditure' is tortuous and full of weak links. We cannot find much comfort here.

Another stabiliser on which some countries have been prepared, and other countries have been forced, to rely is the level of imports. If demand increases within the British economy, one of the first effects is to increase supplies by means of sucking in imports from other countries. This is clearly effective in mopping up very large amounts of expenditure, and the smaller the economy is in relation to the rest of the world the more easily can it be effective. But clearly it is a process with a well-defined limit. It cannot go on beyond the point at which a country has enough reserves to finance the extra imports, or can borrow enough to do so. Either way, there is an ultimate limit beyond which no authorities can go in allowing excess demand to continue.

There is an earlier limit beyond which responsible authorities would be reluctant to go, in that most countries are unwilling to run down their reserves very far except in the direst need, and they are certainly unwilling, even if able, to borrow large amounts abroad, except in the interest of long-term development. Thus this most effective of all stabilisers is strictly limited in its scope for action.

Lastly, it is very likely that a process of rising prices will not uniformly affect all prices. Some are perfectly flexible, others almost completely rigid. This of course applies to incomes as well. Thus, as we have seen, in an inflationary situation the distribution of income is very likely to be altered. Those who are on fixed incomes will inevitably find their real incomes, their purchasing power, squeezed. The amount of consumption which they can finance is thus limited to the amount of assets they can liquidate, plus the declining real income they receive. Others in the community are likely to find their incomes rising in line with prices, while some others will find their money incomes rising faster than prices. This last is especially true of the recipients of profits and dividends, i.e. businesses and equity holders.

Thus within the group of persons some will gain and some will lose, while some will merely hold their own. The distribution of gains and losses depends less on present income than on luck and bargaining power. Thus one cannot assert that the rich will certainly gain and the poor lose, or vice versa. Nonetheless, luck and bargaining power are at least among the reasons why the rich are rich. Hence the redistribution of money incomes is quite likely to result in an increase in incomes in the hands of those most likely to save some of the increase. This will restrain to some extent the rise in consumer expenditure in money terms, and perhaps reduce it in real terms. Whether this happens or not depends of course on the unwillingness of the sections of the community who are being squeezed to liquidate their assets or borrow, and on the willingness of the sections who are growing richer in money terms to save even in the face of rising prices. The effect is thus by no means certain.

Companies, however, are almost certain to gain in money and in real terms. Some of their costs are fixed, while their profit margins can be quite easily maintained in a situation of excess demand. Companies are very likely not to pay out all their extra income in higher dividends but to save certain, perhaps increasing, amounts as ploughed-back profits. If they can resist the temptation to spend these, then demand will be restrained in the aggregate by the redistribution of income in favour of companies.

Thirdly, some countries possess a taxation structure which is progressive. That is to say, a large income is liable to taxation at a higher rate than are lower incomes. Thus if money incomes are generally rising, taxation receipts are likely to be rising at an even faster rate. If the government can resist spending its additional receipts, it will find its deficit falling or its surplus rising, and this too will help to restrain the level of total demand. Unfortunately, it seems that contrary to popular belief, the structure of UK taxation is not very progressive overall, so that the net effect on the budget position of rising prices is small.

But any economy can become sophisticated and conscious of inflation. The author has been present at a seminar at which a Latin American has indeed defined the watershed between slow inflation and fast as the moment when people cease talking about rising prices and start talking about falling value of money. Once that happens they are quite likely to rush to convert cash, and claims to cash such as bank deposits, into real assets. This sort of stampede can lead to a colossal increase in aggregate demand for both assets and current output, and with it an explosion of prices. This indeed has engulfed a number of countries after the first and second world wars.

A steadily rising price level, even though it redistributes income so long as it proceeds, may cause that rise in prices to become cumulative as more and more people climb on to the bandwagon of rising prices, and hence money incomes and costs and prices. As more and more people ensure that their incomes are inflation-proof, the scope for further redistribution against them is of course reduced, and that is precisely the purpose of it.

We are now on the spiral of prices and incomes rising hand in hand. But in that case, the inflationary process loses its stabilising power. When inflation loses its power to squeeze, then creeping inflation may start to gallop.

It would be unwise therefore to rely entirely upon the self-stabilising power of a period of rising prices in a private enterprise economy. Policy is certainly necessary to deal with the problem.

But the above analysis hangs upon an assumption that most prices are flexible, at least upwards. In the nineteenth century and in twentieth-century primary-producing countries, there is perhaps still some truth in this. But in industrialised countries it is very far from the truth.

All sellers ideally wish to control, or at least influence, the prices at which they operate. This is as true of businessmen selling their products as it is of trade unionists selling their labour. They are determined to be in a position to administer the prices at which they offer their wares. This means that when demand falls there is a very strong resistance to following the downward movement of demand with cuts in prices. Equally, when demand increases, there is considerable short-term resistance to rising prices. It is much more likely that in the face of an increase in demand, prices will be held and the order-book allowed to lengthen. Thus queues arise or lengthen but prices do not increase. This is confirmed by an enormous range of investigations into business behaviour and by one's own experience. Businessmen are often greatly inhibited in their attitude to the market by feelings of a 'fair' price, a 'just' price, a 'going' price, and so on.

But this restraint, this inhibition, can be shattered if costs rise. Then there are no inhibitions about at least trying to pass on these price increases to others. Why after all should they, the businessmen, bear them, when the increased costs are not their 'fault'?

No doubt some effort is made to reduce the amount by which prices are increased, by absorbing some of the cost increases in the profit margin, or in greater efforts to increase productivity. But both these roads are limited, and in the end, businessmen convince themselves that it is perfectly proper for them to pass on increased costs in increased prices. Thus it might be fairer to say that higher costs *cause* higher prices, while increased demand merely *permits* them.

But one must note that the very fact of passing on higher costs in itself creates the capacity to bear higher prices. As we have seen, incomes are raised, and with it spending power, so that it becomes peculiarly difficult to isolate price increases which are due to excess demand from those which are due to rising costs. And of course after a time the distinction is almost meaningless. Excess demand may emerge and influence those prices which are flexible, and these happen to be costs for other people. So that excess demand increases prices, and therefore costs, and therefore prices. Cost-push inflation may thus be *analytically* distinguished from the demand-pull inflation which we discussed earlier, but it becomes very difficult in practice to decide which is the more potent factor at work.

Cost-push inflation

Costs of production can be ultimately resolved into wages and salaries, the costs of imported materials and profits. All other costs are intermediate costs which at the economy level disappear. Thus cost inflation – a situation in which rising costs push up prices, rather than rising demand pulling up prices – must imply that one or more of these components has increased.

Let us take the last-named first. It seems unlikely in a situation of not greatly excess demand that businessmen would wish or be able to raise profit margins on their *going* level of output. In other words 'profit inflation' or 'sellers' inflation' is not a very frequent autonomous source of pressure on prices. Interested though businessmen are in raising profits, their complex attitude to business in the main makes them seek greater profits along the road of a larger volume of sales, rather than higher profits on constant sales. Thus competition will restrain profits as a margin of sales, while at the same time urging firms on to raise profits by means of growth.

This is not to suggest that profits will not rise in an inflationary situation. They certainly will, simply because most profit margins are fixed in percentage and not absolute terms. They may even rise relatively to other incomes, since some at least of these are fixed in money terms in the short and medium run.

Indeed, in a situation of pure demand inflation, one would expect profit receivers to gain at the expense of all other income receivers.

But soon wages and salaries would be pushed up too, and, given the relative rigidity of price-fixing procedures, may be pushed up so fast as actually to squeeze profit margins. Then, although aggregate profits may rise, they rise less than in proportion to other incomes, as has indeed been the post-war UK experience.

In other words, prices may be adjusted to demand conditions, thus widening profit margins in periods of excess demand: or more generally to the trend movement in variable costs, in an endeavour to preserve the percentage margin between those costs and prices, and hence to preserve real profit rates. But in any case, profit inflation is unlikely to be an autonomous cause of price increases.

Imported raw materials, our second category, can certainly rise in price for reasons unconnected with the British economy. Prices of these things are determined in world markets and although Britain is a large and important buyer, she is by no means the only one. Thus much of the inflation of the early fifties can be traced to the rise in the sterling cost of imports brought about by the devaluation of sterling in 1949, and the commodity boom of the Korean years. Again, in more recent single years, there has on occasion been pressure on such prices raising our industrial costs.

Over a long period, however, the general trend of imported costs has not been a powerful single inflationary factor, although one has to admit that increases in imported costs may set up a pressure which will take a long time to work its way through the whole economy. Thus we may be suffering from 'imported inflation' some time after the pressure has passed off. Hence our interest here lies in avoiding short-term fluctuations in import prices, even if these take place around a stable trend.

But the greatest pressure in both absolute and relative terms comes from our first cost component – wages and salaries. The *causal* factor at work here is a general desire to share in rising productivity by means of higher money incomes, and to maintain those higher real incomes in the face of rising prices. This, too, demands that money wages should be pushed up.

The *permissive* factor, on the other hand, is the possession of bargaining power, in the market for factor incomes. Such market power is in the hands of employers who find it easy on most occasions to preserve their real profit margins in the face of rising costs. But they have no monopoly of this. Organised trade unionism had, as one of its earliest aims, the desire to break this monopoly, and to redress the balance of power in the labour market. It could be argued that, in the market for labour as a whole (if such can be held to exist), the persistence of full employment for twenty-five years has been even more effective.

But in either case, organised labour does now possess great bargaining power which it is ready, willing, and able to use. It could be held indeed that the structure of the British economy makes it peculiarly susceptible to pressures of this sort. This derives from the popularity of nationally agreed wage rates in preference to rates confined to one area or one industry or even one plant, and the multiplicity of unions that participate in the bargains. Wage rates are agreed, in the bargaining process, 'across the country', without particular regard for present differences in such vital matters as the pressure of demand for the type of labour concerned, or for its product, or the level of profits, or the level of productivity, or for the likely future rate of change of these forces.

Hence increases in money incomes which may exert no pressure on costs in one firm where productivity is rising fast, may raise costs substantially in others where it is not. Prices are thus likely to be pushed up even if profit margins are somewhat squeezed at the same time.

Again the multiplicity of unions involved is very likely to result in a generalisation of the upward pressure on wages, and hence a spread of the pressure on costs into areas or firms which cannot absorb the extra labour costs.

It is difficult therefore to account exactly for the rate of wage increase in any particular situation. A whole galaxy of forces is undoubtedly important, albeit to very varying extents. There is first no doubt a trend factor at work. If all other factors were neutral, it seems certain that money incomes would rise. But what is much more interesting is what other factors can alter, and by how much, the rate of increase relatively to any such trend. Such a factor is the rate of increase of consumer prices.

Wage-earners are concerned to maintain at least, if not to increase, their real standard of living. But the influence seems to be much less than proportional. No doubt the faster the rate of price rise, the more insistent are the wage demands, but there is evidence that in Britain an x per cent increase in consumer prices 'produces' a less than x per cent increase in money wages. In other words, the wage-price spiral, if that were the only force at work, would eventually reduce itself to zero.

But it is hardly likely to be the only force. One must clearly also take into account the pressure of demand for labour, a complex concept influenced by the pressure of demand for commodities in the product market, the level of profits and their expected rate of growth, and the availability of labour both in general, and also in relation to particular types and regions. Measures of this pressure normally take the form of the relationship between the number of men unemployed and the number of unfilled vacancies, although both these variables may be misleading when the pressure of demand is very high.

We are faced here with the need to analyse an almost military situation, in which each of two pressure groups – organised labour and employers – tries to exploit a situation to its own advantage. Economic forces are important, but not final. One can say, however, that the greater is the pressure of demand, the greater the need to hire more labour, probably by the offer of higher wages. At the same time, the greater are the willingness and ability of employers to offer higher wages, because if the pressure of demand is high, the scope for increased profits is greater. So too are the room for passing on higher costs in higher prices, and the real cost of strikes, of labour difficulties, and of the wastage of one's existing labour force if nearby employers offer higher wages.

Indeed, the higher is the level of economic activity relatively to the *total* productive capacity of the economy, the more powerful are all the forces working to raise the rate of increase of money wages, with the exception of the rate of growth of productivity. It is obvious that, with a given rate of rise of money wages, the faster is the rate of growth of productivity, the less is the pressure on labour costs and hence prices. Thus, to the extent that productivity rises faster, with a higher pressure of demand, this latter will be less powerful in tending to increase the rate of rise of wage costs. But the evidence on this proposition is, to say the least, equivocal. The pressure of demand in the UK economy since the war has rarely been steady for any length of time, certainly not long enough to test any proposition about a steady pressure, free from the lagged effects of falling or rising pressure in the recent past.

Thus one must fall back on armchair theorising – and there can be no doubt that *some* level of the pressure of demand will certainly push wage costs up, even if we are not certain or agreed as to what level that is. And secondly, it seems certain that the higher the pressure of demand, the more likely it is that wage costs will rise. But it would be extraordinary if the critical point stayed constant, or could therefore be accurately forecast, or indeed if it were a point at all. And thirdly, it seems certain that the faster the pressure of demand builds up, the more likely are wage costs to rise more.

It is this sort of reasoning that leads to the policy conclusion that we must run the economy with a margin of spare capacity – on which counsel of despair we say more below.

Thus there is a grave danger that the economy becomes doubly inflation-prone when it operates at high levels of output. As we have already seen, any increase in aggregate demand is hazardous, both in itself and because it may filter through the economy and generate further increases in demand. But at high levels of activity there may also be a strong pressure on costs, pushing prices upwards.

It may be held that the pressure on costs is the more insidious. One can after all think of it first of all as the response of the labour market to excess demand, similar to the demand-pull pressure on prices in the goods market. But unfortunately this pressure on costs can start at a level of activity well short of full employment. This is obviously the case where the economy is divided up into fairly specialised regions or sectors, in which demand pressures may be very unequal. Thus it may be that the general level of pressure of demand in the economy is such as to produce something very near absolutely full employment in one or two sectors or one or two regions, but to leave the rest of the economy with a considerable margin of spare capacity.

Nonetheless, such pressure even in these narrow sectors may

be enough to push up costs there very fast, and prices as well, so that the level of prices throughout the economy is raised. And yet the economy as a whole is by no means fully employed. The solution here is clearly a policy of regional development, which will so diversify regions as to make the pressure of demand more even.

To deal with the problem of specialised labour, one needs policies designed both to increase mobility so that trained men are prepared to shift jobs, and to enable them to do so, such as retraining schemes and the like. This sort of policy is obviously preferable to that of lowering the pressure of demand in the whole economy, since this may have to raise the level of unemployment and surplus capacity in the under-employed regions to intolerable heights, before there is any noticeable reduction in the pressure in the overheated regions. Thus there is no simple rule of thumb either to measure or forecast the right pressure of demand.

Another reason why the 'cost-push' variety of inflation is so much more insidious than the pure 'demand-pull' type, lies in the fact that upward pressures of costs are not reversible. All costs, apart from those of some primary products, are much more inflexible downwards than upwards. The price level operates as though it were on some sort of ratchet. Thus we can never be sure that by reducing the pressure of demand, this will do any more than slow down the rate of rise of prices. It is quite uncertain, indeed improbable, that it will actually lower many prices. But unless some prices are lowered, the pressure on wages to enable wage-earners to maintain their standards of living will be weakened, but not eliminated.

What is more, any restraint on price rises can only operate with a long time-lag. Any economic system is a mass of lagged relationships, and indeed these lags are vital in preserving some degree of stability in the whole system. It means, for example, that any inflationary pressure is likely to be voluntarily re-pressed – there is, as it were, a thin crust of price restraint which slows down the speed with which demand pressures are pushed through the economy. This is all to the good, when the only pressure is that from the side of demand, and when or if policy is impotent to deal with it.

But the converse of this is much less attractive. Any policy measures are likely to work with a considerable lag, even in restraining excess demand, while the pressure on costs and prices may persist for many months, if not years, after the originating demand pressure has spent itself.

Stable prices as an objective

At first sight it seems obvious, at least to the man in the street, that, other things being equal, stable prices are better than rising ones. Should price stability then be a goal of economic policy? – a question that has also been posed in Chapter 2 of this book. The answer is yes only if price stability is good in itself, or as a means to something else that is good, and if the economy is not naturally self-stabilising. We have discussed this latter point above. Here, let us look at price stability as a goal in itself, and then as a means.

It could be held that stable prices are desirable in themselves simply because they remove at least one tedious economic uncertainty. 'Getting and spending' are hardly uplifting activities in themselves, and the less time we spend concerned with the mere business of the standard of living, the better.

There is no doubt much in this view. But the case for and against stable prices must really depend on the role of stability in achieving other ends. It might be argued, first that any rate of price rise is bound to degenerate into galloping inflation, and that is destructive of civilised society. It is true that the hyper-inflations of history have developed out of situations in which prices at first rose steadily but fairly gently. There is no evidence, however, that all inflation must become hyper-inflation. We have lived with rising prices for too long, and in too many countries, to need to fear this.

Secondly, it might even be argued that rising prices are positively desirable, through their impact on the distribution of income. Since some prices in any economy are fixed, either by convention or by contract, residual incomes are likely to rise faster than the general level of prices when that general level is itself rising. The most important residual income is profits. Thus it seems likely that in a period of rising prices profits will increase as a proportion of the money national income, and, unless something very peculiar happens to certain types of prices, as a proportion of real national income as well. Hence it has been argued that inflation would stimulate profits and hence investment and the rate of economic growth.

This proposition was reinforced by a belief in the general ebullience and euphoria – albeit quite illusory – of rising money incomes and prices. Money illusion itself might stimulate growth, expansion, investment – and thus to some extent convert 'money' increases into real ones. This has the small rational content that inflation often accompanies a high or rising pressure of demand which in itself justifies further investment.

But demand inflation is fundamentally the proof of inconsistency. It occurs because total demands on resources add up to an amount greater than total available supplies. Thus it cannot sustain itself. Hence this argument – that inflation stimulates growth – implies that somehow or other the profit sector of the community can always keep ahead in the race. That is to say that the proportion of income going to profits is always racing ahead of other incomes in the community, so that in a sense savings and hence resources are being continually 'squeezed' out of the hands of other income receivers. But it is, of course, likely that after some years of inflation most income receivers will have learned their lessons. They too will fight shy of contracts which place them at a disadvantage if prices rise. They too will demand incomes which keep pace with rising prices; but as soon as this happens, the shifts to profits which rising prices ought to produce are thwarted. And then it becomes much more difficult to argue that investment and growth are stimulated through the impact of inflation on profits.

Indeed many commentators would turn these arguments upside down, urging that it is precisely this redistribution of income that inflation brings that is one of its major defects. It does redistribute income, because some prices are rigid and by no means all prices are equally flexible. But this redistribution is totally arbitrary. On the whole it works to the disadvantage of the weak, the unsophisticated, those least likely to be able to suffer any lowering of their living standards, whereas it works in favour of the rich, the wealthy, the sophisticated, those who can look after their material and financial affairs in such a way as will exploit any situation including that of rising prices. Thus we would not want inflation in itself just for the power it has to redistribute incomes. One could argue, of course, that any redistribution which hit the poor to the benefit of the rich could be offset by carefully calculated taxation measures, but in that case there is great danger that the so-called benefit of rising prices in stimulating profits will itself be destroyed. In that case it seems more sensible to aim for no rise in prices.

Many would want to go further than this. They would argue that inflation cheats people's reasonable expectations. All those who hold assets or earn incomes fixed in money terms are relatively impoverished – and in the process, great unhappiness, distress, worry and concern are inflicted on an arbitrarily selected group of, it may be, defenceless individuals. Furthermore, it is no argument to say that, provided rising prices stimulate growth, the losers can *in principle* be more than compensated by the gainers. It needs to be shown that they *are* compensated, without exception or lag or indignity. This is not likely to be so.

Another disadvantage of rising prices stems also from the fact that some prices are more rigid than others. This is simply that a misallocation of resources will continually take place, as the community tends to consume 'too much' of those goods and services and hence of those resources which happen to have fairly rigid prices. And they consume too little of those commodities whose prices rise fastest. In other words, rational calculation of economic costs and benefits, and hence the rational allocation of resources, becomes impossible, or at best very difficult.

But one has to be careful here of arguing about a disadvantage which may be trifling compared with other possibilities. If the measures taken to restrain price rises themselves result in a loss of output or through their impact on investment in a decline in the rate of economic growth, the loss of output from such a policy is final and for ever. British experience, moreover, shows that it can easily amount to a loss in any given year of as much as 2 to 3 per cent of total output, an amount of maybe as much as £5–£800 million. Furthermore, if the rate of growth is retarded we may be faced with the loss year after year of amounts of as much as 1 per cent of the gross national product. It is difficult to believe, on the other hand, that the current loss of output due to the misallocation of resources at any given time which results from inflationary pressures can be nearly as serious as this. In other words, if domestic considerations alone were all-important it would remain an open question to be decided by very intricate analysis which course – of allowing prices to rise or of restraining them by holding back output – would result in the smaller loss of output. The answer is by no means certain.

But, of course, domestic considerations alone are not the end of the problem. The balance of payments of any given country will obviously be affected by the rate of price increase and the level of the pressure of demand. Here one should distinguish between the absolute rise in our prices and the rate at which our prices rise relatively to those of other countries. If our prices rise at all, it is very likely that given the probable values of international elasticities our export receipts will be lower and our import payments higher than they otherwise would have been, and our balance of payments, seldom strong, will be weaker. Thus on balance of payments grounds, we ought to aim at least to keep price increases below those of our competitors, and at best to eliminate even absolute price increases. A weakened balance of trade may have superimposed upon it a weak external capital position if foreigners are unwilling to lend to us because of fears about the exchange rate and if holders of sterling become suspicious of the future of the exchange rate. Thus inflation is quite likely to lead to a very difficult balance of payments condition. It is this above all which has induced successive British governments to apply very fierce restrictive policies frequently since the war – policies which aim immediately to cure a balance of payments deficit but which are ultimately designed among other things to influence the internal level of prices. Thus anti-inflation policy has been dominated by balance of payments policy. In an open economy this is quite likely to be inevitable. In the British case it is certainly so with our reserves at a low level relatively to our international turnover and, in particular, low relatively to overseas holdings of sterling. Nonetheless, we do not need to aim at absolute price stability. To avoid damage to the balance of payments, it would be enough merely to ensure that our prices rose more slowly than those of our major competitors.

Inflation and growth

So far we have been more concerned with the relation between inflation and the level of economic activity, in other words, the level of demand in the goods markets and the labour markets. Empirical studies clearly demonstrate that both wage rates and earnings and hence, at one remove, wage costs and prices are associated, however loosely, with the pressure of the demand for labour. But investigations also show that the rate of change of wage rates is not uniquely related to the degree of pressure, if only because it seems to be connected also with the expected rate of growth of demand for various products, and hence the rate of growth of profits.

Thus to investigate the relationship between inflation and growth is a fairly complex business. One can distinguish at least three quite separate questions. Does faster growth lead to greater inflation? Does faster inflation lead to faster growth? And do attempts to halt inflation inevitably hinder growth? The first pair of propositions suggests that one needs to answer the question, is inflation the price of growth? Must we suffer the damage that inflation does to various income groups in order to enjoy the benefits that economic growth provides for the community as a whole?

The first step in trying to answer this question must inevitably be to distinguish between the growth of capacity and the growth of output. This latter may grow simply because of working more nearly to capacity, even when capacity itself is not growing. In other words, the pressure of demand may be increasing. In this situation it is essentially easy to decide that there is a connection between inflation and 'growth'. An analysis is set out above. But the growth of capacity is a much more complex idea. This must depend upon a growing labour force, or an increase in labour productivity, or both. Other things being equal faster growth ought to lead to a fall in costs, or with any given rate of increase in money wages a slower rate of increase in costs. But rapid growth may well tend to create a sellers' market for labour. Favourable expectations about the future will almost certainly make businessmen more willing to pay increased wages, and indeed perhaps increase their need to do so. So that the rate of growth of money wages may not itself be independent of the expected rate of growth of productivity.

The faster the rate of growth of some sectors of the economy, however, the more uneven are likely to be the rates of growth of different sectors of the economy. If money wages are set by some process which takes account of the national rate of growth one must expect that costs and prices will rise in the more slowly growing sectors, and fall in the more rapidly growing ones. But it is perfectly conceivable that the tone or the norm for wage increases will be set by the fastest-growing sectors. If other sectors try to match the wage increases appropriate to these sectors a wage-wage spiral may well be set up, and certainly rising costs will spread throughout the economy, in particular from sectors of low growth. Indeed, one feels that the faster is growth the greater will be the tension between the slowly growing and fast-growing sectors of the economy. This underlines the need for an incomes policy which we shall examine below.

Another aspect of this relationship between growth and inflation may seem to derive from the fact that in the past attempts in the United Kingdom to halt inflation have often succeeded more conspicuously in halting growth. Most obviously these attempts have held down the rate of growth of output, and on two occasions brought it to a halt. It is more questionable that capacity itself ceased to grow. Certainly net investment rose by a smaller amount than one would have expected it to do otherwise, but it remained high and, for this reason alone, capacity continued to grow. Nonetheless, to the extent that excess capacity emerged, in the form of rising unemployment and idle physical capital, it is clear that some waste of output was being suffered in the effort to halt price increases. In that sense capacity could have grown much faster, had these idle resources been employed in adding to fixed capital. Secondly, it is arguable that restrictive practices and such devices as labour hoarding become more potent in periods when output is being restrained by policy so that, to that extent, both output and capacity are held back.

But it would be going too far to say that this is the inevitable outcome of policy. It is much more the failure of policy. With the present degree of sophistication of our forecasting techniques it is extremely difficult to siphon off exactly the right amount of excess demand. All sorts of time-lags may distort the picture to give a false idea of how much restraint is necessary, and equally all sorts of rigidities may emerge which will make policy much more uncertain. Thus, although we have never succeeded in simply eliminating inflationary pressure, without actually cutting back on the growth of output, it is possible that we will do better in the future. In other words, failure is not inevitable.

Nor is it possible to gain a much clearer picture by comparing the experience of other countries. There is no evidence from international data that faster growth causes, or is caused by, a faster rate of price rise. Both the nature and cause of growth and the causes of price increases are infinitely more complex than any such simple connection.

Policy

The problem of inflation is twofold – that of forces which cause it and forces which propagate it. Thus policy which aims to keep prices stable over a reasonable period of time, without relying on such lucky accidents as falling import prices or abnormally bounteous harvests, ought to aim to deal with both these sorts of factors.

The first aim therefore must be to restrain those factors of demand which might cause a build-up so strong as to threaten rising prices. Thus we must aim at eliminating excess demand, and in particular at rapid increases in the level of demand which may carry the economy beyond full employment. This need is in itself very difficult since our forecasting techniques, to say nothing of the weapons of policy available, are still far too crude to enable us to siphon off just exactly the right amount of spending power. Thus policy is inevitably a somewhat hit-and-miss affair (although its supporters call it rather that of trial and error), but it is clear that the standard weapons of stabilisation policy, of manipulating the budget, of controlling the creation of credit, of regulating interest rates and so on, are easily adaptable to the problem of limiting any upsurge in demand and of restraining any fall-off. In so far as inflation derives solely from the pressure of demand, this should be enough. There is, of course, plenty of room for improvement, in forecasting the turning-points in fluctuations, the time-lags in the system and so on, and equally in improving the speed of action of policy measures and their flexibility. But these defects are not unique in anti-inflation policy. They afflict all economic policy.

But what if the inflation is really basically due to cost-push pressures? Limiting the rate of increase of demand may well slow down the rate of rise of prices and costs but this may be purely a short-term success, if no genuine worthwhile degree of restraint arises until we have an intolerable measure of unemployment. It is likely that we will need other measures to deal with such pressures. The first need is, without a doubt, to ensure that there are no sudden upsurges in demand since these are likely to offer irresistible temptation to both employers and employees to push up incomes.

It may be, however, that overall policy has succeeded in restraining the level of aggregate demand, so that aggregate demand equals aggregate supply. But this, although a necessary condition for the elimination of inflationary pressures, may not be a sufficient one. It is necessary even as part of a policy for holding down pressure on costs, because if excess demand exists in aggregate, earnings may be pushed up at factory or plant level, even although wage rates agreed at national level are not.

If there is no overall excess pressure of demand there may still be pressures on costs. These pressures may be on the costs of imports, or on other prices, or on wages. It is very difficult to know what can be done about 'imported' inflation. Our degree of control over the prices of imports is very limited, and although something could possibly be done by the removal of tariffs on the landed price of imported raw materials, fuels or food, this is a strictly once for all and limited process, and, in the UK, such tariffs are negligible or non-existent.

The scope for operating on other components of costs is fortunately greater, even if infinitely more complicated. Action on prices and wages must certainly be a joint attack. One cannot expect wages to be restrained if prices are not, since that will imply the danger of increases in non-wage incomes, which is socially unjust and certain to weaken resistance to wage demands.

In other words, restraint on wages may well make it easier to hold down price increases while restraint in price increases certainly makes wage restraint easier. Trade unions are readier to co-operate while employers are readier to resist wage demands.

It is conceivable that we could impose direct controls over wages and prices. Such measures would be difficult to operate in a largely free economy, although Belgium, France and the Netherlands have in fact operated them among their anti-inflationary policies. This sort of control has worked with out-standing success in some economies during wartime, but in peacetime the experience of most countries seems to be that everyone wishes to remove the controls as fast as possible and finds it impossible to reimpose them. In the short run at least the need for them is reduced by the very stickiness of prices which we have seen in the past, but this fact in itself, while helpful in the short run, makes life more difficult in the longer run. This is because prices, once they start to rise, may push up other costs and hence other prices for a long time ahead, while one business after another reconsiders its pricing policy and ulti-mately passes on its rising costs. Thus voluntary price restraint may hold the line for some time but ultimately will give way. In that situation a need to prevent *sudden* increases in the level of demand becomes even more important. If the pressure of demand builds up slowly there is more chance of taking action in time, and 'in time' can be defined as the period during which price restraint holds out. But if the rise in demand is large and sudden or prolonged or both, this defence will give way.

In a free economy we will have to rely not on controls but on competition, or intervention, or the pressure of public opinion.

Increased competition can be helpful in a number of ways. First, it can force down profit margins, giving a once and for all gain in lowered prices, which, as they spread throughout the economy in lowered pressure on other costs, may be continued for some time. Secondly, tougher competition could be ex-pected to strengthen management's determination to resist wage demands and to seek out cost reductions. This is a con-tinuing benefit. Thirdly, it could be expected to eliminate the least efficient producers, thereby speeding up the rate of growth of the whole economy as resources are redeployed among the more efficient remainder, and thus, to that extent, helping to restrain increases in costs.

It could be made a more forceful ally by, for example, a tougher line on restrictive practices and various monopolistic restraints. It could be increased by such actions as selective tariff cuts, but the UK balance of payments situation may well make this a dangerous step if it were thought that actual imports would be necessary before prices were lowered. It may be, of course, that the mere threat of such action is enough.

What is certain is that in a free economy any general policy to restrain prices and incomes must have the broad consent of public opinion behind it. Thus it must be possible to mobilise opinion against 'excessive' price increases and income increases. Given that background, it then ought to be possible for the government to exploit the very inflexibility of prices and incomes. It is clearly impossible to expect that the government can determine all of these in their millions, but it certainly ought to be possible for it to intervene in the determination of prices and wages. It could use the weapons of publicity and the climate of favourable opinion; and it can go further and actually intervene in wage and price negotiations.

This is not to suggest that the government can, or need, intervene in every wage and price negotiation. Obviously some wages and some prices are much more important than others. Whether one believes in the concept of the 'wage round' or not, the fact that wage negotiations do not take place simultaneously means that some decisions are likely to set the pattern for later negotiations, thereby adding more fuel to the market pressures that alone might well produce a wage-wage spiral.

One might add here that any measures that can be taken to make wage negotiations more nearly simultaneous would almost certainly reduce wage pressure. This seems at least to have been an important element in whatever success wages policies have enjoyed in, for example, Sweden and the Nether-lands. Its value lies mainly in the possibility of inducing all the negotiators to take an economy-wide view of the situation, and of the effects of their own negotiations. At the same time, it weakens the argument of 'elementary justice' in catching up on others' wage increases which results from the present system of piecemeal bargaining.

Looked at more broadly, it can be seen that both demand inflation and cost inflation are evidence of inconsistency. The former is the result of inconsistent demands in total on resources; the latter the result of inconsistent claims to shares in both total real income and increases therein. This latter is no more surprising than the former. There is no mechanism other than bargaining power for sharing out total national income, and hence no automatic force to ensure that the desired shares add up to the total available. The fact that there is no automatic mechanism to ensure that the partial demands for resources add up to the total available, that is, that we attain and maintain full employment, produced full employment policies, and the whole range of economic stabilisers. But we have as yet no comparable weapons to ensure that income shares are consistent with each other. Simultaneous wage negotiations would at least ensure that the danger of inconsistency – and its outcome, rising prices – is kept in the front of discussion.

But even this will remain extremely difficult to achieve so long as British trade unions remain so numerous. Fewer larger unions are clearly a precondition of more rational bargaining, but one can only be pessimistic about the prospects of reducing the number of unions, especially if it is realised that one of the purposes of such a move is to *reduce* the rate of increase of money wages.

On incomes one must note two quite separate issues – that of general criteria and specific criteria. The general criterion is in principle fairly simple. Incomes per head can be allowed to rise at the annual rate at which productivity increases, without jeopardising overall price stability. In fact of course the economy does not move smoothly forward like this – in some sectors productivity will rise more quickly than the average, and in others more slowly. If then this criterion were to be applied right across the board price stability would only emerge if those industries in which productivity rose faster than average were to lower their prices. That would be necessary in order to offset the effect of price increases in those industries, and there are inevitably some, where productivity rises more slowly than average.

Price cuts are very difficult to impose other than by the pressure of competition, and it may be that this alone is enough. Certainly a tighter attitude to restrictive practices in industry and to monopolistic behaviour in general would increase the chances of such price reductions.

But a general criterion of this sort does nothing to assist in the proper allocation of resources throughout the economy. For this we need specific criteria which will provide grounds for departure from the average 'guiding light'. Such specific criteria would include a great actual or prospective shortage of a certain type of labour, or of labour in a certain area. Again it may be difficult to impose such criteria and one will need all the force of a favourable climate of opinion and sympathetic publicity to ensure that not every case of a wage claim can be shown to be a special case.

In general there are two conflicting views which one might support in deciding on the specific criteria, views which are essentially those about the distribution of relative incomes in the community. One can distinguish between equity on the one hand and 'supply and demand' on the other. The community has fairly firm views about equity and in many cases agreed views, and it may be that this alone is enough. It is surely not the case that the equitable thing to do is to preserve all present margins between incomes.

But one must certainly allow some play to the forces of supply and demand. At any given moment some industries and some areas will probably be short of labour of particular types. It would be difficult and almost certainly wrong to prohibit employers from offering somewhat higher wages than the general criterion would suggest in order to get the labour. But here one must note how important it is to limit such carrots to the minimum incentive necessary; and secondly to break the convention whereby some wage awards are regarded as bellwether in all subsequent wage negotiations. They must not, in other words, set a pattern which if generalised would exceed the overall prescribed wage increase.

Wages are not the only incomes which must be involved in an incomes policy. We must extend such a policy to rents and profits and dividends. In other words, we are taken straight back to restraint of prices. To the extent that wage restraint is matched by price restraint non-wage incomes will themselves be confined to a broadly tolerable rate of increase. But if they are not then fairly vigorous taxation of capital gains is necessary and possibly steep taxation of company profits.

Some would argue that such a policy, in so far as it attempts to thwart market prices, is doomed to failure. But this view underestimates the extent to which prices of both goods and labour are already under human control. They are not, or not often, solely the outcome of impersonal (and irresistible) market forces.

It is of course possible that all this will fail. History offers no precedent for a long period of full employment, fairly steady and rapid growth, free collective bargaining, and price stability. In the past stable prices have been achieved only at the expense of one or more of these. Thus in spite of our best efforts it may well be that we must tolerate rising prices. Is this disastrous? The answer is certainly no if prices rise by no more than, say, 2 or 3 per cent per annum, balance of payments considerations apart. In these circumstances the burden imposed on defenceless fixed income receivers can be fairly easily lightened by social policies while the distortion in the allocation of the resources will be unimportant.

However, we clearly cannot afford to ignore the effect of inflation on the balance of payments. If inflation in the United Kingdom is faster than that of our competitors the effect will certainly be to worsen the balance of payments on current account. But this does not in itself impose an absolute sanction upon us, since our failure to eliminate all price increases is unlikely to be due to some defect in the British character, or even uniquely to British institutions. In that case other countries too can be expected to have rising prices at home. Thus provided we can keep down price increases to something like 2 or 3 per cent the balance of payments should not on average be damaged by this.

But there is no question that the balance of payments represents a much more powerful restraint on growth than does domestic inflation itself. In that case if we fail in eliminating all price increases, and yet desire more rapid growth above all things, it would certainly be more sensible to work for a floating exchange rate as a way of reconciling a stable balance of payments with growth and full employment and free trade unions.

SUGGESTIONS FOR FURTHER READING

J. M. Keynes, *The General Theory of Employment, Interest and Money* (Macmillan, 1936). Chapter 21 – 'The Theory of Prices' – is the first, and classic, description of the Keynesian analysis of price increases. It is, of course, only part of the whole structure of thought which the Keynesian revolution entailed, but it shows how excess demand can be fitted into a system designed to understand deficient demand.

A. J. Brown, *The Great Inflation, 1939–1951* (Oxford University Press, 1955). An excellent analysis of both the theory of inflation and the wartime and early post-war experience of a large number of countries, but completed at a moment when an era was thought to have ended.

T. Wilson, *Inflation* (Blackwell, 1961).

R. J. Ball, *Inflation and the Theory of Money* (Allen and Unwin, 1964).

A. J. Hagger, *The Theory of Inflation* (Melbourne U.P., 1964). *Survey of Economic Theory*, Volume 1 (Macmillan, 1965). These four works all contain good surveys of inflation theory.

OEEC, *The Problem of Rising Prices* (OEEC, Paris, 1961). A very useful integration of demand and cost theories of inflation with the (then) new emphasis on the need to contain autonomous cost increases. It contains an invaluable survey of the experience and policies of the OEEC member countries.

J. C. R. Dow, *The Management of the British Economy, 1945–1960* (NIESR and CUP, 1964). This goes much wider than the problem of inflation, by examining the whole range, tools and success of UK stabilisation policy. Chapter 13 is, however, devoted to purely theoretical considerations.

F. W. Paish, *Studies in an Inflationary Economy* (Macmillan, 1962). Chapters 7 and 17 deal with the U.K. and the latter contains the statement of the 'Paish thesis'.

G. D. N. Worswick and P. H. Ady: *The British Economy in the 1950s*. Chapters 1, 8 and 9 cover the economic history of the period and the use of the major weapons of policy.

6

TAXATION POLICY AND GROWTH

Some seventy years ago the silver-tongued William Jennings Bryan, three times unsuccessful candidate for the Presidency, stormed the country crying that mankind was 'crucified upon a cross of gold'. If such orotundity were still the politician's métier one might say that the 1964 General Election was won on the theme of Britain, broken on a wheel of stagnation and growth. As happens occasionally, economic issues were central. But there is a little more than that to the comparison. Seventy years ago the panacea for what seemed to be the gravest economic problem of shortage of gold was widely held to be Bimetallism which would have eased the shortage by linking gold and silver together: a falsely precise piece of financial engineering with, nonetheless, a grain of sense to it. A crusade against gold could, and did, become a religion of the people. Today's social engineering solution of *taxation*, or as it is often called, *fiscal policy*, is rather more a drawing-room cult, a Gurdjieff to the masses, appealing only to men already intelligent and sophisticated in their understanding of the economy. It is a large part of what is profound in present thinking on how to get Britain off her wheel. But the essential analogy with Bimetallism, I believe, is not strained. Both Bimetallism and Fiscal Policy are in very different ways gimmick solutions and too mechanistic in their presuppositions.

By fiscal policy is meant the government's use of its taxing power to achieve aims beyond the mere raising of revenue and similarly the use of expenditure to promote (subsidise) aims beyond the immediate object of expenditure. One of these aims is economic growth. There are many important and interesting aspects of fiscal policy besides its effect on growth. Many of these can be resolved into various notions about equality or equity: to achieve more equality of income; in a more limited programme to achieve more equality of opportunity (especially by taxing inheritance more severely); or more equality between people of the same 'taxable capacity' (so that, for example, someone is not more lightly taxed only because part of his income accrues as capital gains); or to remove some of the lesser inequalities that lodge in the anomalous interstices of our tax structure (which in particular make the progressiveness of our income taxes very strange). All these are topics which one might have expected to find discussed in an essay on fiscal policy in this book. The excuse one usually gives in these circumstances is the one I must offer: lack of space, and the unfortunate priority we have now to give to economic growth.

The use of fiscal policy to promote growth covers two notions: (a) the smoothing of short-run fluctuations. Although there used to be economists who believed that booms and slumps were a beneficial, even necessary, part of the growth process, so that to iron out fluctuations would lead to less growth in the end (a *reculer pour mieux sauter* theory), few believe it now. So that there is a strong presumption that if *fiscal measures* could promote greater stability in our balance of payments and so eliminate the need to Stop-Go, fiscal policy would have had the indirect effect of raising our average rate of economic growth.

(b) It is also argued that fiscal policy can be used to bring about certain *structural* or long-run changes in the economy which, independently of fluctuations, will lead to higher growth.

Since this chapter is going to be mostly an expression of scepticism, a brief history of how fiscal policy came to displace other mechanisms as the centrepiece of British economic policy will show why I doubt whether it is likely in certain respects to be more successful than they were. What follows falls into four parts: historical; short-run uses of fiscal policy; long-run uses of fiscal policy; and lastly some reflections on the problems that fiscal policy, as at present understood, does not come to terms with.

The historical case for fiscal policy

The emphasis of the 1945 Labour Government's economic policy was almost entirely on fiscal policy. This was to be expected since Keynes had derided the failure of old-fashioned monetary policy to cure slumps and had suggested the use of fiscal measures instead. The older economists' idea of a perfect tax system was the antithesis of fiscal *policy* since its aim was to raise the required revenue with the least disturbance of the behaviour of the taxpayer, hence the search for taxes with the least effect on people's incentives to work and save, and on their patterns of consumption, investment and international trade. As a consequence *neutral* public finance implied a balanced budget. Keynes's justification of an unbalanced budget was the first major challenge to the old orthodoxy: an increase in the budget deficit (the excess of expenditure over revenue) when there was unemployment: the converse if the economy was overstrained, to siphon off inflationary pressures.

It is hardly an over-simplification to say that, apart from tax incentives to investment, this was what fiscal policy meant to the post-war Labour Government: what has been called *budgetary policy*, or decision on the right amount of budget deficit (or surplus) needed to maintain full employment and stable growth. But experience soon suggested that budgetary policy was not enough when there was persistent inflation. In particular, inflation was a major reason why there were balance of payments difficulties. Direct controls, left over from the war, were used to control imports, and so ease the balance of payments. There were also a few monetary measures: the 1949 devaluation, for instance, and capital issues control. Nevertheless, it was budgetary policy which was the heart of economic policy and necessarily become more so when the government began to dismantle direct controls because they were unpopular.

When the Conservatives took power in 1951, there was a reaction against fiscal policy, and a revival of interest in monetary policy, disused since the 1920s. There were many reasons for this: (a) The argument that the Keynesian case against the use of monetary policy in a slump had no relevance to a period of full employment; (b) the belief that monetary policy could be used more frequently and therefore more subtly because in smaller stages to influence the overall level of demand (while the necessary fiscal measures could normally take place once a year, in the Budget); (c) the irrational belief that fiscal policy meant (on average) higher taxes. Succinct characterisation of monetary policy is more difficult, chiefly because of the mystique of high finance which is one of its glories. But in fact it is more sensible to stress the similarities to old-style fiscal policy than the differences. It also, at least in its early revival, was primarily intended to regulate the overall level of demand. It would be silly to try to sketch the *modus operandi* of monetary policy in a chapter on fiscal policy, yet we are interested in why it failed. There are possibly four principal reasons.

(a) Interest rates were a part of the mechanism. A rise in interest rates was once held to discourage investment (and so siphon off inflationary pressures) and vice versa. But changes in interest rates have in fact proved to have had very little effect on the level of economic activity; businessmen's plans are not usually affected by short-run changes in interest rates *unless these are severe or unexpected enough* to damage confidence in the underlying upward economic trend. But this criticism was not fatal. From early in the 1950s many of the publicists for monetary policy revival did not believe it would work through interest rates anyway.

(b) Instead they argued its efficacy was through changes in the *availability* of funds. Bank Rate would affect banks' wish to lend; open market operations, the buying and selling of bills and bonds would affect their ability to do so. (The sale of securities *to* the public *by* the government would withdraw money from the public.) But this expectation has been disproved by events. The war made firms and people save an abnormally high proportion of their incomes so that they ended the war very 'liquid'. For various reasons the economy has effectively stayed liquid* so that most firms simply did not have to notice short-run credit squeezes; and those that happened to be illiquid could usually borrow from those firms and financial institutions well supplied with funds, to tide them over. So monetary policy did not pinch.

This did not mean it was without effect, but instead of working irrestibly, it has rattled confidence. Therefore its operation

* The liquidity of an economy is a compound effect of the volume of money normally kept idle in the bank and the facility with which financial institutions can mobilise these idle funds and make them available where needed. Although liquidity in the first sense has declined generally since 1945, in the second sense it has increased.

has not been the smoothly accelerating and decelerating mechanism which was one of the principal claims of its 1951 protagonists. A small application could have negligible effect: a larger with storm signals flying and alarms buzzing could plunge the economy into a certain measure of unemployment, but more importantly into stagnation: hence 'Stop-Go'. It is possibly odd that there has not been more discussion how liquidity might be drained and monetary policy enabled to be irresistible and gradual. One could try to reduce liquidity directly by various incentives to firms and institutions to become more fully lent ordinarily, or by requiring firms to publish monthly statements of cash balances and money at short notice, or if that failed, by a tax on firms' cash balances, or at a pinch, by the capital levies used by most European countries after the second world war to achieve this. Or one might limit the mobility of funds during credit squeezes by imposing more portfolio requirements on banks and other financial institutions. Or one might try a mixture. This disinclination to discuss reform (on both sides of the Atlantic) is possibly explained by objections (c) and (d).

(c) Had monetary policy worked, it would not have been *selective* enough. What this means is that there was growing disillusionment with the whole 'budgetary' idea, and a belief that an effective economic policy, instead of working on overall demand, ought to work differentially on, *inter alia*, the demand for consumer goods, for investment and for imports. To get the right stabilising effect *and* ensure a high rate of growth one might want to reduce consumption somewhat without depressing investment; or correct a balance of payments crisis by reducing imports (or stimulating exports or encouraging a short-run inflow of capital funds) without depressing business activity at home. The most trenchant criticism of monetary policy was that, affecting only the price or availability of *investible* funds (except for an effect on consumption through hire purchase), it only operated on *investment*. (If it were to have an effect on other consumption it would be because higher interest rates encourage more saving and so less consumption; but there is no evidence that on balance the volume of savings is affected by such interest rate changes.) *Prima facie*, the enormous variety of possible fiscal measures which make for so much difficulty when one comes to try to weld them together into a fiscal manifold, was evidence that fiscal policy could be more selective in the ways that were needed.

(d) But there was another reason why monetary policy became, frankly, boring. The immediate post-war belief that a slump was imminent and the consequent preoccupation with preventing unemployment gave way to concern about inflation. During the 1950s interest wandered to the more profound question of considering how Britain could achieve a higher, while still stable, rate of economic growth. This meant a new field for economic policy: correction of long-run underlying faults that were obstacles to growth; the inefficiency of firms particularly in respect of investment, failure to export and to modernise in various ways, the tendency to hoard labour. Plainly traditional monetary policy had no relevance here (though the selective credit control possible when the banks are in part nationalised, as in France, could be relevant). Most of these arguments about obstacles to growth boil down to one of two kinds. Sometimes it is said that many firms are inefficient even within their own terms of reference: they are not acting so as to maximise profits in the shareholders' interest. In other instances there seems to be a genuine conflict between the efficiency of the firm and the public interest. As something quicker than educational reform and without the odium of more direct intervention, fiscal policy seemed to have an obvious role as a remover of these kinds of obstacles: both, by tax inducement and penalty, to make firms behave more in the shareholders' interest, and to encourage them again, by tax inducement (rather than penalty), to close the gap between their own and the public interest.

Apart then from the disbelief in the efficacy of interest rates which was replaced by a belief in controlling the economy through changes in the availability of funds, there are therefore three reasons why monetary policy is out of vogue. There is the belief that it has been defeated by the effective liquidity of the economy. And that it cannot be used selectively to affect *inter alia* consumption, investment and the balance of payments separately. Lastly monetary policy cannot be used in British conditions to sweep away obstacles to growth.

Short-run fiscal policy

As has been mentioned already, the relevance to growth of fiscal measures to smooth short-run economic fluctuations is the belief that a steadier rate of growth will normally be a faster one. In the past those economists who have doubted this have given one or more of these reasons: (a) A fast rate of growth depends on technical innovation, new ideas, new products. Such new ideas come only from time to time and the economy may have to pause occasionally for the fertility of its inventors to catch up with economic progress. This is no longer true today, whatever may have been the case with railways, bicycles or sewing-machines. Technical progress and growth are interdependent. One feeds the other. A slow-moving economy is likelier to have a dearth of ideas than a fast one. (b) Sometimes it is argued that businessmen need the jolt of bad times to stimulate them. There is no evidence for this. (c) More commonly recently, it has been argued that the economy needs to stop for a while so that an unemployment level of 3 to 5 per cent may have a loosening effect on the economy. Employers who have been hoarding labour in good times which might have been employed more profitably elsewhere will let it go. And the same may be true of other resources. Again the evidence does not support the view that this happens to any important extent during a recession.

On the other hand, the opposing arguments for thinking steadier growth should increase the speed of growth are more persuasive: the view, discussed in Chapter 3, that many of the obstacles to growth will vanish if only the economy can gather momentum. But irrespective of the merits of that thesis one can argue that continuous growth is likely to accelerate somewhat because it is likely to build up the confidence of businessmen. Their investment plans will be less harassed by uncertainty. And it will be easier to work indicative planning because greater certainty and confidence mean it is easier to relate the plans of the different industries and firms of the economy. So there should also be a growth bonus from this.

The most useful distinction to be made between sorts of fiscal policy is between measures applied *ad hoc* and automatic stabilisers. Whatever the form of *ad hoc* measures they are applied as and to the extent that the authorities feel fit. Their use implies reaction to circumstances as they arise and therefore a special continuing exercise of judgement. Though it is the government that prearranges the way in which automatic stabilisers operate, they are linked to some kind of index. A movement in an index of unemployment for instance could induce a countering response in the stabilisers automatically.

The two most important stability problems in Britain are first in the general level of economic activity, particularly in employment, and secondly in the balance of payments. This provides another basis for distinguishing measures.

(a) *Ad hoc fiscal measures*, affecting the *general level of economic activity*. The point is that these need to be more selective than old-fashioned budgetary policies. This is the role in which fiscal policy is intended most obviously to replace monetary policy. A good system would be one in which there were flexible fiscal regulators which could be used instantaneously to control the level of consumption and investment. Of course, one could attempt a much more selective control than this, being prepared to vary the fiscal regulators from industry to industry so that, for example, one might try to choke off demand for an industry which might be over-expanded, perhaps the car industry, while stimulating the demand for another industry where there is excess capacity. But for the moment let us be less ambitious.

Consumption. This is the most important regulator of all since, when there is inflationary pressure, it is consumption that one usually wants to restrain. One method would be to be able to vary income tax rates, say the standard rate, easily. This would be impossible at the moment not so much because of the convention, which could be easily altered, that such changes are only made in a Budget, but because of the inability of the Inland Revenue to make rapid changes in tax coding. I find it implausible that a determined effort could not be made to programme the income tax codes for a computer in such a way that the implications, say, of a sixpenny change in the standard rate could be worked out very quickly; and the actual codes could be made more comprehensive in such a way that it would be easy to recognise the new code applicable to any given taxpayer for PAYE purposes after such a tax change. (Investigation of the possibility of doing this should anyway be given a high priority in any programme of fiscal reform.)

The disadvantage of using income tax as a regulator, apart from the present inflexibility of the tax, and the opposition of the Inland Revenue, is that it misses the consumption of those who do not pay tax and it is also a tax on savings. (The chances are that the higher the income group, the more a cut in expenditure following such a tax change will take the form of a cut in savings rather than in consumption.) This ought to mean merely that a larger increase in tax rates is needed to get a desired reduction in total consumption and vice versa.

Perhaps the closest alternative to varying the income tax rates themselves is to be able to change the National Insurance contribution rates similarly. Apparently this would be administratively difficult at present. But if National Insurance contributions could be assimilated to the PAYE system, then it would be comparatively easy to work as a regulator. Another advantage would be that, since part is paid by the employer and part by the employee, matters can be arranged so that this regulator seems to bite at the same time into both wages and profits. The chief drawback is that it is regressive, falling alike on all virtually irrespective of income. Depending on which way one looks at it, it has the opposite vice or virtue to changes in the income tax rates. (However, the odiousness of regressiveness in a regulator is much less than that of regressive ordinary taxation. A regulator, if successful, does not alter the amount of income someone gets, only its reception over time. Yet in so far as this interference is a disutility, its impact is regressive.)

A somewhat similar regulator would be a special variable payroll tax. This could be made a flat rate per head or could be proportional (or indeed progressive with) the amount of wage or salary paid. But since it would, at least in the first instance, be paid out of profits, it is less clear that it would have as much effect on consumption. (In fact, Mr Selwyn Lloyd in the 1961 Budget took powers to impose a version of this tax, from mixed short- and long-run motives. But the very suggestion was met by a howl of protest from the FBI and the tax has not been used. We will return to consider the long-run case for it below.)

Among the alternatives to changing income tax rates are introducing general sales tax as a regulator, to replace the arbitrariness of purchase tax which does not cover all goods anyway. This has the advantage that it is apparently much easier to administer such a system, and also that *prima facie* it is 100 per cent a tax on consumption and not on savings; but, as we shall see, this may be an illusion. The chief disadvantage compared with the use of income tax is that it, like the last measure, is regressive, falling with greater impact on the lower income groups (though attempts can be made to give sales taxes a progressive character, at the expense of greater complexity), and that it would mean the introduction of yet another tax. (It is also argued by 'shifters', about whom we will have more to say later, that increases in the regulator would be passed on in higher prices, while cuts would not cause lower prices. Therefore, more inflationary pressure.)

A general sales tax of this kind, although it has had much support in official circles, was opposed successfully by the Customs and Excise again on grounds of great administrative inconvenience. The Customs and Excise own scheme, adopted in the 1961 Budget, was that the government should have the power to change all existing tax rates on consumption, including purchase taxes and taxes on tobacco and alcohol, by up to 10 per cent in one year. Perhaps the chief argument against this is that, besides narrowing the tax basis and so requiring a greater increase in tax rates to get a given change in total consumption, it can be regarded as somewhat unfair to producers (and consumers) of goods happening to be taxed in this way. (Again, the loss is not to any marked extent in the amount sold and bought, but in the pattern of sales and purchases over time, which inflicts costs upon both producer and consumer which need not be negligible.)

Investment – This needs little discussion. Whatever system may be adopted to promote long-run investment may be modified to act as a short-run regulator also, with the general reservation to be discussed at the end of this section. Long-run inducements to investment will be discussed in the next section.

Stabilising the balance of payments – There is nothing for me to add here to what Maurice Scott has said in his essay. Tariffs and export subsidies can be used to correct balance of payments difficulties by stimulating exports and import substitutes while repressing imports.

(b) *Automatic stabilisers* have been advocated strongly in many quarters recently. The criticism is made very reasonably, notably by Friedman in America and by commentators like Maddison, Dow, Little and Macrae in Britain, that the authorities tend to *apply* regulators, monetary and fiscal, at the wrong moment and by the wrong amount. There is a long tale of instances when they have applied the brake when they should have put their foot on the accelerator and vice versa, arguably making the fluctuations bigger rather than smaller. One reason for the ham-fistedness is bad information, last year's Bradshaw; and in so far as that is the trouble, an automatic stabiliser, except of the naïvest type, would be no better since it too would be linked to bad data. But there are other reasons. It is said, and there is evidence for it, that it is much more difficult to take a decision, a collective decision, between various ministers, officials and servants of the Bank of England, when the events are crowding on the decision-makers. Secondly, it is argued that simply in the process of making a decision all sorts of subsidiary factors affect what is decided: political pressures, the imminence of an election, etc. The point there is that it would be easier for a Prime Minister or Chancellor to stand up to such pressures if stabilisation happened automatically. A third argument is that there is an inevitable tendency, when decisions are taken *ad hoc*, for delay to creep in as people wait and see. This means that, in the end, the measures have to be more drastic; while in practice under an automatic system it is much easier to arrange matters so that there are more immediate and therefore gradual changes in the regulators.

In principle, any of the *ad hoc* regulators given above could be adapted to become automatic, but a more subtle and imaginative notion was in fact suggested in the 1944 White Paper on Employment Policy, and since then by J. K. Galbraith in *The Affluent Society*. This has the great virtue that it appears in the most compelling way to be related to the problem of stabilising consumption through stabilising incomes and employment. The principle would be that the dole would vary in inverse relationship to the number employed. A high level of unemployment might go with unemployment benefit which, as far as possible, was equal to the average earnings of the employed. (Indeed, it should be possible to relate the benefit to the earnings of the individual.) A low level of unemployment would mean a low rate of benefit. To avoid the obvious disadvantage that this would encourage people not to work, the progressiveness of the dole would have to be carefully chosen. (For example, suppose there is 10 per cent unemployment and the basic dole is £10 per week. Even at that rate we may suppose that 1 per cent of the labour force would rather return to work than stay idle; but 9 per cent unemployment might reduce the dole to say £8 10s., and so on.) The actual figures would have to be chosen with care as a first venture and adjusted in the light of experience. There would be some progression which would not run the risk of encouraging large-scale idleness.

The great advantage of the scheme which should commend itself to a socialist government is that it would be an *automatic stabiliser*, acting as a built-in cure for recession. Unemployment would lead to a much less than proportional fall in national income: a self-correcting mechanism. The chief argument against it is that it would be inflationary in two senses; first, when there was unemployment unless measures were taken to encourage the movement of labour from declining industries (which should be done), and, second, because it would tend to encourage full employment. There seems to be overwhelming evidence now, despite the reluctance of many to admit it, that there is connection between rising money wages and full employment. When there is full employment, wages rise faster with inflationary consequences. Hence arguments that the economy needs perhaps from 2 to 4 per cent unemployment to be able to grow with acceptably stable prices. But there is another way out of the dilemma which might be commended. There might be an automatic convention that as unemployment fell below 1½–2 per cent, there would be a rise in social security contributions *pari passu* with further falls in unemployment, so as to cream off the inflationary pressure that way and counteract the pressure for wages increases. (To the argument that this would increase inflationary pressure all the more, all one can say is that, if it was widely understood by the trade unions that this was a price to be paid for full employment, this should tend to dampen the pressure behind wage increases; and, if as is intended, social security contributions are related to the amount of wages paid, management, knowing that concessions would be followed by further increases in their costs, might stiffen their resistance.)

There is a wide range of choice between regulators of consumption. My own preference would be for the ambitious variable unemployment benefit as a basis with changes in income tax rates, if this can be made administratively possible, to support it. If that is ruled out, the second best alternative would be to use national insurance contributions and social security payments, principally because it would seem unnecessarily complicated to introduce a general sales tax as well into our tax system; moreover, the payroll and purchase tax regulators do have serious disadvantages, the first of falling primarily on profits, not consumption, and the second of being obviously and curiously inequitable because of the limited range of products affected.

Balance of payments – One can also devise stabilisers to correct this. One is discussed by the author in another article, published in 1964 in *Labour's New Frontiers*.

There would therefore seem to be almost an embarrassing number of fiscal measures which could be used as the centrepiece of economic policy and which have, apparently, the great advantage over monetary policy in that they could be used more *selectively* as between consumption and investment, the level of activity at home and the balance of payments. But, as we saw, this was not the only disadvantage of monetary policy as it developed in practice during the 1960s. There was also the liquidity of the economy which defeated monetary policy. How does fiscal policy stand in relation to that?

For various reasons the development of the theory of monetary policy has been such that, under the influence of Lord Keynes, great attention has been paid to the phenomena that cause 'liquidity'. In a world in which there was no uncertainty it would be an irrational man who would hold on to more money than he needed for transactions purposes, since money, both notes and cash balances at the bank, earns him nothing, whereas if he lends the money he can ordinarily earn interest. The reasons a rational man or firm holds money are what Keynes called speculative or precautionary, as a hedge against falls in the value of assets alternative to money, or to be ready for an opportunity for a quick profit or for various emergencies.

In practice it is hard to believe that people are *rational*, since the average man with a bank account tends to hold more money in current account than he reasonably needs to meet emergencies, and the same applies to a great many firms which have high idle cash balances. But whatever the reasons for holding this money idle, we have seen that, when the emergency of a monetary credit squeeze arises, these idle balances are mobilised to defeat it, to enable firms and people to maintain the level of transactions (investment and consumption) that was theirs before the squeeze began and which it was the object of the government to reduce to ease inflationary pressure. The rehabilitation of monetary policy would depend on measures to reduce the normal level of liquidity.

As it happens also for historical reasons the development of the theory of fiscal policy has given almost no attention to the phenomena of confidence which are the essence of the question of liquidity. This is perhaps a pity because it has led to some neglect of the implications of liquidity for fiscal policy. What reasons are there to suppose that firms and people will not draw on their idle balances (or their savings) in order to defeat an attempted contraction in demand imposed by fiscal policy also? It might be argued that, whereas firms are prepared to draw down their balances or borrow to meet shortage of funds caused by monetary policy, their reaction to tax changes will be based on a different ethic; and simply because they are *tax* changes they will yield to them. Even if fiscal policy should be more effective in its first few applications for this reason, it is hard to believe that firms will not learn their power. It might also be argued that, even if firms are able to withstand attempts to make them alter their short-run investment plans for this reason, tax regulators will still be effective against consumption. Even this seems to me no more than a half-truth. If one knew that although the standard rate of income tax or the general sales tax had gone up now, yet there was a probability that the rise would be reversed in about six months' time, would one not tend to maintain one's consumption at the expense of one's bank balance, or one's normal net addition to savings, *if one could afford it*? Short-run fluctuations in spending habits are extremely inconvenient (and likely to be unpopular with one's wife). Therefore the chances are that short-run regulation of consumption will work only inasmuch as it is borne by people who have no idle balances or are not regular savers, that is, generally, the poor. And the poor are, in this sense, a diminishing class. Even the poor borrow on hire purchase and, in so far as dealers allow people to postpone payment during short-term difficulty, as is both humane and profitable, many of the poor can take a cut in income without a proportional, or perhaps any, cut in consumption. Furthermore, is there not a chance that as people come to expect regulatory policies they will tend to accumulate sufficient liquidity if they have not it already?

And it is the fact that recent government measures, including this one, have paid virtually no attention to the problem of draining liquidity that makes one so pessimistic that fiscal policy will have the effects the optimists and even the sober men expect. Since this was first written the experience of the import surcharge levied in October 1964 would seem to confirm this view. It is generally recognised to have been a failure but the moral has not been drawn. Because they have been promised that import levies would not last, firms either continued to import as before, or ran down stocks in the belief that one or other of these policies would be less disruptive on production and profits in the end than succumbing straightforwardly to the government's policy. What made it possible for them to do this was sufficient liquidity in the economy.

These reflections suggest that the use of short-run fiscal policy may be little more effective than short-run monetary policy if the liquidity of the economy is not tackled directly. But if it can be and *is* tackled, then fiscal policy is likely to be more effective, mainly because it is more selective. There is one way in which a direct attack can be made on liquidity, and this is simply by having such large changes in the short-run regulators that the cash balances are too small and the regulators really begin to bite. (The possibility of doing this with monetary policy, implying very high interest rates and much larger-scale open market operations, is generally ruled out on the grounds of the greater cost of the national debt.)

It might be thought that getting rid of liquidity was simply a matter of implementing one or two of the measures mentioned earlier in this chapter, but liquidity is a price people are prepared to pay for, *inter alia*, not having to cut their consumption (or investment or import) plans when the government implements fiscal or, for that matter, monetary policy. If the cost to them, either in profits or in psychic terms, of changing those plans is high, as it would seem to be, then the severity of fiscal policy which will persuade them to do without liquidity will have to be correspondingly high also. However, in respect of consumption, the evidence is that people tend, on average, to keep money in the bank to meet emergencies irrespective of alternative uses of that money and the profit to be gained from investing it; but the amount they hold usually rises with prosperity and the chances are that they will draw down on this, if they have it, to meet a fiscal credit squeeze. Now the dilemma is that in the battle between government and the rest, there may be no resting place. Given the liquidity of the economy at a moment in time, there are always measures the government can take to reduce that liquidity. Alternatively there is always a change in tax rates in any given situation which will defeat liquidity and impose the government's will. But if the psychic and real costs of being defeated are great enough, there will be an increase in the normal level of liquidity to meet the next squeeze. So a running battle between the government and the rest may develop. Clearly it will hardly go on forever: whatever the psychic and real costs, there is some degree of liquidity which would be too expensive to attempt. But there is a danger that in the process, as firms and people strive to strengthen their normal liquidity position, this will only be done at the cost of some real investment, and thus at the cost of economic growth. The implication of this is not that the liquidity problem is intractable but it would have to be considered very carefully before action is taken.

Long-term fiscal policy

As has already been explained, the distinction is one of methods, not aims. By long-term measures one means changes that one thinks will be sustained for a long period, more like cosmetic surgery than cosmetics. It will be convenient to divide discussion into three parts; into measures concerned with the efficiency of individuals, the efficiency of firms, and some problems of efficiency connected with relations between firms.

The attention we will give to each will be grossly disproportion-
ate: by far the most is given to the second just because of the
crucial role of business efficiency collectively on growth.

Personal taxation – Until not so many years ago, and for many
people still, a discussion of the growth effects of fiscal policy
would give first place to personal taxation. A change in the form
and level of taxation is asserted to affect people's incentives to
work and save, and the distribution of their capital between
more and less risky investments. From our point of view there
are two ways in which such matters may be relevant. There
are the growth effects of changes in taxation introduced primarily on other grounds; and one could also try for tax changes
whose first object would be to affect these incentives. But there
is a real difficulty in reaching conclusions. Tax changes can cut
both ways. To take the example of an increase in the progressiveness of the income tax: one can argue this will reduce
the incentive to work because the same effort will be rewarded
by less post-tax income and also that the richer a person is the
more he will lose by the change and therefore the less he will
bother to work. But this argument is no stronger than its basic
hypothesis that people work less if they get less for what they
do. But there is evidence that some people react by working
harder so that they regain what they feel is a desirable or necessary post-tax income.

The same happens with changes in capital taxation. A rise
makes some people save less, others are provoked into saving
more to achieve or maintain a given level of wealth (in some
cases it may be to set enough aside to live as they plan to live
after retirement). Different temperaments react in opposite
ways to tax changes and it is virtually impossible to make an
overall prediction. Such evidence as there is generally supports
the idea that the relatively small changes in taxes and tax
rates which Chancellors normally introduce have negligible net
effects on these incentives. (This is not to deny that a thorough-
paced reform such as the substitution of an expenditure tax for
income tax, and the consequential exemption of all saving from
taxation, would not encourage saving. It would.) Yet there is
perhaps one kind of change where one might venture a prediction. If a capital gains tax were introduced without full loss
offsets (so that the Exchequer gains from a man's winnings, but

does not share equally when he loses), such a tax will discourage people from making as risky investments as before. The main reason why the attractiveness of such investments falls is that a man will make less for himself if the gamble pays off, but if it fails, his loss will not be correspondingly less. One can imagine a determined gambler inflamed by the tax into making still greater gambles with a smaller chance of achieving a larger jackpot. But most people who provide what is sometimes called 'venture capital' are not gamblers in this sense, neither are the 'riskiest' investments of all the most socially rewarding, so that this is unlikely to be the average reaction. (However, if losses are fully offset the analysis is more complicated.)

If one can draw any conclusions from this, they are that one should not, perhaps, be too worried about the disincentive effects, at least in the long run, of tax changes which do not lead to a substantially big change in the incidence of taxation on any class of people; and that there is no obvious change in tax structure which would pay off in increased incentives to work, save, or engage in riskier investment. The underlying message is that it is a mistake to fasten on incentives to individuals: the fundamental decision-making unit is not so much the person as the firm and it is the firm's behaviour that one needs to affect to make a difference to growth. It is the environment provided by the firm, its *élan* and management skill, which is a much more important incentive to the persons working for it, especially the management, than any changes in tax rates. And, as far as savings are concerned, there have been many demonstrations that it would take a very large change in tax structure to get a large change in the volume of savings, even making optimistic assumptions about the reactions to such changes on incentives. Much more important for savings is budgetary policy: the government's ability to alter aggregate savings by overall fiscal policy, an increase in budget surplus or a reduction in deficit being an increase in savings and vice versa. As for the alleged need to attract more private 'venture' capital into riskier investments and away from dull certainties, this raises a great many complicated issues, but even here the best future for policy probably rests with influencing the firm rather than the person.

Firms' efficiency – Here again it is convenient to categorise: there are measures which involve thorough reorganisation of company taxation and those affecting particular aspects only. The usual charge made is that firms are inefficient in certain respects of which the most important are: (i) they do not invest enough; (ii) they do not invest in the most profitable fashion; (iii) in particular they should allow for more rapid obsolescence; (iv) they should undertake more labour-saving investment; (v) they should invest more in technical progress. A criticism of a different kind, in that it relates to investment less directly, is that they tend not to export enough (and import too much). It is usually implied that it would be profitable, and so in the interests of shareholders, to be more efficient in these respects; but occasionally there is a real clash between the interest of the firms and the public interest. An example, as we shall see, is investment in technical progress, where often it pays the firm to do less research than would be in the national interest. (With export subsidies and import taxes there is yet another reason for government action; disinclination to adjust exchange rates directly because of international agreements and strong feeling at home and abroad, and also a preference for more oblique methods.)

All measures to be examined involve a shift of the burden of taxation from investment, or from particular kinds of investment (ii to v listed above), or from exports. The criteria by which the measures should be judged are: whether they need an uncommonly sensitive decision-making procedure in firms to respond to them; whether they have regrettable side effects; and whether in fact they do fall on those the government wants to bear them, or whether in practice their effects are shifted away to people quite different or irrelevant. Another point is whether there is great variation in the degree of firms' inefficiency; the right tax inducement to make one firm more efficient may over- or under-stimulate others. It is usually assumed that, in practice, such differences do not matter. (Giving a tax incentive to persuade an efficient firm which is already doing all the investment profitable for it to do, to invest more, probably implies a judgement that waste from this cause is of small importance compared with the overall benefit, though there are subtler justifications.)

Let us begin with some piecemeal proposals. There are first the *initial* allowances which go back to the post-war Labour Government and the *investment* allowances introduced by R. A.

Butler in 1954. There is no need for us to go into details. As far as we are concerned they are subsidies to firms related to the quantity of investment undertaken. We are not now interested in them as short-run regulators but as long-run inducements to firms to increase investment. Their protagonists claim that they are direct inducements to invest more, and therefore also to some extent to substitute capital for labour (and also that conventionally firms do not pass on reductions in them in the form of higher prices to customers). The main argument against them is that, although we have experienced very high rates of subsidy in this form compared with most other countries, nevertheless the ratio of investment to national income has remained comparatively low. There are fast-growing firms who in effect pay no company taxation at all because of the rebates gained on account of investment done. If one asks why this method, in spite of high rates, does not seem to have succeeded one finds there is much evidence to suggest that many firms do not take investment allowances into account at all when making investments. The evidence that there is this obtuseness has received wide attention recently, being reported by NIESR and NEDC, but there is in fact published evidence to the same effect going back at least to the mid-fifties, which has largely been neglected. Firms make the investment they want to make, irrespective, and treat any rebates in the form of investment and initial allowances as a bonanza. Indeed, it is an *already efficient* firm whose investment appraisal is developed enough to be sensitive to the really rather subtle implications. This means their effect is not only limited to a proportion of firms but touches those only whose investment might be expected to be efficient anyway. (It encourages them to make investments which would be unprofitable if there were no tax inducement.) There is a simpler argument for these allowances and that is that by making the tax burden lighter, they increase firms' capacity for self-finance, but the significance of this is probably small since there is little evidence to suggest that the rate of growth of companies and their investment is usually affected by scarcity of funds. The argument that firms already have to be efficient to be prompted to invest more because of these allowances seems to me to be extremely damaging. *A fortiori* this point militates against the more subtle effects of these allowances: the suggestion that by

making the employment of labour relatively dearer than investment in capital, it will make British industry more labour-
saving. And even more so against allowances which are still
more complicated in the same sort of way: for example, Nicholas
Kaldor's suggestion that there should be obsolescence taxes on
old equipment to complement the accelerated depreciation on
new; or the idea that there should be special investment allowances for 'science based investment' (whatever that might
mean), or for any other category of investment which is thought
specially desirable.

The same goes for *payroll taxes*: whatever their other justification, to believe that they will encourage firms to invest more in
labour-saving equipment just because of a small difference in
the relative prices of labour and capital, is to overrate the
subtlety with which most investment decisions are made: crude
rates of return, pay-off periods, etc., are not designed to reflect
these nuances. The same does not apply to export subsidies, or,
if it could be imagined, long-maintained taxes on imports, since
most firms' procedures allow for differences in the prices of outputs or of raw materials, but the objection to overt export subsidies is, of course, GATT and other international agreements.
The more one tries to complicate the incentive pattern by
applying various taxes and incentives, the more essential it is
that firms should have sophisticated present value forms of
investment appraisal as a basis for introducing the complications. Therefore the type of fiscal policy must await a revolution
in firms' efficiency to be highly effective and cannot itself be the
cause of such a revolution.

The other main proposals suggest more comprehensive
changes in the system of company taxation. To begin with the
least radical. British general company taxation has been made
up of two parts: (a) income taxation at the standard rate which
harks back to the old fiction that companies are, in some sense,
people, and in any case assimilates the taxation of companies
to that of persons; (b) profits tax in addition. One possibility
which has been tried in the past is to have different rates of
profit tax on distributed and undistributed profits. The case for
having a higher rate on *retained profits* is that this acts as a very
crude form of capital gains tax. When profits are ploughed back
the market value of shares rises, and capital gains accrue to

shareholders, so that to impose an additional tax on retained profits will reduce both appreciation and gains so that it is tantamount to a tax on gains. But since we are to have a capital gains tax anyway, the case for this crude approximation lapses. The case for a higher rate on distributed profits is mainly to encourage retention and so investment. (All retained profits will be saved and invested in working or fixed capital. Only a proportion of distributed profits will be saved, the rest spent. However, the argument is weakened to the extent that shareholders live off capital gains, or refrain from saving because of capital appreciation.) The differential profit rates would encourage boards of directors to limit dividends and plough back; so that overall investment in the economy would increase. The case for the same rates of profits tax on both was principally that retention in this way would encourage uneconomic investment while larger dividend distributions would return the capital to the market where shareholders would allocate it in the most profitable way, therefore increasing the net return on the country's investment.

Neither argument has turned out well. Again the villain is the management's lack of subtlety. The evidence suggests that the amount of profits paid out in dividends depends on total profits less total taxes (including profits taxes, investment allowances, etc.). Differential profits tax rates have little or no effect as such. (It may be unfair to blame management's inefficiency, its insensitivity to tax rate changes. What management may be sensitive to is the idea that their obligation to shareholders is such they ought to pay what they feel to be the right dividend to shareholders, irrespective of tax rate differentials.) The case against equal tax rates is similar: the evidence that the shareholder is a better judge of the most profitable investment than the retaining company is, simply does not exist. In conclusion the case for having a differential profits tax to stimulate investment is an exceedingly weak one. (One must be careful to distinguish between a change in tax structure which alters the difference between the rates paid on the two and one which alters the aggregate paid in profits tax.)

The argument for a lower tax rate on undistributed profits has recurred in a different form as the *corporation tax*. The basic idea of this tax is that one will abolish income taxation paid by companies. Instead it will be paid directly by the shareholder on distributed profits. All profits will be subject to a corporation tax. Hence the effect will be the same as a differential profits tax. The arguments for this version are: it will greatly increase the potential gap between the effective tax rates that can be laid on distributed and undistributed profits. It has been alleged that a really wide difference would persuade firms to distribute less and invest more. (The interest of the City, as soon as the advent of a corporation tax was announced in October 1964, in the difference this was likely to make to the aggregate company tax rate payable suggests that this *might* be over-optimistic.) But here surely one must think of something else: if a wide spread is needed to get a sizeable shift in aggregate from distribution to retention, then for a great many more responsive firms the tax differential will be such as to encourage them to retain much more and invest it. Therefore there is a real danger that the most responsive, which may also be the most efficient firms, will over-invest internally, and so give substance to the arguments of those who claim that any differential will not lead to the most efficient allocation of investible funds.

A further argument is that the tax will create an illusion: because income taxation is now paid by shareholders instead of by firms, firms will be prepared to accept a lower rate of return on capital and therefore will be prepared to invest more until all projects at the new lower rate have been exhausted. This suggests a curious logic on the part of boards of directors: it should hardly escape them that there is no real change and that the only difference in this respect is the mechanism by which tax is collected. They should realise also that their market position will suffer if shareholders get a lower real rate of return on their capital than before (which must be what the proposition implies.) (They should also realise that since capital gains are to be taxed, a firm will have to secure a higher real rate of capital appreciation to give the same satisfaction to shareholders.) Otherwise the arguments are very much the same as for a differential profits tax. (There are minor anomalies which replacement of income by corporation tax will effect, but these are technical and comparatively trivial; and the major change in the treatment of Overseas Trading Corporations which raises separate issues not discussed here.)

It would therefore seem that all that the corporation tax form of the proposal adds is the possibility of greater differentiation and the illusion argument. There is another argument we shall come to consider when we discuss tax 'shifting' at the end of this section, but nevertheless I find it hard to escape the conclusion that the present Labour Government is wedded to a major tax reconstruction few of the alleged benefits of which could not be achieved by a simple differential profits tax system, and the stimulating effect upon investment of which is dubious.

The other major category of radical proposals all imply some shifting of taxation from profits (investment) elsewhere. Most make the assumption that roughly the same aggregate revenue will be raised. Thus the shift must be from capital to other factors of production used by the firm; or the attempt is made to shift some of the incidence away from the firm altogether. The best known of these proposals are the various forms of *value added tax*. The most favoured form is one where the basis of tax is widened from profits to profits *plus* wages *plus* imports. The idea is that a firm should be taxed on the value it has added to the raw materials and services it has bought. (Imports are included because they are other firms' outputs, they originate abroad and have not been already taxed domestically.) Compared with ordinary company taxation, it encourages firms to economise on labour and imports; and since, in the form usually advocated there is no tax on depreciation, some of the tax is taken off investment as such, and it should encourage more investment. It is believed that by comparison with differential profits tax, investment allowances and corporation taxes, it would have this effect since for accounting reasons, the taxes on labour and imports would be levied before profits were calculated.

An interesting variation on this is Professor Nevin's *factor tax* which broadens the base still further and levies a tax on all a firm's inputs, raw materials, services, imports, but exempts profits altogether from taxation. Since the base is still broader the rate of tax on each input can be lower to achieve the same aggregate revenue. If the aim is to encourage investment, then there is much to be said for exempting profits from taxation altogether. (This does not mean that shareholders will get away with it, since most proposals imply that they will be taxed at income tax and surtax rate in the ordinary manner; however, if it is decided to raise more money than at present through company taxation, income tax rates in general can be lowered.) Nevin also argues that his system, unlike all others, encourages firms to economise on all inputs; for example, to cut down on expense accounts since these would be subject to tax. There would seem to be much to be said for Nevin's proposal if it were not that it implied the *cascade* principle. Every input is taxed, therefore the tax element in the final sales price depends on the number of firms the product has passed through since the original input entered the chain of production. This, like the similar principle, applied as in Germany to the value added tax, encourages vertical integration of firms to cut out inter-firm sales and so reduce the tax burden. Here the argument usually ends since it seems to be assumed that the elimination of small firms and the tendency towards combination are necessarily deplorable. Whatever case is made out politically, as so often, it is difficult to argue one way or another on economic grounds; whether the competition between firms or the economics of scale arising from merger are more important for efficiency.

A strong argument for all these variants of value added tax, and there are others, is that it is easy to combine them with export incentives. Rebates may be given on all goods exported of all taxes paid at every stage of production before export, so that the actual exporter would be able to claim back on all the taxes paid at earlier stages. This would amount to a large export incentive and is also within the rules of GATT, but there are difficulties. It might be supposed that producers at early stages of production might not allow the final exporter to recoup all the benefit and so try to arrange things that they get some of it. But it is arguable that would be impossible for intermediate producers supplying for both home and foreign sales to charge a higher price for inputs designed for exports; and that even if there should be some effect of this kind, nevertheless the overwhelming proportion of the benefit will accrue to the exporter. (The exception is the exporter who is a merchant and not a producer. If he gets the rebate, then, because there is likely to be strong competition between merchants, one might find them paying negative commission to get export business.) Simply because it is within the rules of GATT for an export subsidy to be fixed in this way, this is perhaps the only firm recommendation we can draw from the arguments of this section. It can hardly be denied that, on the argument as it has developed at present and before we introduce the complications of the next paragraph, this would be an appreciable stimulus to exports. It would be big enough to be noticed by relatively insensitive decision-making procedures. Because it would be reflected in costs of production it could be taken into account of easily in most firms' investment appraisals.

But before trying to draw some other tentative conclusions, there is a major problem which must be thrashed out. Much of the ingenuity that has been spilt over tax proposals has come from making different hypotheses about tax *shifting*. For example, it is said that any tax on sales will not be reflected in lower profits but will be passed on in the form of higher prices. Quite apart from the impetus price rises give to inflation, this will become a tax on consumption if it sticks, and so in a sense a tax on incomes. Indeed, it has been said, not implausibly, that all taxes are in the end borne by consumers. This is an area where more knowledge has dispelled some naïve ideas but has made explanation more difficult. For example, the whole question of the ability of firms to pass on increases in profits tax in higher prices raises many difficult questions. The latest American research suggests that in the US companies have been able to shift profits tax increases 100 per cent upwards, but have not shifted decreases downwards; and most research in the United Kingdom also suggests considerable shifting. (Although tax rates have risen, net profit rates have not fallen or have not fallen much so that gross profit rates must have risen which implies shifting forwards in terms of higher prices, or backwards in lower costs.) But there are many possible explanations of this. (One *can* deny that there has been any real shifting at all by maintaining that it is the productivity of capital that has risen and that in some sense capital 'deserves' a higher rate of return.)

This is another point in the argument where one may slump irreversibly into gloom. The powers of resistance to all long-run fiscal measures might be too great. Slowly the shifting would take place to restore something like the *status quo*. (And it is not only fiscal policy to promote growth that meets this kind of resistance. Increases in the progressiveness of the income tax were meant to make for more equality; but this has been countered largely by countervailing increases in the progressiveness of the salaries paid and also by expense accounts and other non-pecuniary benefits. This has not meant that there has been no equalisation of incomes from this cause but that one powerful group, managers and professional men, may have been able to opt out. Collectively they happen to have had the economic power to do this, and a sense of what is due to them.) One would be wrong to suggest that all groups have this power of resisting taxation. Many are too weak.

But whatever gloom one may feel about the shifting problem in general, there are specific applications of it which seem illicit. For example, it is often deduced from the fact that increases in profits tax rates are normally associated with price rises, while cuts in profits tax rates are not usually followed by price cuts, that firms would respond to a replacement of the present company income plus profits tax system by raising prices. And several writers have ruled out the *value added tax* almost entirely on similar grounds. And indeed Mr Scott, in Chapter 4 of this book, disagrees with me over this point. He believes that a value added tax might not improve the long-run balance of payments situation because the bad inflationary effect might outweigh the good export incentive effect. The case for accepting this line of argument is strong since examination of the evidence does bear out that, in the past, firms have responded to tax changes in this way. Nevertheless, I think there is here a fallacy of compounding. What we have observed in the past is businessmen reacting on different occasions sometimes to a rise and sometimes to a fall in company taxation. This is how the Richardson Committee, set up to inquire into the matter, reported most businessmen as prophesying would happen. But surely the circumstances here would be quite different. They are being offered a package deal, the *substitution* of one system of company taxation for another which happens to involve a cut in income tax and a rise in a new tax, value added tax. Past evidence for reaction to piecemeal changes is surely totally irrelevant. And businessmen's first thoughts on their reaction may reflect a distrust of change, or else a lack of comprehension of the package deal. (Perhaps more serious, these firms who lose by the change – there are bound to be some – will raise prices and other prices may follow sympathetically by what is known as the ratchet effect. This would have to be watched carefully.) So it can be argued that, while the problem of shifting is a real one, most of the hypotheses about what shifts are, when taken out of their context, unreliable predictors. To argue that businessmen will react in old ways to transparently new situations is a gross underestimation of their intelligence, or a complete failure by the government to explain that it is a new situation. What is more, it is unlikely that businessmen would feel that they would want to react in such a way as to defeat a tax whose sole purpose, *prima facie*, is to increase exports. Such a subsidy is not analogous to an increase in the rate of tax on distributed profits which is intended to reduce the incomes of specific collections of people, mostly British nationals, the shareholders, and for whom all companies feel some responsibility. Hence my belief that a value added tax might stimulate exports.

Despite the difficulty of drawing firm conclusions in this subject, I believe that three results emerge from this discussion.

(1) It is surely foolish to design tax systems which require great sophistication in businessmen's decision-making procedures.

(2) One cannot hope to encourage investment except by reducing taxation on profits in aggregate and this can only be done, given the obligation to raise as much revenue, by shifting company taxes on to other inputs as do the various forms of value added tax. But one should not expect a very large effect on investment from this.

(3) Exports are much easier to encourage, and the value added taxes provide an internationally acceptable way of doing this. Given that a tax which would actively encourage concentration is probably unacceptable, it would seem to me that the strongest case is for a value added tax. Arguments derived from past experience of shifting should not be given too much weight.

The interaction of firms and the economy – Firms may be efficient according to their own lights and yet interact with each other and the rest of the economy so as to get less than the most efficient result in terms of growth for the economy. The clearest example of such divergence between private and public interest is restrictive practices and monopolies; but fiscal policy would seem to have no function there. In this short section two areas are considered briefly where it has.

(a) *Scientific and technological research by firms.* The most profitable amount of research for a firm will often be less than would be best in the national interest. In spite of the safeguards against poaching ideas given by such things as the patent laws, a firm with a new idea will find that some of the benefits pass to its competitors. This is because no law can really give anyone a monopoly of an idea. When something new appears it is usually possible for other firms to work away and produce something sufficiently different not to contravene the patent laws but which is a marketable modification of the same basic idea. This means, first, that it pays many firms, especially small ones, not to do their own research, but to wait around and poach, edging round those patent laws, the research done by other firms. Second, the research firms will find research less profitable than would otherwise be the case since they will incur most of the costs while the poachers filch some of the benefits. Therefore they do less research; but from society's point of view, the research pays off whoever gets the benefit. Since laws cannot be framed to avoid the difficulty one way of closing the gap between the social and private rate of return from this type of research would be for the government to levy a tax perhaps proportional to turnover or some other acceptable measure. This tax could be paid back as a bonus to firms who have done successful research of a kind from which other firms might be expected to benefit. Both examples depend on the idea that the social consequences of private actions may ramify.

(b) *Interaction between firms adding to inflation.* Standard budgetary policy to control the level of demand can be used to contain the kind of inflation really caused simply by excess money supply. But this, it is generally agreed, is not the chief source of inflationary pressure now: commonly called 'cost' inflation, a better analysis suggests that such an inflation is spurred on by 'emulation'. For example, an industry's wages rise because of an increased demand for, or productivity of, labour in it. People in other industries notice they are slipping behind, and present and gain a wage claim to maintain parity. Both employees, by their demands, and employers, by their concessions, make this possible.

There has been one ingenious suggestion of a tax to check the process. In it profits tax (but it could as well be value added tax) for the firm is geared to the rise or fall in the firm's average prices during the year. A given fall might earn exemption from tax altogether. Conversely a sharp price rise would earn a high rate of tax. The incidence of the tax would be graded between the two extremes. (The scheme's author, Maurice Scott, has suggested that firms might be allowed to opt out if they paid a standard rate of profits tax at a higher rate than now. This might help firms with peculiar difficulties, but if they went out or in they would have to stay that way for a given number of years, to avoid firms annually choosing to stay in or out, depending on which was cheaper for them.) The biggest snag would be to allow for quality changes. If quality rises as price rises, then there may not be a real price rise at all. This difficulty has raised considerable opposition to the proposal: the measurement of quality changes is notoriously difficult. But the new Prices and Incomes Board will inevitably have to face this problem anyway, when it gives or withholds its imprimatur on price increases. It must have some criterion for what constitutes a justifiable price increase. If that is so, a profits tax geared to inflation of this kind would be a great administrative aid to the Board. It would help it to enforce its views better than mere disapproval, however trumpeted. (The Board would exempt firms from the incidence of the tax in so far as they thought the price increase justified by a quality change.)

Similar arguments based on divergence between social and private interest can be developed to justify subsidisation in respect of exports (where the exchange rates are wrong); traffic congestion in cities (where vehicles pay less than social cost); general congestion in cities (where citizens pay less than it costs to provide social overheads). But, before becoming too enthusiastic, one should remember the problems of the insensitivity of firms' decision-making procedures to given taxation differences; or the question of shifting which may blunt or distort the effect of subsidies.

(c) *Reflections on the possible failure of fiscal policy.* There is a famous passage in *War and Peace* where Tolstoy, describing the battle of Austerlitz, ruminates on the problems of causation and power in history. In the middle of the battle there is a scene of confusion near the village of Schön Grabern where the great general, Prince Bagration, and his staff are gathered. No one knows exactly what is happening in the battle, least of all Bagration. Yet all his staff behave as if he knew, as if the battle were going as he planned it, as if he were in control. Not only do they behave as if this were true, it is a necessary myth that they should believe it. Bagration will be blamed for the defeat which in Tolstoy's view was really the upshot of the chaotic intermingling of individuals reacting to emergencies as they erupted at their feet.

In this chapter various reasons have been given for scepticism about the great, and especially the immediate, superiority of fiscal policy over monetary policy: (1) that 'liquidity' may present as many problems for fiscal measures as for monetary; (2) that much of it presupposes more subtle decision-making procedures than obtain except in the most efficient business; (3) that the power to shift taxes makes the effect of incentives less sure. The moral should not be, I hope, to abandon the problem of control which would be nothing short of ridiculous, but to do four things: not to attempt too complicated measures, to take independent measures to reduce liquidity, to study the workings of confidence in the context of fiscal policy, and, in the short run, to realise that success depends on the co-operation of most of the forces concerned, and that co-operation depends on persuasion that the measures adopted are really in the national interest which depends generally on rational argument.

Inevitably this will seem too glib a solution to the administrative problem of economic control. If you cannot *force* someone to do what you want, *persuade* them or vice versa. So there is a tendency to oscillate between two naïve views: the force of such direct measures as monetary or fiscal policy where the crowning naïvety is, to use a tarnished metaphor which makes clearer the mechanistic presuppositions of so much economic philosophy, to believe that the point is 'in whose hands are the levers of economic power?' There has been a fatal tendency to believe that there are 'commanding heights of the economy'. Who commands them, commands the battle. Rationalists – and most socialist economic thinkers, perhaps one ought to say simply most economists, are rationalists – are perhaps too inclined to believe in the sovereignty of the Cabinet or, if they read their Crossman, of the Prime Minister.

Those who have argued the need to control, reform, or re-man the Civil Service before radical policies can be effected, have probably done a disservice by perceiving the problems of control but prescribing an impossible cure. Between the hands on these levers and the people, is the machinery connecting the two. Replace this, repair that, and it will all work. That is also too mechanistic a view. The platitude surely is that while a left-wing government, or any innovating government, may win a majority of votes, it never has a majority of power. The old Marxist line was that economic power, wealth, was the real power and that the majority of that was always in the hands, and therefore the nation was always in the hands, of a minority. A more correct version is, using the simple sociological notion of a 'role' and the equally simple one that any one man has many roles, that while in some roles (very often those roles in which he is not at all involved professionally) he may think and vote like a socialist, his mind is liable to be made up very differently in his principal roles, especially his job. There he will be strongly conditioned by his environment and its traditions, especially in a country where 'on the job' training is the norm and it is rare to find objective, detached vocational education to train that spirit of critical judgement which a great stream of commentators in various ways from Arnold down to Leavis and Hoggart have believed essential. Consequently a radical businessman or civil servant, equipped with his acquired practical knowledge, will usually have very different views, usually more cautious, on what is politically possible and desirable in and for his role as businessman or civil servant, than a radical government will. New ideas must be explained to him. It may be unnecessary to convert him to the truth of a new scheme, but he should at least be convinced, if he is a civil servant, that it is workable and not dangerous; if a businessman, that it does not, except for some very clear reason he is prepared to accept, conflict with his own or his firm's self-interest.

But the alternative naïvety which comes from believing that everything can be achieved by *reason* (or is it *persuasion*?) is too well known to be elaborated, though it seems to inspire many of the most hopeful supporters of indicative planning. That is an explanatory process and it would be ridiculous that there are not important conflicts of interest based on misunderstanding removable by 'good men and true round a table'. Yet there are bound to be conflicts that getting round a table cannot resolve, inefficiencies that councils cannot burn away with sweetness and light. Regulations, inducements, controls are needed.

The moral is that a socialist government to effect its policies must work through people who, whatever their ideological pre-conceptions, whether they are regarded as innovators or not in their principal roles, are deeply embedded in a role-bound tradition of thought; neither need this be a bad thing. It is only bad if the practitioners are not subjected to pertinent informed criticism from within or without which they, or the more en-lightened among them, respect. So much current criticism of institutions is not that well informed. And there is no escape from this dilemma, except understanding. As a distinguished American literary critic has said of the rationalism of another, 'the true business of literature, as of all intellect, critical or creative, is to remind the powers that be, simple and corrupt as they are, of the turbulence they have to control.'

When we have digested this, perhaps it will be time to get down to grounding policies for economic control on to theories of government and firms' administrative behaviour.

SUGGESTIONS FOR FURTHER READING

The strength and fallacies of the older neutral approach to fiscal policy is well discussed in J. Burkhead, 'The Balanced Budget', *Quarterly Journal of Economics* (1954.)

The experience of monetary policy in the 1950s has been analysed in the Radcliffe Report: *Report of the Committee on the Working of the Monetary System*, Cmnd. 827; and more recently and historically as well as analytically by J. C. R. Dow, *The*

Management of the British Economy 1945–60 (Cambridge University Press, 1964). A much more exhaustive analysis of monetary policy, including some ideas for its reform, can be found in the large number of research studies done for the US *Commission on Money and Credit* and published for them by Prentice Hall, 1963–64.

The case for replacing monetary policy by fiscal policy has been put by Dow in the book mentioned above, and also in his three articles on 'Fiscal Policy and Monetary Policy as Instruments of Economic Control' in the *Westminster Bank Review* (1960); but the *locus classicus* of the case for fiscal policy is I. M. D. Little's 'Fiscal Policy' in G. D. N. Worswick and P. Ady, *The British Economy in the Nineteen-Fifties* (Oxford University Press, 1962). Most of the short-run measures advocated are discussed by Dow or Little.

There is an interesting discussion on the events leading up to the adoption of changes in purchase tax and the payroll tax as short-term regulators in S. Brittan, *The Treasury under the Tories* (Penguin Books, 1964).

The arch advocate of automatic (monetary) stabilisers is the great American economist, Milton Friedman. His *Programme for Monetary Stability* (Fordham UP, 1960) is a readable attack on the ham-fistedness of *ad hoc* policies and a reasoned case for stabilisers. A similar case against *ad hoc* measures has been made by Dow and Little (op. cit.) and also A. Maddison, *Economic Growth in the West* (Allen and Unwin, 1964).

A discussion of the effect of automatic stabilisers in the British context is by P. H. Pearse in the *Review of Economic Studies* (1962), which, however, is moderately mathematical.

The most readable discussion of the monetary problem of liquidity which got to the heart of the matter was by Sir Roy Harrod, 'Is the Money Supply Important?', *Westminster Bank Review* (November 1959). There is a more extended treatment by M. Gaskin in *Oxford Economic Papers* (October 1960).

Much has been written on specific long-run fiscal measures. The most systematic discussion of tax reform was N. Kaldor's *Expenditure Tax* (Duckworth, 1955), a brilliant suggestion that the whole tax structure should be reworked, replacing taxation on income by taxation on expenditure as the nub of the system. Unfortunately, the administrative upheaval required seems to rule it out as practical politics. W. Vickery's *Agenda for Progressive Taxation* (Ronald Press, 1947) has many ideas that are still relevant. Almost all other proposals have been discussed piecemeal. The argument that changes in tax structure will have little effect on the volume of savings is in R. A. Musgrave's paper in *Proceedings of the American Economic Association* (1963, p. 325).

There are interesting discussions by Kaldor of the reform of company taxation in *The Expenditure Tax* and also in the minority submission to the report of the *Royal Commission on the Taxation of Incomes and Profits*, Cmnd. 9474, 1955; R. Turvey, 'A Tax System without Company Taxation', *Lloyds Bank Review* (January 1963); E. Nevin, 'Taxation for Growth: A Factor Tax', *Westminster Bank Review* (November 1963); D. K. Stout and others discuss the value added tax in the *British Tax Review* (September–October 1963).

The opposing view on the value added tax is put by N. Kaldor in an essay in his *Essays in Economic Policy: I* (Duckworth, 1964) which, in my view, relies on an inappropriate use of the shifting argument. Kaldor has also discussed shifting in the *Expenditure Tax*. The most detailed study is American: M. Krzyzaniak and R. A. Musgrave, *The Shifting of the Corporation Income Tax* (Johns Hopkins Press, 1963). Maurice Scott's argument for a tax against inflation is to be found in the *Economic Journal* (June 1961).

The best analysis of the causes of British inflation, with the implication that simple overall budgetary policies will not do, is R. J. Ball, *Inflation and the Theory of Money* (Allen and Unwin, 1964).

The book referred to on page 175, *Labour's New Frontiers*, is edited by P. G. Hall and published by André Deutsch.

7

PLANNING AND THE MACHINERY
OF POLICY

Introduction

The concept of economic planning may be given a wide variety
of different interpretations. In the most general sense, it may be
used to refer to any conscious and systematic attempt by governments to influence the values or rates of change of particular
economic variables. On this interpretation, all governments
engage in planning. In the advanced economies, every administration is committed in principle to realising the objectives of
high and stable employment, reasonable price stability, and
equilibrium in the balance of payments. This implies the need
to forecast future events, and to take corrective action when the
situation seems to require it. In this broad sense, planning is
not a controversial matter.

This, however, does not take us very far. The notion that Dr
Erhard and Mr Harold Wilson are equally committed to
economic planning, in the same sense of the term, is an attractive one, since it appeals both to the love of paradox and to the
desire to believe that all rational men are in agreement on
fundamental issues. There is also some truth in it, since the
ways in which governments and parties choose to portray their
policies often obscure basic similarities of ends and means. But
even if we consider only the particular objectives of economic
policy which have been mentioned above, there are important
differences between the ways in which governments have chosen
to interpret and to carry out their agreed responsibilities. These
differences mainly concern two closely related aspects of
economic policy: first, the extent to which objectives should be
specified explicitly and in detail; and, second, the executive or
policy measures which governments are prepared to use in the
pursuit of these objectives.

A further difference appears when we consider in addition the other objectives of economic policy which have been outlined in Chapter 2. This difference relates to the range of objectives for which governments are (or should be) prepared to assume responsibility. In particular, neither economists nor practical men are agreed on how far a high rate of economic growth is something for which governments can and should plan, in the same sense in which they may be said to plan to avoid inflation or to secure a surplus on the balance of payments.

Thus, if we start from our first broad interpretation of economic planning, it is possible to imagine a politico-economic spectrum with the most ardent believers in planning at one end and the most confirmed non-believers at the other. The main distinguishing characteristics of the two groups relate to the three issues that have been referred to. The planners are willing to assign to governments a wider range of responsibilities for fulfilling particular broad objectives; they are more ready to prescribe in detail what it is that governments should try to accomplish under the heading of each of these objectives; and they are usually prepared to advocate the use of a wider range of particular instruments of policy. In contrast, non-believers may assume one or other of two defensive positions. On the one hand, they often argue that governments are powerless to achieve the objectives which the planners want them to adopt, or that the instruments of policy which the planners favour would be inefficient or futile in practice. On the other hand, non-believers may concede that government action may sometimes be reasonably effective in both respects, but maintain that the price of achieving economic success in this way, in terms of the extension of central power and the loss of individual freedom which they think would be involved, is far too high to be worth paying.

In practice, as has been argued in Chapter 2, there is a close correspondence between judgements of fact and judgements of value. There is thus a natural tendency for those who think that more ambitious economic planning would be politically harmful to believe also that it would have little or no effect on the rate of growth, or in realising other objectives. Conversely, the advocates of planning are not only more optimistic about its usefulness with respect to economic goals, but tend to be far more sceptical about the dangers which are alleged to arise from it.

Economic planning in our first broad sense is therefore inevitable in the modern world. The interesting and controversial issues concern the scope of planning and the form which it should take. We shall return to this below. Before doing so, it is appropriate to refer to another sense in which the concept of planning is often used.

On this second interpretation, economic planning is regarded as an alternative to the pricing system as a means of allocating both productive resources and the output of goods and services. Quantitative or regulatory planning of this type has three main aspects which may be distinguished. First, at the national level it involves the imposition of a set of multiple interrelated objectives with respect to the growth and composition of output and expenditure: plans are laid down for industries and enterprises, and an attempt is made to draw up these plans in such a way that they are consistent with each other and with the overall growth objective. Second, the realisation of such a complex of objectives may demand a far-reaching set of sanctions and controls over the decisions of particular units – departments, firms, households and workers – within the economic system. The instruments of policy which the government is able and willing to use must be more numerous and far-reaching than in a less centralised system. Third, in the choice of instruments, regulatory planning implies the use of physical controls – such as licensing, rationing, allocation by quota, price controls, and direction of resources – rather than reliance on the effects of price changes to secure the outcomes that are desired.

There is an obvious correspondence between degrees of commitment to regulatory planning, in this sense, and advocacy of economic planning in the much broader and less clearly defined sense which we have outlined earlier. Nevertheless, the distinction between the two senses of planning is by no means trivial, and the correspondence is not exact.

The reason for this becomes clear if we examine the second spectrum of doctrines (to continue the metaphor), ranging from detailed regulatory planning at the one extreme to unqualified advocacy of *laissez-faire* at the other. This choice, between planning and the use of the price mechanism, is often treated as having a logical correspondence with three other forms of anti-thesis: between socialism and capitalism; between authoritarian regimes and democracy; and within the context of a modern Western mixed economy, between left-wing and right-wing governments. Although this way of looking at the relationships has a certain validity, it is in some respects over-simplified and misleading.

(a) Let us consider first the degree of correspondence between regulatory economic planning and socialism. It is true that planning of the Soviet type, with objectives and targets specified in great detail and a very wide range of executive sanctions, is incompatible with maintaining a free-enterprise system. On the other hand, there is no logical necessity for a socialist society, in which public ownership predominates, to make use of this type of planning. In recent years the Russian authorities have placed increasing reliance on prices as an allocative device, and it is likely that this tendency will continue. Simi-larly, there was a sharp change in Yugoslavia towards a decentralised system, with much greater use of price incentives and wider scope for individual choice and decision, after the palpable failure of early post-war attempts to operate a highly detailed system of central planning. Subject to certain con-straints concerning the distribution of property and wealth, it is open to a socialist society to make as full use of the pricing system as it chooses. Indeed, twenty to thirty years ago it was quite a common argument among economists that an important element in the case for socialism was that it would enable the price system to function more effectively than it could possibly be made to do under modern capitalist conditions.

If we consider less comprehensive forms of intervention than Soviet-type planning, then it is clear that these are compatible with a free-enterprise system. Thus our third aspect of economic planning – a preference for using direct controls rather than the pricing system – is not necessarily associated with socialism or socialist parties. As we shall see below, it is arguable whether it is even closely linked to the division between left and right in politics.

(b) Similar considerations apply to the antithesis between authoritarian systems and democracy on the Western model. Again, it is clear that Soviet-type planning would be incom-

PLANNING AND THE MACHINERY OF POLICY

patible with parliamentary democracy in peacetime. There are two distinct reasons for this. First, it has consistently emphasised capital investment and military preparedness at the expense of current consumption, to an extent which would have been unthinkable for any government faced with a genuine opposition which could replace it after free elections. Further, the execution of plans has involved a degree of ruthlessness and interference with personal liberty which would also have been impossible for a regime dependent on popular votes and support. However, there is nothing self-contradictory in the notion of an authoritarian society making considerable use of prices as an allocative device. A strong emphasis on investment and military expenditure could be secured through a system of incentives, positive and negative, which left residual discretion to producers and consumers in making their decisions with respect to output, expenditure, and places of work. Whether more direct instruments of policy should be used is to some extent a question of convenience, of means more than ends.

Again, if we turn to the more limited forms of regulatory planning which involves the use of direct controls rather than prices, it is obvious that these are compatible with parliamentary democracy. There is no reason why a democratic system should not maintain building licences (as in Holland), control capital issues (as in France), impose quantitative import restrictions (as in Australia, and until recently the United Kingdom), fix rent ceilings (as in France and Britain), or make use of a wide variety of other means of control which may appear to its rulers to be more effective or acceptable than the alternative of allowing or causing prices to change.

(c) Finally, if we confine the analysis to Western democratic societies, there is no exact correspondence between the spectrum of political attitudes, from left to right, and the degree of commitment to direct methods of economic planning. In the British case this identification has been too readily made, for two related reasons.

First, the attitudes which the two main parties have been ready to strike while in opposition have been taken more seriously than is warranted. Here, as in other respects, the behaviour of parties when in office is a good deal more similar than a study of campaign speeches would suggest.

Second, the identification has been based on a natural but mistaken interpretation of recent history. The Labour governments of 1945–51 felt obliged to maintain a considerable apparatus of direct controls and restrictions. Because the early years of Conservative governments after 1951 coincided with the general dismantling of licensing, rationing and other direct controls, the change has been attributed to the particular set of political beliefs held by these governments. Closer study of events suggests that in fact the coincidence was no more than that, and the differences between the two main parties with respect to these issues, though significant in one or two areas of policy such as the balance of payments, were for the most part extremely unimportant.

More generally, an analysis of the powers which modern British governments possess to intervene directly in the management of economic affairs, and of the way in which these powers have in fact been used, would suggest that even under Conservative governments there is no marked reluctance to use direct methods, and little sign of doctrinaire bias towards relying on the price system. This is entirely consistent with the history and traditions of the Conservative Party.

The same broad conclusion could be drawn from international comparisons, though any extended discussion of this topic is outside the scope of this essay. The ways in which Western democratic governments have chosen to regulate the economy, and the kind of direct interventions or controls which they have decided to adopt, can be best explained by reference to national traditions and individual circumstances rather than the political labels of their governments. Thus for example the evolution of French planning, and the methods of influencing economic events and decisions which have been developed in conjunction with it, cannot be attributed to the political complexion of the various governments with which they have been associated in time. They can be understood more readily in terms of the well-established tradition in France of centralised administration and government initiative, and the special problems which faced the French economy in the early post-war years. Again, the administration of the United States, unlike the British Labour Government, is opposed to nationalisation and uncommitted to economic planning; yet it maintains compulsory military service, while the British Government relies on securing enough voluntary recruits for the armed services through the working of the price system in an uncontrolled labour market.

Thus it can be seen that advocacy of regulatory forms of planning does not necessarily imply a determinate position on the usual political spectrum. The reason for this is that the choice between influencing events and decisions through the market mechanism, on the one hand, or by more direct means of control on the other, is partly a matter of convenience and assessment of circumstances, of means rather than ends. (This is not to deny that in some cases the choice may involve important questions of principle, as with the right of workers to choose their own jobs.)

On this way of looking at the matter, the antithesis between economic planning, in a broad sense of the term, and a recognition of the functions and uses of the price system, is false. It is entirely consistent (and in many ways sensible) to maintain that in Britain today there is a case *both* for more economic planning *and* for greater readiness to make use of the price system in particular contexts. Again, it should not be taken for granted that a belief in economic planning necessarily implies that the central government must acquire and use a new set of powers which it does not at present have. An alternative and more satisfactory way of stating the position has been put by Mr Robert Neild: 'To plan is simply to use existing powers more efficiently; it means looking ahead and using them with sense of design.'

Thus, although our second interpretation of economic planning is a perfectly legitimate one, it is not very helpful for our purposes. We are thus brought back to the more general way of formulating the issues with which we began. Granted that governments will and must engage in economic planning, the interesting and controversial questions concern the scope and methods of planning. In particular, we must consider what it is that may be implied by the notion of planning in order to increase the rate of economic growth, and whether it is plausible to expect that the rate of growth can in fact be influenced significantly in this way. In doing so, it is helpful to start by looking at the forms of planning which have been introduced in this country and in France.

Planning for growth: the French and British experience

An excellent summary of what is implied by planning in this context has been given in a paper by Mr C. T. Saunders. He distinguishes three necessary ingredients, in the following terms.

'(a) General acceptance of a set of specific objectives for the economy as a whole, expressed quantitatively and related to a time-period;

'(b) commitment of government and industry to a set of policies for various sectors of economic life and society, consciously and explicitly geared to each other and to the objectives for the economy as a whole; this implies a quantitative estimate of potential resources and a social choice about the ways they should be used;

'(c) administrative and executive machinery for achieving the objectives.'

It is convenient to begin the process of illustrating and elucidating this summary by referring to the origins and early activities of the recently established British planning organisation.

The decision to create such a body was taken in 1961 by the then Chancellor of the Exchequer, Mr Selwyn Lloyd. The National Economic Development Council was formed in February 1962. It consisted of three ministers from economic departments, including the Chancellor of the Exchequer, who acted as chairman of the Council; six businessmen from private industry; six trade union representatives; the chairmen of two of the nationalised industries; and two independent members. The Council was provided with its own staff, known collectively as the National Economic Development Office, and the head of the Office, who was given the title of Director-General, was also a member of the Council. Formally, all Council members were appointed by the Chancellor, though in the case of the trade union members the choice was actually made by the General Council of the Trades Union Congress.

The main work of the organisation during its first year consisted in the preparation and publication of two documents dealing with the growth problems of the British economy. The first of them was called *Growth of the United Kingdom Economy,*

1961–66. There are three features of this publication which are of particular interest in relation to the type of economic planning with which we are now concerned.

First it laid down a specific figure for the rate of growth – an average annual increase in total output of 4 per cent between the years 1961 and 1966. This was chosen as a 'reasonably ambitious' target; it was used as a working assumption in the calculations made by the Office; and it was eventually accepted by the government as a formal objective of policy.

Second, the study presented in outline form a set of national accounts for the British economy in 1966, in which the assumption of a 4 per cent rate of growth was incorporated. The possible implications of a growth rate were thus analysed in quantitative terms, within the framework of an economic model constructed for this purpose.

Third, the work of preparing the study involved consultations with a number of industries, covering a wide range of activities and about 40 per cent of the British national product. These consultations, though necessarily rather hasty and experimental, were an important innovation in British practice. They had three interrelated purposes.

(a) They were a means both of acquainting industry with the preliminary results of work on the model for 1966, and of obtaining information and opinions which were of value in improving the model. In any serious and sustained attempt to carry out economic planning, such interchanges will certainly have to become more detailed and more formalised.

(b) The consultations were designed to throw light on the feasibility of the chosen rate of growth. In particular, four possible limiting factors or constraints were examined. The rate of *savings* might be such a factor, since the projected increase in investment required for an acceleration of growth might imply an unacceptable reduction in private and public consumption. Information provided by industry was used in investigating this possibility. The *balance of payments* situation was a second potential constraint. Here again the evidence and opinions of industries were relevant, particularly in relation to export prospects; though the difficulties of this type of forecasting are obvious. Particular *shortages of capacity* might have been another limiting factor, and on this question the industry inquiries were especially useful. Finally, the industries were consulted about prospective requirements for *labour* in general, and skilled labour in particular.

(c) The consultations also dealt with the question of how to increase the rate of growth of productivity in the industries affected. An inquiry of this kind cannot result in easy or rapid conclusions; and in the time available the analysis was inevitably superficial. Nevertheless, this type of consultation illustrates the possibility, to which we shall refer again below, of using the machinery of economic planning as a means to improving the efficiency of particular sectors of the economy.

These features of the early work of NEDC throw light on the nature of economic planning in the sense in which we are now using the term. A number of related basic ingredients or elements can be distinguished. The first, and perhaps the most significant, is *a conscious extension of the time-horizon of economic policy decisions*. It is a legitimate criticism of British economic policy since the war that it has concentrated on immediate issues and responded to short-term pressures, to the almost complete neglect of longer-term problems. The establishment of NEDC, and the effects of its early work, have already done something to correct this myopic tendency.

A second and clearly related element of planning is *the use of quantitative economic models* in the analysis of future possibilities, and as a framework for decisions of policy. There is, of course, no exact correspondence between model-building and planning; economic models have a wide variety of uses and applications, and short-term models for purposes of forecasting were used in Britain before. However, the extension of model-building to inquire into the development of the economy over a period of years has been a relatively new development.

Third, the work of NEDC has resulted in the deliberate adoption of a *specific growth objective*. It would be misleading to suggest that this was entirely a matter of the Council's initiative: the decision to create NEDC was itself the outcome of the government's concern about the United Kingdom's rate of growth; and the 4 per cent target would have had little significance if the government had refused to take it seriously. The point, however, is that a growth objective was adopted in Britain partly as the result of the establishment of a planning agency, and that this was a natural and predictable sequence of events.

Fourth, the initial work of NEDC has led to the creation, though necessarily in a rudimentary and experimental form, of what may be termed *machinery of confrontation*. In any form of economic planning for growth, however limited the objectives and forms of intervention may be, some kind of confrontation procedure is a necessary element. The main purpose is simple: it is to ensure that the official projections of the planning agency should both influence and be influenced by discussions with people outside the government machine, and in particular, with representatives of industry. The procedure may also be used to pursue other ends, but this is a primary and indispensable function.

The creation of a planning agency, together with the combination of the four elements which have just been described, may be said to constitute what is sometimes called *indicative planning*. It can be seen to involve the adoption of certain broad objectives for the economy, a concerted analysis of the possible implications of these, and of ways of realising them, and thus a set of conditional predictions about the future course of economic events. It also implies some attempt to influence the decisions of different economic agents – such as government departments, industries and firms, particular interests or social groups – in such a way as to help to ensure that the objectives are secured. In so far as the means of influence extend beyond publicity and persuasion, however, it becomes doubtful whether the term indicative planning remains appropriate.

Indicative planning as we have outlined it does not comprise the work that has been undertaken by NEDC in inquiring into particular ways of increasing efficiency as a means to faster growth. As we have seen, this question was tentatively explored in the early consultations with industry; and more recently the establishment of Joint Economic Development Committees in a number of industries, under the auspices of NEDC, has enabled such work to be undertaken in a more formal and permanent way. A further illustration of this type of activity is the second report of NEDC, which was called *Conditions Favourable to Faster Growth*.

This took the form of a brief review of a number of measures of policy by which growth could be stimulated, such as better provision for training, more effective policies for regional development, taxation reforms, and an incomes policy. The approach was a straightforward and pragmatic one, and the argument was presented with due caution in statesmanlike official prose. Moreover, neither the list of topics nor the conclusions were especially novel. Despite these apparent limitations, however, there is no doubt that publications of this kind can fulfil useful purposes. They can serve as a means both of keeping the issues alive and in the forefront of ministers' attention, and of educating and influencing public opinion. By doing so, they can help to ensure that the growth objective is treated seriously, as a continuing commitment. It has sometimes been suggested that the main role of a body such as the NEDC is to act as a kind of standing royal commission on ways of improving the performance of the economy. This clearly implies a duty to suggest possible courses of action, and inquire into particular measures of policy.

Whether or not the exercise of this function should be described as economic planning is a debatable question. Professor Thomas Wilson has recently suggested, as one of two possible interpretations of the notion of planning, a conscious attempt by the state 'to ensure that the general environment is favourable to growth'. (His alternative interpretation is that planning means the specification, in more or less detail, of target objectives for the economy.) From our point of view here, however, this is not very helpful. It is an odd use of language to describe particular measures designed to improve efficiency – such as a reform of company law, or legislation against restrictive practices, or spending more money on technical education – as themselves constituting economic planning; and it has no clear relation to any of the elements of planning which have been defined above.

A more satisfactory alternative is to regard both the analysis and the execution of such measures as part of the process of planning, but only in so far as they are undertaken through machinery specially created for the task of economic planning in the sense already described. Thus, we do not regard specific policies for growth as in themselves an ingredient of planning. But it is a legitimate function of planning agencies to consider and recommend such policies; and they may be carried out as an integral part of a general strategy for raising the rate of growth, in which an economic plan is the central feature. We have thus identified a further element in the set of activities which it is convenient to describe as economic planning.

The decision to create the NEDC, and the kind of planning that has been undertaken in Britain as a consequence of that decision, have been considerably influenced by French practice. The present French system is the outcome of a process of evolution which has been going on for almost twenty years, and it is still changing and developing. Thus any description of the system must relate to a particular period only; there is no given and unique set of procedures which may be said to constitute French planning. However, precisely as a result of this long experience there are certain features of the system which are firmly established, and which are unlikely to change substantially as future plans are prepared. It is therefore useful to consider the most recent of the plans to be completed and put into operation, the Fourth Plan, which covered the period 1961–65, and to look at some of the points of resemblance and contrast with Britain.

From the earliest preliminary work to final acceptance, the preparation of the Fourth Plan took more than three years. Even if some of the early and concluding stages are omitted as relatively unimportant, more than two years' work was involved. Two phases can be distinguished, each of which can in turn be divided into three separate stages.

In the earlier phase, the first stage consisted in the construction of models of the economy both in the long term, for a period of about fifteen years ahead, and for the terminal year of the Plan, which was 1965. These were used to analyse in a preliminary way the possible implications of different hypothetical growth rates over the period of the Plan. This work was carried out by the specialised economic and statistical services of government departments, reporting to the Commissariat Général du Plan. As a result of it, certain tentative recommendations could be made by officials concerning the range of growth targets within which it would be feasible to choose a specific rate.

At the second stage, this analysis was submitted to a

consultative body, including representatives of industry and independent experts, and roughly corresponding to the NEDC, the Conseil Economique et Social. As a result of this examination, a number of recommendations were made. These affected not merely the target rate of growth, but also other objectives of policy. In particular, it was urged that in deciding what use should be made of higher output, due regard should be paid to the claims of social investment and consumption, as distinct from personal consumption: France should avoid the creation of an affluent society of the kind described by Professor Galbraith, a *civilisation des gadgets*.

Following the work of the Conseil, the government issued a set of directives setting out in general terms the objectives of the Plan, and specifying a growth rate of 5 to $5\frac{1}{2}$ per cent. On the basis of these directives and the earlier work of model-building, a new set of projections for 1965 was drawn up by officials, and this became the main working document issued by the Commissariat Général du Plan to those who were to take part in the second phase of preparing the Plan.

The main work during this second phase was undertaken by the various Commissions de Modernisation. The original Commissions were established as part of the machinery of preparation for the first Plan in 1946. By 1960 there were twenty-five of them, divided into two broad categories. Twenty Commissions corresponded to the main sectors of the economy, while the remaining five were concerned with particular topics, each dealing with the economy as a whole – finance, manpower, research, productivity, and regional development. They were composed of businessmen, trade unionists, civil servants, and independent experts (though trade union participation was very limited). Altogether more than 3,000 people were involved in the work, as members either of the Commissions themselves or of sub-committees established by them, and the process of consultation and inquiry lasted over six months. At the end of this period the Commissions had reported to the Commissariat, which was now in a position to draw up a full revised version of the Plan for resubmission to the government.

The aims of these discussions and consultations are precisely the same as they were in the industrial inquiries set in motion in 1962 by the NEDC. They are to examine critically the initial projections prepared by the Commissariat, both for the economy as a whole and for particular sectors within it; to inquire into some of the detailed implications for individual industries and activities; to provide further data which can be used to improve the quality of estimates originally made at the centre; and to investigate ways of improving efficiency and thus realising the broad objectives of the Plan. All these aims are closely interrelated, and can be pursued simultaneously in a single process of review. The obvious difference between France and Britain relates to the scale of the work, the elaboration of institutions and procedures to deal with it, and the far more highly organised character of the machinery for confrontation. This is, of course, largely explained by the fact that France has now had long experience in operating planning procedures, so that there has been time to develop new methods and institutions and get them to the stage where their activities are taken for granted and their functioning can become almost a matter of routine.

After the reports of the Commissions had been digested, two final stages remained in preparing the Plan. First, the government decided the particular rate of growth to be adopted, and the final draft of the Plan was prepared in the light of this decision. This draft was then submitted to the Conseil Economique et Social and to a rather similarly constituted body, the Conseil Supérieur du Plan. Lastly, the amended draft was submitted to Parliament, and published, with further minor amendments, after it had been formally approved by both Chambers.

It can be seen from this account that the French system contains the basic elements that have been mentioned above: it combines model-building and a very full process of consultation, the synthesis of which we have described as indicative planning. Further, the consultative process makes provision for inquiries into ways of raising productivity and removing obstacles to growth, which are carried out through the institutions specifically established for purposes of planning. But much more is involved than this. Although the French system is often described as one of indicative planning, it goes considerably further than such a description would suggest, both in conception and in means of execution. In particular, there are two aspects of it which do not emerge clearly from a chronological review of procedure, and which will be considered in turn.

First, the Plan is very much more than a set of growth targets for the economy and the productive sectors into which it can be divided. It also incorporates a number of other ingredients. (a) As we have seen, it embodies objectives which are related to the composition and quality of consumption, as well as to the growth of output. The growth targets are thus a framework for broad decisions about the character of national economic life, which introduce social and political as well as more narrowly economic considerations. (b) The choice of growth rates is itself related to an analysis of other economic objectives, such as price stability and a reasonable balance of payments. (c) The Plan deals not only with industries and specific economic problems such as finance or productivity, but also, and in considerable detail, with regional problems. The system of projections has now been extended to cover individual regions, and the government's strategy for altering and determining the relative expansion of different parts of the country is both formulated and expressed within the Plan. (d) Attention is given to a variety of ways in which the government can take action to raise efficiency, and the Plan contains a general statement of intention with respect to some of these. This may cover such questions as tax reform or measures to deal with restrictive practices. (e) The Plan also contains broad statements of intention with respect to the distribution of incomes, and the relative share of increases in output which ought to go to various social and economic groups.

Thus it can be seen that in the course of time the French planning system has been extended to cover virtually the whole range of broad government decisions of economic and social policy. The responsibility for formulating policies in detail, and for carrying them out, remains as before with the government and individual industries; the planning machinery has no executive functions. But the Plan has grown to become the main expression of the government's general economic strategy, of which the growth objectives are only a part. Similarly, the institutions which take part in the preparation of the Plan, such as the Modernisation Commissions and the Conseil Economique et Social, are not concerned only with the analysis of growth projections; their terms of reference may include advising or expressing opinions on other aspects of policy. This extension of the scope of planning, and of the functions of planning agencies outside the machinery of government, is an important aspect of what has come to be called the *économie concertée*.

The second respect in which French planning oversteps the bounds of indicative planning, as we have defined the term, is in its use of means of enforcement. This has led some French commentators to describe the system as 'active' or 'normative' planning. As we have just noted, the planning machinery as such has no executive functions; but the Plan itself provides for or has come to imply the use of a variety of controls or inducements, the exercise of which may be regarded as a part of the planning process.

Some of these instruments of policy are of a general character, affecting all firms and enterprises. Thus, for example, there are inducements to firms to locate their new activities in particular areas, and to move out of Paris. These have a close and obvious correspondence with similar British devices; the only difference, which recent developments in this country seem to have removed, is that problems of regional development were brought into the framework of a plan for the economy as a whole. Again, particular tax or credit policies designed to improve efficiency or increase exports are general in their effects and often have their counterparts in other countries, including the United Kingdom.

In addition, however, there is the problem of trying to ensure consistency between the objectives of the Plan and the decisions of individual firms. This arises primarily in relation to decisions to invest in order to increase capacity. Broad targets for the output of particular sectors are established in the course of preparing the Plan; but decisions about increasing capacity in privately owned industries remain with individual firms, so that it is easy to imagine a situation in which the total result of these separate decisions would be to create a level of capacity which exceeded or fell short of the objective. This is a special case of the general point made in a recent PEP study, that 'the

French plans are worked out in terms of industries but implemented via the individual firm'. Neither the methods of implementation nor the official doctrine underlying them seem to be entirely clear.

A fair summary of the position may be as follows. Responsibility for its decisions rests with the firm: the Plan makes no attempt to set targets for individual businesses. Thus there is a real possibility that inconsistency will arise between the targets established in the Plan and the collective outcome of particular business decisions. This possibility, however, is much reduced by three considerations. (a) Firms themselves have been represented, through the Modernisation Commissions, in drawing up the targets. The strength of this influence on them will clearly depend on the efficiency and representative character of each Commission, and these vary a good deal. (b) It is clearly in the interest of firms, especially the big and prominent ones, to maintain good relations with the government machine as a whole. (c) The French administration can influence the decisions of firms through its control of the capital market. Not only has official sanction to be obtained for new issues, but nationalised credit agencies have a leading position in the monetary system. For this there is of course no British counterpart.

It is thus clear that French practice embraces a good deal more than purely indicative planning. In fact, this is inevitable. Although one can make out a case for restricting the central government's activities to setting broad objectives which are analysed and agreed in concert with industry, it is hard to imagine any modern government choosing to interpret its responsibilities in quite so limited a way. Moreover, as we have seen, some of the instruments of policy which have been adopted as part of the Plan have close equivalents in this country. But the question of how detailed planning should be, and how far it should or inevitably will lead to new forms of intervention affecting individual firms, is a genuine and important one. We shall refer to it briefly in the following section.

Some of the points of contrast between French and British practice have already been noted. A number of further observations on this are in order.

One difference which emerges is that the central planning agency and co-ordinating body in France, the Commissariat

Général du Plan, is a government department staffed entirely with officials. In contrast, the planning staff in this country were initially assigned to the National Economic Development Office, reporting to the Council, and the staff were drawn from business and universities as well as government departments. Since the October 1964 election, however, the British system has been altered in a way that brings it more closely in line with the French, as the forecasting and model-building side of the NEDC has been largely incorporated into the new Department of Economic Affairs.

Despite this loss of part of its functions, however, the Office remains and the Council therefore still retains a staff of its own. This is a potentially useful feature of the present British system. The old Economic Planning Board, which was created in 1947 by Sir Stafford Cripps and survived until the NEDC came into existence and supplanted it, was a useless body largely because it had no staff of its own. As a result of having the Office, the Council is in a position to get its own reasonably independent briefing, to have inquiries conducted into subjects which it chooses, and to receive stimulus and independent suggestions for work from the Office itself. Since effective planning requires understanding and independent initiative from outside representative bodies such as the NEDC, this is all to the good. Further, it means that the NEDC can be used as an active channel of communication between government and industry. The need for such an intermediary has not been felt in France, where relations between businessmen and government departments appear to be closer and based on a greater degree of mutual understanding. In the British situation, the creation and preservation of the NEDO has probably been wise.

An important respect in which Britain is more favourably placed than France is that trade union participation in the machinery of planning is much greater. The original Modernisation Commissions in France had a strong technocratic bias, which to some extent remains. Thus the contribution which it was felt that labour representatives could make was limited, and less importance was attached to union participation than could ever have been the case in Britain, where in contrast to France there is a single and powerful trade union movement with a long tradition of consultative work of this kind.

Partly as a result of this difference, and partly also because of the much greater dependence of the United Kingdom on foreign trade and the endemic problems of the British balance of payments, incomes policy has been considered as an issue in this country whereas in France it has been until recently neglected. This again may be regarded as an advantage; and while it is by no means clear that the adoption of planning will enable an incomes policy to be introduced, still less to be operated successfully, the existence and earlier activities of the NEDC were certainly helpful to the progress made in the early part of 1965.

On the other side of the coin, a conspicuous weakness of the British system is the relative absence so far of any counterpart to the Modernisation Commissions. The task of creating effective machinery of confrontation, which will also be able to initiate and carry through useful inquiries on specialised problems, has scarcely begun, and its magnitude does not seem to have been fully appreciated. Despite predictably wide differences in their quality and usefulness, the Commissions and the working parties to which they have given rise have been a considerable achievement in the French system. Their present success can be largely explained by the long experience of this type of work which has now been gained in France. It is also possible, however, that certain features of present British institutions will make the task of creating equally effective machinery more difficult than was the case in France.

While it is true that there is well-established machinery for bargaining and consultation, this has been developed in response to quite different and unrelated needs, and may not be easily adaptable to the purpose of planning. On the union side, experience and concern have been largely confined to issues of wages and conditions; and individual unions, as distinct from the Trades Union Congress itself, have done little to develop specialist economic or statistical services. On the other side, neither employers' associations nor trade associations are suitable as intermediaries or as exclusive sources of membership for planning committees: their purposes are equally unrelated; they are by no means always representative of their industries; and their specialist services, if anything, are more rudimentary than those of the unions. Thus in developing effective machinery of confrontation, peculiar problems may arise in Britain from the existence of well-established bodies which it is impossible to ignore but difficult to make use of. Earlier British experience, as with the Economic Planning Board and the Development Councils which were set up in several industries during the late nineteen-forties, is by no means encouraging.

A final difference between the two countries is that the French system has by now the very great advantage that it is an accepted part of the process of decision-making, with a clearly articulated set of procedures and institutions. Those who participate in French planning know what they are doing and why they are doing it. This stage has not yet been reached in Britain, and it will require a determined effort of leadership, and a number of related institutional innovations and reforms, before it is achieved.

Our analysis in this section has not led to any neat and simple definition of economic planning, but rather to a general description of its main features in a democratic society in which private enterprise is predominant. We must now consider whether there is reason to expect that planning of this kind may help to ensure a higher rate of economic growth.

The effects of economic planning on the rate of growth

The factors which determine the rate of growth of an economy, and still more the relative importance of different factors, are very much a matter of dispute. Economists differ widely in their assessment of the usefulness and desirability of planning, and there is no conclusive evidence which can be used to establish its effects. All that can be done here is to list some of the reasons which may be advanced to suggest that planning may have significant effects, either favourable or unfavourable.

Before we consider these, it should be mentioned that the case for or against planning does not necessarily stand or fall by them. It is possible to advocate planning or to oppose it on grounds which are wholly or partly unconnected with a judgement concerning its effect on growth. Thus one might concede a certain very limited favourable effect, but argue that the political dangers arising from its use were too great for these effects to compensate for them. Conversely, one can find other arguments in favour of planning. In a recent paper on the French system by M. Pierre Massé, the present Director-General of the Commissariat Général du Plan, three broad justifications (*légitimations*) are put forward. Under none of these headings is the rate of growth explicitly referred to; and though it can be held to be implicit in all of them, it is clear that the author's case does not rest entirely on this consideration. However, the main argument for planning in Britain has been that it may be a means to raising the rate of growth, and it is with this aspect that we are especially concerned in this chapter.

There are six principal reasons for believing that economic planning may contribute to raising the rate of growth of the economy. Although they are connected with each other, it is convenient to list them separately.

First, a commitment to planning helps to ensure that in framing its general economic policies the government will assign due weight to the particular objective of maintaining a high rate of growth. This may effect decisions in two ways. (a) As has been seen in Chapter 2 above, conflict may arise between growth and other objectives of policy. A government which is consciously trying to plan for a higher rate of growth may place greater emphasis on this, on the occasions when a conflict is seen to arise, than would otherwise have been the case. (b) As we have seen, the decision to engage in planning may affect the government's willingness to consider specific measures designed to improve economic performance, and its ability to carry these out.

It is arguable that in both these respects the role of planning is a secondary one. Most governments are concerned about the rate of growth, but not all of them believe in planning. Moreover, the willingness to undertake planning, and the effectiveness with which it is done, are in the first instance a result rather than a cause of the government's readiness to accept the growth objective. However, the commitment to planning, once made, may have further effects of its own. It involves the creation of new institutions, both inside and outside the government machine, which have a vested interest in the success of policies for growth, and which can exert pressure on the government in various ways. Again, a commitment to a specific growth target implies that failure to achieve it will affect the government's prestige in an obvious and damaging way.

Second, the existence of a plan provides a context in which other decisions of policy, and in particular, decisions about the regulation of demand and the balance of payments, can be taken in better perspective. Unless the authorities are prepared to think in terms of the growth potential of the economy over a period of years, fiscal and monetary policies may be unduly short-sighted and have unintended and harmful effects. British experience since the war provides some evidence for this. The effect of measures to control demand in the short run, based very largely on short-term analysis and considerations, was probably to make the rate of growth of output more unstable than it need have been. The economy has passed through successive alternating phases, in which the growth of output has first exceeded the underlying rate of growth of potential output, and then fallen short of it. A greater explicit concern with the rate of growth over a longer period might have helped governments to frame policies which would have reduced fluctuations, and thus made for a steadier growth of output; and this in turn, by reducing uncertainty and increasing business confidence that demand would continue to grow, might well have had a favourable effect on the growth potential itself.

Third, the process of confrontation may also have a favourable effect on business confidence and expectations, and thus on decisions to invest. This can happen in a number of different ways. (a) Confrontation can become a means of convincing both sides of industry that the government means business, and that it takes the objective of a higher growth rate seriously, as a basic and continuing responsibility. (b) Joint analysis of the possible implications of a higher rate of growth may help to convince people that it is a feasible and realistic objective, and not just a useless set of figures invented for propaganda purposes by government departments. (c) By taking part in the planning machinery and becoming aware of the issues which are raised by planning, businesses themselves may be encouraged to look ahead in a more systematic way, and to plan their own activities more coherently and explicitly. Some firms already do this, and it was partly pressure from business which induced a Conservative Government to create the NEDC; but there is also evidence that many businesses in Britain have a very restricted time-horizon, and that methods of longer-term planning could be greatly improved. (d) Confrontation makes available to business the government's own forecasts and analysis, thus providing them with what M. Pierre Massé has termed 'generalised market research'. This may help to reduce uncertainty and to make business plans firmer and more realistic.

Each of the three related factors so far listed may affect the climate of business expectations, and thus the rate of investment and the rate of growth of output per head. The causal process which may be involved here has been analysed in Chapter 3 of this book.

Fourth, planning may help to promote faster growth by ensuring that the plans of individual industries and sectors are consciously related to one another. In this way something can be done to anticipate and avoid particular shortages of capacity or bottlenecks. Such constraints may have an unfavourable effect on growth either directly or indirectly. In the first case output may be affected by shortages of goods or services which cannot easily be imported, such as electric power. In the second case, the effect of shortages is on the balance of payments, by increasing imports and reducing the supply of exports. This in turn may make it more difficult for the government to maintain the rate of growth of demand and output.

In so far as planning helps to bring about a clearer and more realistic assessment of future possibilities, it will also help to avoid the opposite danger of wasted and misdirected investment. Thus the effect on the growth potential of a given rate of investment may be greater.

Fifth, economic planning provides a framework for the government's decisions about the policies to be followed by its own departments and agencies and by public corporations. Some decisions of policy clearly have long-term implications. An obvious illustration is the complex of decisions which together constitute public policy towards the related issues of transport planning, the distribution of industry, regional economic balance, and the general physical environment of cities and countryside. It is impossible to formulate a coherent set of policies unless the long-term implications of different alternatives are analysed; and this in turn requires an explicit assessment of future developments, and consistent working assumptions about the economic environment. Similar considerations apply to other areas of policy, such as health, education, and the social services. The difficulty of making good long-term predictions is not a valid reason for inaction or failure to plan, since any set of policies implies corresponding assumptions about the future, even if these have never been consciously formulated or investigated.

In the case of the nationalised industries also, the role of the government in framing and co-ordinating policy with respect to pricing and investment can only be carried out effectively in the context of an agreed general plan. The unsatisfactory record of successive British governments in their dealings with the nationalised industries has not been due to lack of planning alone; the way in which the government departments concerned have chosen to interpret their responsibilities has been largely to blame. But it is clear that important decisions have been taken on the basis of hasty and short-sighted assessments, as with the initial railway modernisation plan and the decision to expand the atomic power programme after Suez. Further, no general guidance was given to the industries about the rate of growth which they should assume in planning their investment, nor on the pricing policies which would influence their relative shares of future demand. Although economic planning is by no means a sufficient condition for better decisions in this sector of the economy, it is in some respects a necessary one.

Sixth, economic planning may, over a period of time, help to create a social environment which is more favourable to economic growth. M. Massé, in the paper already referred to, has described the first justification of French planning as being to symbolise *la conscience du développement*: to create a more general awareness of the meaning and the possibility of growth, and of the benefits and opportunities which it can yield. This in turn may lead to a greater understanding of, and readiness to accept, policies which are intended to improve economic performance.

We must now consider the contrary argument, that the effects of economic planning on the rate of growth are likely to be unimportant or even unfavourable.

Some writers have argued that the kind of planning which

we have described is little more than a hoax: the authorities invent a target rate of growth, and then set out to create the impression that it is practicable, under the illusion that if they succeed in persuading enough people of this the target will in some mysterious way be attained. Since however (it is argued) nothing has really been changed by promulgating a set of bogus projections, there is no reason to suppose that the growth rate will be in any way affected by it. Thus, even if planning has no other harmful effects, resort to it betrays a credulous and irresponsible state of mind, and is therefore to be deplored on much the same grounds as an enthusiasm for astrology or witch-doctors.

This is much too simple a view. It is clear from what has already been said that planning is not just a matter of incantations and propaganda. On the contrary, it is a complicated business, and for this very reason it is difficult to do well. In so far as sceptics emphasise the problems of planning – the limitations of our knowledge of the economic system, the difficulty of making good predictions, and of creating machinery of planning adequate for its task – they are on firm but largely undisputed ground. Moreover, the potential usefulness of even well-conducted planning as a means to raising the growth rate is open to question, and is a matter on which reasonable men will certainly continue to disagree. But as we have seen, there are good reasons for believing that in some respects at least economic planning may be favourable to growth; and it is very much more than a ritual exercise.

It has also been argued, however, that planning may have definitely unfavourable effects. The argument here falls under four main headings. Each of them concerns the possible consequences of planning for individual industries and firms.

First, it is held that planning procedures may encourage the growth of restrictive practices within industries, and in particular, that they will promote market-sharing agreements between firms. Two separate issues arise here: first, whether planning will have the results thus attributed to it, and second, whether restrictive practices have on balance a harmful or favourable effect on growth.

On the first point, the evidence is inevitably not very clear. It is however a reasonable presumption that this may happen.

If businessmen are meeting in industrial committees, to analyse and try to form a common view about the demand for their industry's products, this can easily lead to an agreement about future market shares, especially where the number of firms involved is small. Some observers claim to have detected evidence of this in France.

The second issue is of course very much disputed. Some restrictive agreements have been defended on the grounds that they reduce uncertainty, and thus have good effects on the level and pattern of investment; all of them can be attacked because they reduce competition and may thus remove an important stimulus to businesses to improve their efficiency. If one inclines to the second view, however, this is not necessarily a conclusive reason for rejecting planning. First, one could hold that on balance the effects of planning would be favourable, despite its tendency to reduce competition. Second, the introduction of planning could be accompanied by stricter measures to deal with restrictive practices; there are various ways in which existing British legislation could be tightened up. A further change which would have a similar effect, and which is desirable in its own right, is a reform of British company law which would force companies to disclose much more about their activities than they are at present obliged to do. Both these measures could of course be undertaken quite independently of any economic plan, and they have indeed been recommended by opponents of planning. Our point is that they would do much to counter any possibly harmful effects of planning on competition and growth.

Second, it can be argued that planning also tends to restrict competition by promoting mergers and consolidation within industry. Again, there does not seem to be any very clear evidence on the matter, but it is easy to see that this might be the case. From the viewpoint of those concerned in the administration of planning it is a great convenience to have only a few firms to deal with. Further, the big firms have articulate bureaucracies which can deal with government officials more easily and thus reduce the inevitable problems of communication and mutual comprehension. These advantages of big business may reinforce the disposition, shared by many administrators in business and government alike, to believe that there is a close correspondence between size and efficiency. Thus the planning process may have three possibly undesirable results: it may result in mergers, or a reduction in the number of firms in an industry, even where this could not easily be justified on technical grounds; by doing so, it may impair growth by weakening competition; and it may lead to an undesirable concentration of power within industry in the hands of the large firms who are better able to conduct negotiations with the government.

As against this, a number of counter-arguments can be made. The effects of concentrating output in a small number of firms – assuming that this in fact occurs – may often be favourable rather than unfavourable. Again, if the government is concerned about the possibly undesirable effects of mergers and concentration, it can take legislative action, either to prevent these in certain circumstances or to provide for a full review in each specific case. Finally, if there is a general awareness that this particular trend may be encouraged by planning, and that its effects may be harmful, this itself may be a partial safeguard against an uncritical tendency to equate size and concentration with efficiency.

Third, there is said to be a danger that once it embarks on economic planning the government will try to do too much, and will intervene in the affairs of individual firms in ways which will be damaging to growth. In doing so, it may also make use of physical controls, such as licensing or quota allocations, in ways that are damaging to efficiency and growth and unduly restrictive of individual freedom.

In some formulations, this argument seems to depend in part on one or both of two serious misconceptions. First, as we have seen in the opening section of this chapter, it is wrong to think of economic planning, in the sense in which we are now using the term, as having any necessary connection with a reliance on physical controls rather than price changes as an instrument of policy. In any case, all governments make some use of physical controls, whether or not they engage in economic planning. Second, it should be recognised that every democratic government already intervenes in a variety of ways in the affairs of particular firms and industries; in Britain, such interventions have been commonplace for the past half-century. The problems which arise from this are inescapable in the modern world, and again have no necessary connection with planning. Thus it would be quite misleading to imply that, when a society undertakes economic planning, it is thereby abandoning some luxuriant *laissez-faire* Garden of Eden for the austere and formal geometric patterns of a State Park of Rest and Culture.

Nevertheless, planning does give rise to some new problems in the relationship between government and private business. In particular, the possibility arises of a conflict of views about the future level of demand, both at home and abroad, and thus about the extent of the investment currently required in order to create the capacity to meet it. In such a case, there are a number of broad alternatives which the government can adopt.

First, it can try to ensure that industry targets are reached by prescribing more detailed targets for particular firms, with rewards for success and penalties for failure. The arguments against this are well known and decisive. Such an extension of planning is not seriously proposed in any democratic country, and need not concern us here.

Second, the government can decide as a matter of principle that the final responsibility for choice should be left with business. This can be defended on three grounds: that business bears the financial risks involved in a decision to invest; that the judgement of private firms is likely to be better than that of the government in matters concerning their own products; and that it would be politically embarrassing for the government to have enforced its own views if these proved in the event to be mistaken. On the other hand, it can be argued that to adopt this procedure in every case would imply too narrow a conception of the responsibilities of government.

An alternative is for the government to reduce the risks to business by providing insurance or financial aid. This can be done through loans, subsidies, specific grants, or guarantees; and there are of course many precedents. The objection to such a procedure is that it may involve the government in making payments to firms to persuade them to undertake commitments which they would have been prepared to assume in any case. Not only is this a wasteful use of public money, but there is a possibility that, in order to get help from the state, businesses will find it to their advantage to express pessimistic views, and to exaggerate the difficulties and risks of accepting projections made in the plan. This increases the danger that the business representatives in industry planning commissions will treat the commissions mainly as a means of lobbying for particular sectional benefits.

Finally, the government may assume the risk more directly, by itself either undertaking or sharing in the developments that are thought to be needed. This may be done through specially created state enterprises, or through some form of equity participation – possibly of a temporary kind – in joint enterprises. There may be room for a variety of possible arrangements here.

The choice between these last three alternatives must clearly depend on circumstances; there is no point in trying to lay down simple dogmatic rules for universal application. But it can reasonably be concluded that the special problems which planning may create with respect to relations between government and industry are not necessarily intractable. There is no reason to suppose that by having recourse to planning the government will find itself driven to take measures which will slow down growth, through excessive interference with the autonomy of firms.

All the same, we cannot conclude that the danger of excessive interference is unreal. The fact that planning need not give rise to this does not mean that in practice, in current British conditions, it will not. Again, though planning does not entail increasing reliance on direct controls, this is what may actually happen, to an undesirable or at least highly debatable extent. As yet it is doubtful whether experience here or abroad provides any firm basis for a conclusion on these issues.

The *fourth* and last argument against planning is that if industries accept growth projections which turn out to be unrealistically high this will lead to over-investment and excess capacity. This argument has some force, but a number of considerations can be brought against it. (a) In a growing economy, excess capacity cannot last for ever, and unless very bad mistakes are made the waste involved is not likely to be serious. (b) In so far as the effect of planning is to provide businesses with new and more complete information on which to base projections of demand, it is likely to make for a better rather than a worse adjustment of capacity to future demand. (c) The risks of under-investing are also significant, particularly in the British case where the effects may be felt on the balance of payments, by increasing the demand for imports and reducing the supply of exports. (d) To some extent at least, growth is a cumulative process, in which business expectations and investment play an important role. Unless firms are prepared to take the risks of expansion, it may be difficult or impossible to secure a higher rate of growth.

The effects of economic planning on the rate of growth are thus uncertain and open to dispute. It is clear that the potential effects, whether favourable or unfavourable, will depend on the form of planning that is adopted. Thus the simpler form of indicative planning, which implies no more than published projections and some form of consultative machinery for discussing these, has limited possibilities for good or harm. Planning of a more ambitious and far-reaching kind carries with it greater opportunities and possibly also corresponding risks.

In our view the balance of the argument, particularly in the British case, is favourable to planning. Although no one can say how much the rate of growth in recent years has been affected by the failure to relate decisions more systematically to the growth potential of the economy, it is at least a reasonable conjecture that the effects have been significant. Thus the need for at any rate some limited indicative planning is apparent. It is possible to go further than this, however, and argue that it would be a mistake for planning to be confined within the limits of what we have called pure indicative planning. More positive forms of intervention are certainly required in the public sector if the government is to carry out its responsibilities effectively. In the private sector, we have already noted that direct forms of government intervention are numerous, varied and long-established. To try to bring such interventions within the framework of a plan need not imply either a big extension of government powers or an increasing resort to direct controls; on the other hand, it should help to promote a more consistent and far-sighted use of existing powers. We have also seen that the machinery of planning may be of value in furthering specific measures to increase efficiency. Finally, the possible dangers of an extension of economic planning beyond its pure indicative form need not be serious if they are realised and a conscious attempt is made to avoid or minimise them.

Our conclusion therefore is that economic planning in Britain has a potentially valuable role as part of a general set of policies to increase the rate of growth. As yet, however, it is still in the early and formative stage in this country: it has become respectable, but it has not yet become effective. In the final section of this chapter, we shall refer briefly to some of the changes that may be needed if planning is to become an established and useful element in the process of formulating economic policy.

The future of economic planning in Britain

It is convenient here to distinguish the issues which are current and immediate from those which relate to the longer term. The *immediate* prospects for planning have naturally been affected by the election of a Labour Government and the advent of an extremely serious crisis in the balance of payments.

The change of government has led to consequential changes in the machinery of planning. As we have seen above, the NEDC and its supporting Office, together with the 'little Neddies' for particular industries, have been continued; though the Council itself was reconstructed, and most of the staff and functions of the Economic Directorate of the Office were absorbed into the new Department of Economic Affairs.

The decision to create this new department, and to place it under a very senior Minister, has been a significant innovation. The Department has in effect taken over from NEDC and the Treasury the main responsibility for preparing a national plan, while in conjunction with the Board of Trade and other departments it has the directing responsibility in preparing regional plans which are to be embodied within the national plan. Two related consequences follow from this: first, the function of being a 'lobby for growth', which has with some justice been ascribed to the NEDC, is now within the terms of reference of a leading department; and second, the responsibility for the general direction of economic policy is no longer vested exclusively in the Treasury, but is shared between two departments whose concerns, though broadly distinct, overlap considerably in several areas of policy.

It is of course too early to judge whether this particular arrangement will prove to be a sensible one. Whatever its effects, however, the main object is clear. It is to ensure that due weight is given to the growth objective in formulating general economic policy, and that decisions are made with regard to their possible long-term consequences for the growth of the economy and its constituent regions. Thus the creation of this new machinery can be interpreted as a way of trying to improve methods of planning in order to secure a higher rate of growth.

While in administrative matters the new government has shown a firm commitment to the idea of planning, and a determination to find ways of improving the machinery of preparing and executing plans, the latest balance of payments crisis has created some new dilemmas for economic policy, and has led to speculation that for the time being at least, planning for growth may have to be suspended. In particular, it can be argued that the original target set by NEDC has been proved to be unrealistic; that even if this does not discredit the whole notion of planning, it is a good reason why governments should be cautious about any future commitment of this kind; and that for the time being any notions about accelerating the rate of growth of output must be set aside, as irrelevant until the balance of payments situation has been restored. Consideration of such issues lies outside the scope of this chapter, but a few points are relevant here.

First, the question of how to deal with current British balance of payments problems has quite obviously been posed in a particularly acute and urgent form. The main issues are discussed elsewhere in this book, especially in Chapter 4. It should be noted, however, that decisions about these problems have an immediate bearing on the long-term plans that may be drawn up for industries. This applies particularly to those sectors of the economy in which protective measures of one kind or another are in force or under consideration, and are advocated with reference to the supposed needs of the balance of payments. The main examples are agriculture, coal-mining, cotton and jute textiles, aircraft, shipbuilding, and parts of the electronics industry. Future government policies towards these and other industries, which will partly or even largely determine their output, should be framed in relation to, and consistently with, a clearly defined strategy for dealing with the balance of payments. This point has already been emphasised on page 123 above.

Second, the argument that because of balance of payments difficulties a slower rate of growth may be desirable, or regrettably unavoidable, needs to be stated more precisely. A high rate of growth of output *in line with the output potential* of the economy, and thus associated with a rapid increase in output per head, is not necessarily unfavourable to the balance of payments: recent historical experience suggests that the converse is true. On the other hand, an increase in output *in relation to the output potential*, and associated with an increase in the pressure of demand, is likely to have unfavourable effects on the current balance; and these may be more pronounced if the increase takes place when the pressure of demand is already high. Thus the statement that for balance of payments reasons a lower rate of growth must be accepted refers to the second situation, and implies that the pressure of demand will have to be reduced. It does not imply that measures to increase the output potential of the economy should be postponed.

Further, even if the case for a lower pressure of demand is accepted (and there are of course arguments on the other side), it does not in the least follow that economic planning must be put into suspense. On the contrary, it has already been seen that a valid criticism of previous restrictive measures was that they were adopted with too little concern for the future growth potential of the economy. If a period of restriction is *not* accompanied by a plan for growth in the longer term, there is a danger that past history will be repeated, and that the effect on expectations and investment will reduce future output potential. The two sets of decisions, immediate and longer term, should be consciously and quite explicitly related. The need for this is part of the case for economic planning.

In the *longer period*, the prospects for planning will mainly depend on the determination with which British governments pursue a number of related objectives. Some of these concern the general management of the economy, and have already been briefly referred to in the previous section of this chapter.

In addition, there are two other areas of policy which may be mentioned in conclusion.

The first of these is industrial planning. As we have seen, the machinery of confrontation is still in a rather rudimentary form, simply because it has had so little time in which to develop. There is clear evidence of the Labour Government's determination to increase the scope of this machinery. What is not so clear is whether this will result in anything more than a proliferation of ineffectual committees. This is of course not entirely within the control of the government, but a good deal can be done to ensure that these bodies have useful work to do and actually perform it. This implies careful choice of membership, readiness to consider ideas and suggestions arising from the committees, and above all, a willingness on the government's part to reveal and discuss its own plans, both for the general management of the economy and for the industries concerned, with a much greater degree of clarity and candour than has been usual in the past. We shall revert to this latter point below.

Second, there is the machinery of government itself. The failures and weaknesses of British policy in recent years cannot be explained entirely by chance and bad luck. In part, they were due to bad management, and this in turn can be largely attributed to a failure to adapt methods of decision-making to modern needs and possibilities. Higher standards of management are needed in the public sector; and within government departments, a number of reforms are needed in order to ensure that the quality of the advice which ministers receive is improved. Although some very welcome changes have recently been made with respect to training and recruitment in the Civil Service, there is still a long way to go.

Although detailed questions of administrative reform are not our concern here, there is one particular and very serious defect of British governmental processes which deserves to be treated, because it has particular relevance to economic planning. This is the extraordinary and unjustifiable secrecy with which decisions are surrounded. 'Never apologise, never explain' has become the chief precept of British governments, regardless of party; and though this is no doubt a good recipe for a certain disagreeable kind of personal success, its influence on public life is degrading and its effects on the quality of governmental decisions have certainly been harmful. More important for our immediate purpose here, it is inconsistent with any serious attempt to engage in economic planning in a free society. The success of the kind of planning which we have described in this chapter depends to a considerable extent on understanding and consent; and this in turn depends on clear, frank and articulate explanations of the policies that are adopted and the reasons for them. It is impossible to achieve this so long as the principal concern of ministers and officials is to maintain at all costs the boring and useless pretence that British government departments can never make a mistake.

It is often suggested that methods of decision-making in democracies must necessarily be slow and inefficient, and also that economic planning, in so far as it may lead to more efficient methods, can only do so at the cost of greater centralisation and a further concentration of power in the hands of the government. Thus (it is said) democratic procedures tend to be inefficient, and planning tends to be anti-democratic. Although a case can be made out for both these positions, there are strong arguments, particularly in Britain today, for holding the converse to be true.

In the first place, there can be little doubt that if British governments were made more fully accountable for their actions this would lead to an improvement in the quality of decisions. There are certain institutional changes which would help to bring this about, and which would make for more democratic as well as more efficient methods of government. Indeed, in this instance the improvement in efficiency would be the direct consequence of a more democratic procedure; the two goals are by no means necessarily in conflict.

Second, a reform of this kind would certainly help to make economic planning work successfully; for as we have seen it may be a necessary condition of success that there should be much fuller and franker explanations of government policy. In addition, however, planning of the kind that we have described also depends for its success on the progress made in realising another democratic goal, namely a wider participation in decision-making and in the formulation of government policy. Here again there need be no conflict between better economic performance and more democratic procedures; the second can be a means of realising the first. Further, the object and effect of planning, in this respect at least, is to promote a freer and more open society.

In this chapter we have naturally been concerned with the possible effects of economic planning, in the sense in which we have defined the term, on the rate of growth of the British economy. We have argued that these effects are uncertain, but that for a number of reasons it can be expected that planning will have a favourable influence on growth. But the case for planning does not depend only on this conclusion. In France, the advocates of the Plan have increasingly come to regard it, not just as a means to increasing output over time, but rather as a design for gradually changing and enriching the quality of French national life. Although such notions come less readily to Anglo-Saxon ways of thinking, and are not always easy to relate to the detailed technicalities of economic policy, they embody an important truth. The case for economic planning is that it may help to create a better society, and not merely a richer one.

SUGGESTIONS FOR FURTHER READING

General – Three publications may be mentioned here. First in chronological order is J. E. Meade, *Planning and the Price Mechanism* (Allen and Unwin, 1948). Though inevitably somewhat dated, this is a lucid and balanced analysis. As the title implies, planning is treated as an alternative to the use of the pricing system, so that the approach differs from the one used here. Second, there is Thomas Wilson, *Planning and Growth* (Macmillan, 1964), particularly Chapter 1. This is referred to on page 210 of this chapter. Third, there is an excellent paper by C. T. Saunders on British economic planning in the *Weltwirtschaftliches Archiv* (1964, first issue). The paper is in English. The quotation on page 206 of this chapter is taken from it, and the subsequent argument has been influenced by it at several points.

In addition, some interesting observations on planning are contained in Angus Maddison, *Economic Growth in the West* (Allen and Unwin, 1964), pp. 151–5, and in J. C. R. Dow, *The Management of the British Economy* (Cambridge University Press, 1964), Chapter XVI.

French planning – A good short survey is contained in a PEP pamphlet, *French Planning: Some Lessons for Britain* (*Planning*, Vol. XXIX, No. 475). The quotation on page 216 of this chapter is taken from it. The main work of reference here is John and Anne-Marie Hackett, *Economic Planning in France* (Allen and Unwin, 1963). A shorter and more personal general survey is Pierre Bauchet, *Economic Planning: the French Experience* (Heinemann, 1964). There is an interesting interpretative account of the system by the present Commissaire-Général du Plan, M. Pierre Massé, in the issue of the *Weltwirtschaftliches Archiv* referred to above. This paper is in French, and is mentioned on pages 220 and 223 of this chapter. A highly sceptical view of French planning can be found in the chapter by Vera Lutz in *Economic Miracles*, edited by Josselyn Hennessey (André Deutsch, 1964).

British planning – The main sources here are: the two NEDC publications referred to in this chapter, which are *Growth of the United Kingdom Economy to 1966* and *Conditions Favourable to Faster Growth* (both HMSO, 1963); and *The National Plan* (Cmnd. 2764, HMSO, September 1965), which appeared too late to be considered in this chapter.

Two recent and contrasting papers on planning in the UK are Sir Robert Shone, 'Problems of Planning for Economic Growth in a Mixed Economy', *Economic Journal*, March 1965; and John Brunner, *The National Plan* (Institute of Economic Affairs, 1965).

8

EDUCATION, TRAINING
AND GROWTH

Introduction

The overall growth of the British economy since 1948 or so has
been handicapped by labour and skill shortages at the period of
peak demand. There has also allegedly been difficulty in moving
labour from low-productivity sectors to high-productivity sectors. Special measures may be adopted to speed this process by
the location of new plants in areas where declining industries
are found, and providing facilities for retraining the redundant
labour which is to be absorbed by the growing industries.
Various other measures such as compulsory transfer of pension
rights, more rented housing, a cheaper means of buying and
selling houses, and a tax on the use of labour may all assist the
movement of labour from one industry to another. But, undoubtedly, labour mobility is not enough; the skill-intensity of
the whole labour force should be deepened, through education
and training. Initially, however, an increase in education and
training reduces the labour force by withdrawing people from
the labour market. If the school-leaving age is raised by a year,
then half a million or more juveniles are taken from the 25
million working force – a fall of 2 per cent. This suggests that
education and training will tend to intensify the labour shortage.

Yet, obviously, training is a substitute for sheer numbers;
quality replaces quantity. Economising in labour itself is a
technique that has to be learned. All managements must have
added inducements to economise in the use of labour. The payroll tax is one instance of a device to induce managements to
save labour. But they also need to be trained how to do this, in
addition to the incentive of a rising wage-bill. The experience

of productivity teams, and the gap between best- and worst-practice firms, suggest that there is considerable scope for management to learn how to reduce its labour requirements.

Further, as is argued below, the fastest-growing industries, like chemicals, engineering and vehicles, tend to be the most skill-intensive. This suggests that the limitation on their growth rate is more likely to be the shortage of skilled workers than a labour shortage in general. The problem that faces these industries is the elimination of skill shortages, and this is achieved only in part by upgrading and training of their own labour force. For the greater part these industries rely upon the technical education system for their skilled labour force.

In addition, however, some of these industries tend to be heavy users of complex machinery as well. There is, therefore, a relationship between skill-intensive processes and the use of capital involving a complex technology, as might be expected. The dichotomy between labour-intensive and capital-intensive industries can be supplemented by a further – and partly overlapping – dichotomy between skill-intensive and skill-shallow industries. Any attempt to overcome the labour shortage by the use of machinery embodying an advanced technology is likely to intensify the demand for skills, and partly to defeat its own aims by creating skill shortages in place of more general shortages of labour. This process may be seen to have been developing during the last decade when investment has been rising as a proportion of GNP, the capital-output has been rising, and skill shortages have been intensifying.

These three considerations suggest that education and training may be a way of relieving some at least of the pressure on the labour market, which has been a major cause of the failure of the British economy to grow faster. In addition the development of a more educated and resilient population probably has longer-term effects of a profound kind.

In an article recently published in the National Institute *Economic Review*, Messrs Godley and Shepherd estimated that over the ten-year period from 1952 to 1962 the underlying rate of growth of output per head rose from 1·8 per cent a year to 2·5 per cent. It may be asked how far this rise in the underlying rate of growth of output per head can be attributed to education and training.

The connection between education and the economy

We do not know the answer to this question, for although most people would agree that education has something to do with growth, the difficulty is to pin down the connection exactly. The most precise connection is between the skills of the labour force and the schools and colleges that train people in skills. A production engineer, a veterinary surgeon, an architect, all have a direct and clearly necessary function in the productive process. If their skills are not available production will obviously be lower than it would otherwise be.

The more skilled people of the right type who are available, the greater will be the productive capacity of the economy. These examples have been chosen from skills which are in sectors that contribute obviously and directly to the growth of the economy. But what of the doctor? He makes the growth of the Health Service possible and so (indirectly at least) adds to the productive capacity of the economy and, in so far as the Health Service output enters into the GNP, he adds to the GNP. But he is less obviously *productive* than an engineer.

Let us take the argument further – what of the woman graduate, perhaps a doctor, who is married and raising a family? What *economic* use is her degree? How does it add to the productive capacity of the economy to educate her and her daughters? It may be a civilised thing to do; it may be a thing worthwhile in itself; but it does not self-evidently add to growth.

These philistine points need to be made, for it is all too easy a doctrine to say that education causes growth, and that therefore the more education there is, the faster will be the potential growth rate. Much education is not of this growth-oriented kind – music and the arts being only at the extreme of a whole genus of 'useless' skills – and, indeed, some of the attitudes that schools and colleges inculcate may be positively deleterious to growth. Alfred Marshall regarded the public schools as the places where promising entrepreneurial stock was brainwashed into becoming civil servants and administrators. The commercial rise of the nonconformists in England, we are told, was due in part to their exclusion from the ecclesiastically controlled schools and colleges of the day. More education does not

necessarily mean faster growth. In general, however, it probably does.

The USSR poured resources into education and training as
well as into physical capital, and its reserves of skilled manpower have clearly been a major factor in accelerating its
growth rate. The USA imported many skilled people from
Europe during the nineteenth century, and then educated
generation after generation of Americans to a high level. The
resources of skill and trained talent upon which the American
economy has been able to draw have undoubtedly been a major
element in its potential for growth.

There are two common characteristics of the education system of the USA and the USSR. In both of them technical and
vocational skills are given great attention and prestige – no less
than that given to the highly academic subject. And in both of
them, the emphasis has been upon educating the whole nation,
rather than a small elite class. Consequently, talent has been
able to emerge from almost any source, and there seems little
doubt that there is a broad executive capacity which is not so
evident in other countries. Psychological research suggests, too,
that 'talent' is primarily a social phenomenon; it multiplies in
favourable conditions; and it seems fairly certain that 'favourable conditions' implies broad avenues of education rather than
narrow ladders.

In Denmark, Germany and Japan a different situation seems
to have prevailed. Their deeply stratified educational systems
remained, and in all of them the prestige of the classical curri-
culum was in no whit diminished by the importance attached
to technical education which in all three countries, however,
was held to be a major force in take-off. Danish agriculture
benefited from the rural folk high schools of the mid-nineteenth
century; German industry, in the period 1840–90 (especially in
chemicals and engineering) relied upon advanced technological
training and research; and the Japanese deliberately trained
their workers during the Meiji period to enable Western industry to be emulated. Let it not be thought, however, that mass
education on the US or Soviet models was a precondition of
education's playing a major role in the development of these
three countries.

It is also worth remembering that only in the most implausible circumstances could education become a substitute for physical accumulation – notably, if techniques were developed which were skill-intensive and labour-intensive, but most skill-intensive techniques are capital-intensive. Unfortunately, many of the arguments used to demonstrate the role that education has played in economic growth have emphasised its independent contribution when its place is more properly to be seen as complementary to other factors – notably the development of technology and high levels of physical investment – in the generation of economic development. One method of argument that has had great vogue has been the so-called 'human capital' approach. The use of the Cobb-Douglas function, and its variants, has led to the view that after the contributions of capital and labour have been deducted from growth, there is a sizeable residual. This residual is held to be caused, for the greater part, by education. There are two steps to this argument – neither of them wholly satisfactory. The first is the acceptance of a production function of a Cobb-Douglas type, relying as it does on assumptions of perfect competition and full employment and drawing attention to the substitutability of factors rather than to their complementarity. The second step is that the contribution of education is deduced from the fact that the earnings of the educated are greater than those of the uneducated. If the labour market is working perfectly this would indicate of course (after standardising for innate ability, social class and other factors) that education led to the higher incomes of the educated. But the labour market does not work perfectly. Incomes are conventionally determined. There is a constellation of social class, parental income-group, access to education, access to good jobs; and a correlation of position in the income hierarchy with social position. If two men lift potatoes all day and sell them by the roadside, and one has worked twice as long as the other and lifted twice as many potatoes as the other, he will earn twice as much (assuming a perfect market, free and identical land, costless seed and forks, spades and other implements). But it is a far cry from this to say that the productivity of education is to be measured by the income differential of educated people. For what you are doing in part at least is measuring social inequality, not economic productivity. It might be done in real terms, if index-number problems could be overcome, or it might be done if the labour market were perfect, but to measure the returns to education is more difficult – even – than to measure the returns to physical capital. Globally, it cannot be done satisfactorily.

What can be done is to present an argument couched in less global terms, but which draws attention to those parts of the economy where education has a role to play in solving certain key problems which seem to limit growth. For the part that education plays is probably complementary to the part that is played by capital and by technology. The problem (from the point of view of those bent on raising the growth rate) is to get the balance between technology (in the broadest sense), physical capital, and education and training right.

In this chapter, we attempt, first, to make certain suggestions with regard to higher education and research. The next section deals with middle-level manpower. In the last section, some general observations are made on the education system as a whole. Two major conclusions are drawn. The first is that the substantial expansion of the education system – especially on the technical side – since the early 1950s has already added to the productive powers of the economy, and that in the next few years there are reasons to hope for a really big breakthrough on this front, when those who have recently entered industry rise to responsible executive posts. Clearly, too, the faster the promotion rates of these young educated people, the more quickly the effects of their education are likely to be felt. In the second place, the argument here means that an acceleration of the technical education programme, building on a sound basis of a widespread general education, is likely to pay off fairly quickly.

High-level skills and research

In this section an attempt will be made to trace a connection between research, high-level skills, and technological development.

In recent years, there has been a considerable growth of outlays on higher education. In 1960–61 £100m. was spent. In 1964–65 equivalent outlays were over £200m. At the last count, nearly 300,000 students over the age of eighteen were involved in full-time education, and there were many more taking part-time courses, compared with only a quarter of this number in 1938. Over half a million people, for example, were thought to be engaged in correspondence courses in a recent year.

In addition research, which is integrally linked to the development of high-level skills, has been increasing in volume. In 1959 outlays on research were running at about £500m. compared with less than half this amount at the end of the 1940s. Of this the government spent about £150m., the universities about £25m., and industry nearly £300m. The bigger part of this was for defence purposes, but even so a high proportion of research was for industrial purposes.

About one-twentieth of the working population have high-level skills derived from higher education. In the 1961 census, 1,090,000 members of the working population were shown as having completed higher education. Of these the biggest group was the teachers (360,000) followed by 350,000 miscellaneous arts and commerce graduates and 310,000 scientists and technologists working in administration, business and industry, and what is interesting is that about a quarter of these qualified people, and the majority of scientists and technologists, have been educated in part-time further education.

Until recently, the full-time education system, at the higher levels, has been a small enterprise, producing teachers and comparatively few other people. Consequently, the recent rapid growth of full-time advanced education is a new thing (historically speaking) in the British economy, and its effects may not be felt until its products are in their late thirties and early forties.

Two other things may be said with certainty. The first is that the reasonably fast growth of higher education in recent years, and the somewhat faster growth that is now being planned, will lead to a rise in the number of these highly qualified people in the labour force. Allowing for withdrawals through sickness, retirement and emigration, the numbers should build up to over 2 million, and possibly to $2\frac{1}{2}$ million, over the next ten to fifteen years or so. The labour force at the same time is likely to grow by only 3 million or so. Consequently, something nearer one-tenth of the labour force will have completed higher education compared with one-twentieth now, and a great proportion of them will have followed full-time courses rather than part-time courses. The second forecast that may be made with confidence is that the demand for these high-level skills is likely to grow at a rate at least as fast as that shown by the supply. This is for a number of reasons. Education will take about 700,000 or more of them – twice as many as at present. The projections for the growth of the service industries and trades, where many qualified people are employed, suggest that their output will grow considerably as a proportion of GNP. The fastest-growing industries – chemicals and engineering – use the largest numbers of highly qualified people, and, in addition, many other industries are becoming more science-based, and so there will be a rising demand for scientists and engineers. Research itself, in the universities or research establishments, is growing faster than the number of good graduates from the universities, so that the demand for the most highly qualified people is likely to rise fastest of all.

This being said in general terms, what we cannot say in detail (except for teachers) is what the demand for any single category of qualified people is likely to look like, nor how far a kind of Say's law for graduates may be operating. Some of the evidence for the employment of arts graduates suggests that the supply may in some sense be creating its own demand. Self-evidently, in full employment, all graduates will be employed, and it will not necessarily be because their degree is 'useful' but because, in conditions of labour shortage, all hands are useful. Their relative salaries may suffer as their scarcity diminishes. In the short run their differentials are convention-ally established, and will remain fixed, but in the long run it is probable that it is only if demand for their services rises as its supply does that their salaries will not fall, relative to those of other people. Most people would judge that the employment opportunities for most graduates are likely to improve, but the detailed forecasts needed to substantiate this judgement require an assessment of the future course of salary levels. All forecasts for manpower requirements stumble at this point. It is not known how far the relationship between output and require-ment for skills is technologically determined, and how far, with shifting wage relativities, it is in fact possible to combine different kinds of skills (and different kinds of capital) to produce the same output. The presumption is that on the whole there is no fixed technological determinism operating on the levels and types of skill required, in all industries, though there may be in some. But how far there is substitutability of skill levels and types in response to wage changes and skill shortages is not known. The UK Government has tried forecasting the industrial requirements for highly qualified scientists and engineers on a variety of assumptions. A 1956 ten-year forecast assumed a simple proportionate connection between the rate of growth of industrial output and the rate of employment of scientists. 'In the event,' Moser and Layard say, 'the index of industrial production rose between 1956 and 1959 . . . by an average of 2·1 per cent. At the same time, the number of scientists and engineers grew by an average of 8·5 per cent per annum.' Two obvious fallacies in this method are that rising industrial output masks different rates of growth of different sectors. If shipbuilding goes down and electronics go up, the rise in the demand for engineers and scientists will be bigger than the average rise in output for the economy as a whole. Further, if the situation in the base-year was sub-optimal, a greater availability of scientists and engineers could lead to a rapid manning-up of industry to achieve desired levels of skill-use.

A second UK long-term forecast of the requirements for scientists and engineers was made in 1961 for 1970 and it tried to take account of these objections to the first method by making a rather primitive sectoral forecast of industrial output for 1970, and then took present 'best-practice' firms as a criterion of what an average firm would be like at the end of the decade ahead. Here again, the forecast has already been proven to be far too low.

Sophisticated techniques for manpower forecasting have been tried elsewhere, but they have not had much greater success. Consequently, as in so much else, the economist advising on growth policy has to argue from first principles on insufficient evidence.

If we put the question – what do these highly qualified people do? – a sensible sort of answer emerges. At present, of scientists and technologists in manufacturing industry, 40 per cent are directly involved in the production process, 40 per cent are engaged in research and development, and 20 per cent manage. Where is the fastest expansion likely to be in require-ments for skilled people, especially on the service side? The answer seems clear – management at all levels. The develop-ment of research in industry is unlikely to be so rapid that it absorbs a growing proportion of scientists and engineers, and the production process relies chiefly upon people trained in middle skills. High-level skilled people are useful chiefly in managerial and supervisory grades. Now this is highly sig-nificant, because the connection between research and the adoption of the most advanced technology possible is probably linked to two further things. One is that somewhat elusive factor, the calibre of the management, its open-mindedness and its willingness to face up to change. The other is the rate of physical investment. If management and investment are the key factors, it follows that a common scientific and technological background between general management, production super-visors and the research and development department may well be one of the most effective methods of closing the gap which undoubtedly exists between research on the one hand and its incorporation into the productive process on the other, and in accelerating the write-off of obsolescent equipment. In other words, a greater degree of responsiveness to technical change may well come from a rise in the number of managers with a highly trained (scientific, engineering or even just university) background than from manipulations of the rate of write-off of capital for tax purposes, or other measures of fiscal policy designed to accelerate the adoption of new techniques by the use of new equipment. A skilled university-trained engineer is, perhaps, more likely to adjust to a high rate of scrapping old equipment than somebody who has just 'learned the business' man and boy, if only because the graduate will be more likely to be in touch with new developments.

The evidence is strong that there is a high correlation be-tween research and growth – Freeman found a high correlation between research expenditure and rate of growth of output per man in seventeen industries, between 1935 and 1958. The big-gest research industries are chemicals, and those making capital goods. These are also, of course, easily the fastest-growing industries in our economy. The relationship between the backgrounds of managers and their attitudes to new techniques is less well-established; the most authoritative investigation – that by Carter and Williams – is somewhat inconclusive on this point.

But other evidence suggests that these industries which spend most on research are also the most skill-using industries. In 1959, in the US chemical industry, 9·6 per cent of the total labour force were engineers and scientists, compared with 1·6 per cent in the labour force as a whole. In other industries the figures for engineers and scientists were 4·2 per cent in machinery, 7·7 per cent in electrical equipment, and 7·5 per cent in petroleum refinery, and these few were the fastest-growing industries in the US. In the most thorough analysis yet published of the relationships between skills, research outlays and the rate of growth, the National Science Foundation found that in the US aircraft, missiles and space-craft industry, 12·3 per cent of the personnel in 1960 were scientists and engineers and that it was expected that this proportion would grow to 21 per cent in 1970. The factors leading to this growth of skill intensity, during a period when output is expected to grow by 50 per cent and total employment by 29 per cent, were the growing complexity of product, the amount of research per product, and the rapidity with which technological innovations had to be introduced.

Since there is reason to expect that industry as a whole will share (though to a far lesser extent) these three characteristics, it would be reasonable to assume that those links between the rate of growth of output and the demand for skills which have been found in this industry will characterise industry as a whole.

A further relevant consideration is that the larger firms are overwhelmingly those that engage in research and development. In 1961, of 11,600 firms doing research and development work in the US 86 per cent of the expenditure was by the 391 companies employing more than 5,000 employees. The increasing size of the firms in growing industries therefore increases the likelihood of research becoming an important activity, and of their requirements for high-level skills accelerating faster than output. It therefore seems probable that research and skill-intensity are concentrated in big firms in the leading growth industries. Two problems present themselves – how fast can the other industries, especially those where smaller firms predominate, be brought up to the level of the firms in the leading sectors, and how the rate of growth of the leading sectors themselves can be accelerated.

One popular answer is more competition. Yet it seems unlikely that chemicals and engineering are more highly competitive than the rest of British industry – indeed, the reverse is probably the case – and the argument for bigger firms is an argument for mergers and amalgamations, rather than for competition, to replace market-sharing agreements. Another popular answer is industrial co-operation in research and training.

There is some evidence on the effectiveness of research associations for whole industries which can provide research results on a contract basis. It is commonly thought that many of them are comparatively ineffectual. Research associations account for only a small proportion of total research and development outlays, and only nine associations (in the early 1960s) spent more than £250,000 a year. Government research, too, that was directly relevant to industry was comparatively small in total – certainly less than £15m. a year was spent. The bulk of research and development is therefore concentrated in large firms in a few growth industries – notably chemicals and engineering – which also are big employers of highly skilled people.

What are the implications of this for policy? First, that to bring other industries up to the level of adoption of new techniques and new processes maintained by these leading sectors is going to be no easy task. Feeding in new management skills is likely to be the quickest method, since that seems the most likely way that new rates of investment and obsolescence will be adopted, and more skilled workers trained and recruited. Can a big effort in management education help this? Or must we wait for a slow process of take-over of small firms by bigger firms, of partial nationalisation of key firms and – imperceptibly like some slow ocean swell – for the advance of B.Sc.s and B. Techs. to the boards of British firms? Certainly there seems little likelihood that co-operative or government-sponsored research, even if it can be quickly generated, will enter the productive process rapidly unless the firms have managements and research departments which are 'technologically receptive'. The rate of build-up of higher education among people in business and industry is likely to be a factor in developing this receptiveness. Therefore, perhaps the main effect of high-level education on economic growth may be its effect in generating an appetite for technological change. This, in turn, is far more likely to happen in industries where output is expanding rapidly, and management is therefore adaptable, partly because the numbers of people engaged in management are increasing, and new capital is being added to the stock already at work.

The more the appetite for new technology develops, so will the demand for production workers who have middle-level technological skills. It is to these that we now turn.

Industrial training and retraining

The most obvious direct connection between economic growth and the education and training system is industrial training and retraining. Industry itself undertakes considerable programmes of training, ranging from courses of executive development at staff colleges of its own (and at the highest level the Henley Staff College) to short initiation courses of one or two days' duration for operatives, to teach them the simple repetitive operations they will have to do. The major contribution of business and industry to the provision of a skilled labour force lies, however, midway between these two points, and represents the chaotic structure of further education and training for middle-level skills which has developed from the old apprenticeship system.

There are three main characteristics of this work. In the first place, there are the professional and semi-professional types of training which have developed (like the law and accountancy) along the lines of articled clerkships, associated with correspondence and evening courses, leading to a recognised qualification. There are a great many bodies giving qualifications of this sort, and many thousands of people are studying hard to acquire these qualifications.

In the second place, the higher-level engineering and technological skills have evolved from the apprenticeship pattern to the sandwich course principle which is the basis for the work of the degrees in Technology and of some engineering degrees in the Technological Universities and the Regional and Area Technical Colleges. This work has expanded quickly in the last ten years, and improved greatly in quality. During the period 1958–64, 3,000 Diplomas in Technology were awarded, and the rate of increase over the six years was very rapid. Other (lower) qualifications were awarded in correspondingly greater numbers.

Thirdly, the old craftsmen apprenticeships are entering a period of change, for a number of reasons. The rise in the school-leaving age (over a third of fifteen-year-olds voluntarily stay on at school until eighteen or later, and in 1971 the school-leaving age is to be raised to sixteen) has made anything more than a four- or five-year apprenticeship impracticable. The development of part-time day release – which the Henniker-Heaton Report is likely to accelerate, with its target of a further 250,000 students in part-time day release in 1970 – enables many thousands of boys and girls to supplement their learning-on-the-job with education in the local technical college. Part-time day release is an extremely inefficient system, and it should be replaced by full-time courses or by block-release. The tendency is for this to happen.

More and more boys and girls are going to full-time or part-time courses in the technical colleges, and in addition, the bigger firms have well-established training departments, which co-operate with the local authority colleges. Now, under the Industrial Training Act, there is a Central Training Council, and a number of Industrial Training Boards for each industry, which impose a levy on firms to finance training arrangements, remitting the levy in accordance to the efforts made by the firm themselves. Ten years ago, much of this rapid growth of technical education and training would have seemed almost impossible. A number of fundamental issues are raised by these developments. In the first place, it is now widely realised that the imparting of skills is itself a skilled procedure, that not everybody can do it and that probably somebody who is fully engaged himself in the production process is not the best person to accept full responsibility for training others. Therefore, training is increasingly a specialised function in all but the smallest firms, and more and more of it is in fact conducted in the local authority colleges. But, of course, such training outside the firm may not be as directly relevant to the firm's needs as it would like it to be. Each firm has its own idiosyncrasies.

However this may be, the general interest is served by training which it not too specific to the firm, since initial training serves industry as a whole, as well as the firm the new entrant goes into. Labour turnover figures suggest that most training given by firms must eventually benefit other firms, as the trained labour is gradually absorbed by other firms.

Further, the rapid rate of technical change that is associated with economic growth will make skill redundancy an increasing problem. It is probable that those who have been taught at least some elements of the fundamentals of those skills will be more adaptable to change, and likely to be more easily and quickly retrained.

Retraining is likely to be a matter of growing concern. It therefore deserves special consideration here. It seems probable that the agencies for retraining the older worker need to be built on the existing adult education agencies. These are, besides voluntary bodies like the WEA, the technical colleges and the correspondence colleges. There may well be a possibility of developing the radio and the television as media for retraining, used in co-operation with the correspondence colleges.

Earlier, the conclusion was reached that the bulk of the use of high-level skills will be concentrated in the growth industries, which are also science-based and capital-intensive. But the requirements for training and the development of middle-level skills extend to the whole economy. Nevertheless, it seems that the demand for middle-level manpower is to some degree a function of the use of high-level manpower.

There are four major needs if the economy is to make the best use of the increasing flow of educated and trained manpower. The first is for extensive managerial education, which needs a considerable development, especially at the level of the small business and the lower supervisory grades. It should be concerned not only with managerial decision-making processes, labour relations, salesmanship and the other aspects of management that the best courses are already designed to help, but with a range of technological skills which will enable the latest technologies to be more rapidly understood and adopted.

Secondly, there is a need for the more highly skilled technologists to be kept in continuous and rapid contact with the development of research into new processes and new products. The place of the Technological Universities and the regional and area technical colleges in this respect is of crucial importance. This should become an easier task as the level of management improves, and its understanding of the possibilities of modern techniques, since more managers will then go out and look for research results instead of having these reluctantly thrust upon them.

The third level – middle-level skilled manpower as it might be called – is of tremendous importance. It is here that the collaboration between technical colleges on the one hand and industry and business on the other needs to be at its closest. It is also a field where rapid change is occurring.

Here and at the fourth level – initial training for new semi-skilled entrants to industry, and for those who have just changed their occupation – there is much that the government can do. The growth industries constitute the biggest single source of initial training and retraining, and therefore it may be easier to accelerate their programmes than to initiate programmes in industries which have a more stagnant technology.

The Industrial Training Boards, if properly developed, provide wide scope for this level of training. What may be needed in addition are tax-incentives for additional training facilities – perhaps along the lines of initial write-offs for capital goods. It might be, for example, that training costs should be not only a legitimate business expense, but should count double for tax purposes in the year in which they have been incurred. In addition, there is a strong case for extra incentives to the entrants themselves to become trained. Thus a tax on untrained entrants to employment might itself be a powerful inducement to employers not to hire untrained entrants. The whole question of grants to people who undertake courses of training needs to be re-examined.

One major difficulty that faces forward planning for training is the problem of the development areas where growth is the most urgently needed. There are now facilities for training people who are unemployed or threatened with unemployment in these areas, but two questions arise. First, how far can the training for new jobs be undertaken in advance of the creation of the new job – how far, that is, can training be a lead factor? Here the correct answer is probably a cautious one – generalised unspecific training undoubtedly has its uses, but the main need is to tie initial training into the employment-creating investment, if it is to be fully effective. Secondly, however, a high and general level of education, especially on the technical side, will undoubtedly be an incentive for new industrial development in a depressed area, since the initial training of workers at all levels will be easier. In addition, a good local education system is a factor in determining the drawing-power of a locality to a business thinking of moving or developing a branch. It is striking, however, that the depressed areas are precisely those where the educational standards are (generally speaking) fairly low – where fewer children stay on at school after fifteen, where entry rates to higher education are lowest, and where the proportions of slum schools are highest. It therefore follows that a redirection of educational effort towards these areas could play a part in creating better conditions for development.

In addition, in so far as the development of modern industry requires fairly close co-operation between universities (especially technical universities) and industry, the decision to locate so many new universities in and around London and the Midlands may have been a foolish one. As higher education is expanding rapidly, the opportunity should have been taken earlier to develop new universities in areas like the North-east, where it was left to the Labour Government to found a technological university, though four had been founded earlier in the London area.

The education system

The rapid expansion of higher education (which is a prerequisite for many aspects of rapid technological and managerial improvement) relies upon the expansion of the education system as a whole. For, to get ten people out of the university system, there have to be twenty to thirty people in the academic parts of the secondary education system. To make the secondary education system viable, the primary schools have to be adequate. So that, in this limited sense, an increase in the numbers of engineers – say – usually entails the expansion of the system as a whole. Nowhere is this more clear than in the teacher-training system. Education has a large feed-back; it is itself the largest single consumer of skills – a third of the highly qualified people in the country are teachers.

Further, at the level below the high-level skills there is a bigger demand for skilled people. For every scientist or engineer rather more than one more middle-skilled man is needed. This in itself will require a still bigger expansion of the technical education system. At the level below this a whole range of developments in training for relatively low-level skills may be foreseen. To take one example, the new examination for foremen – the National Examination in Supervisory Studies – will develop the courses in foremanship which, at a crucial level of management, could lead to considerable improvements in industrial attitudes to productivity which no amount of exhortation by industrialists and politicians could effect. The general standard of the craft skills will also be raised by the courses now being developed under the Industrial Training Act.

Two consequences derive from this. In the first place, the expansion of the supply of trained people at all levels is a function of the expansion of the whole education system. Secondly, the fact that the general level of the education system has risen – and it has risen – means that the level of attainment of the parts of the system specifically concerned with training can also rise.

Could one, perhaps, go further? Would it be possible to say that the manifest improvement of the education system since 1944 – and especially since the early 1950s – has other consequences of a more indirect nature which will raise the general level of achievement? The answer to this is 'yes'. There is now a sufficient body of evidence to suggest that adequate home background, plus adequate schooling, will actually raise 'intelligence' (however measured) and other social skills. The numbers of illiterates and semi-literates, for example, have declined dramatically in the past decade, and the average level of reading has improved considerably. This has coincided with an improvement in young people's physical condition which should have made the population at large far more resilient and prepared for change than it has ever been in the past. There are two caveats. The first is that large parts of the population – those roughly over thirty – have a considerable educational lag compared with the younger generations. It is true that so-called informal education – TV and Penguins – is in many respects more effective than formal education, and that over one million people are enrolled at evening classes, so that to some extent the lag is being overcome, but the people who make use of this informal education are likely to be those who have already had more than the minimum education, for there is considerable evidence that the appetite for education grows by what it feeds on. Consequently, if we look at the *flow* of educated people into the economy the situation looks far more favourable than if we look at the *stock* of educated people.

In the second place we must beware that the education that people get is not of a kind that positively unfits them for creative and useful work. This is not so remote an eventuality as it seems. There is a danger in this country of a considerable number of arts graduates, with no clear job in view, becoming what they would regard as a drug on the market – feeling that their only possibility of a job was in school-teaching which (quite rightly) they believe they would be no good at. The danger is of a kind of structural unemployment because there is no clear avenue for their talents at an appropriate price, and it may be a considerable one.

That being said, however, it is fairly clear that the contemporary education system is evolving in such a way that a great deal more talent is being liberated than in the past. The evidence of the results of the comprehensive schools, for example, in dealing with children from the middle range of ability is indeed impressive. Some primary schools have raised the standards of the slower learners to a quite remarkable height. There is reason to hope that good, modern schools will be increasingly successful with many children who were wholly or in part rejected by the education system in the past. This means two things – first, there will be more and more talented people able to go on to advanced and middle-level courses, and second, that the general level of resilience and creative ability should rise fairly quickly.

If we attempt to give some quantitative estimates of this progress, the statistics must be very rough. The real break-through in education seems to have been in the middle 1950s. By the end of the 1940s the schools were only just recovering from the disruptions of the war. In 1938, about one in seven or so of the age-group 15–20 entering the labour force probably had some kind of sixth-form (or its equivalent in technical education) experience, though often for only one year. Probably about one in twenty went on to higher education of some kind, full or part-time. In the working force as a whole in 1938, of those aged 60 (who would have left school before the Boer War) only about one in twenty would have had any kind of post-14 education, and about one in fifty would have had a degree. Those aged forty fell midway between the people aged twenty and people aged sixty, as the expansion of secondary education had been a fairly linear one.

If we take 1964, the sixty-year-olds represent the education system as it was during and immediately after the first world war.

TABLE I. PERCENTAGE OF THOSE IN THE LABOUR FORCE WITH SOME EDUCATION BEYOND THE MINIMUM*

Year	*Age in that year*		
	20	40	60
1938	15	8	5
1964	25	15	6
1980	60	20	12

* This table is calculated roughly from the appropriate year of output for the education system adjusted for female participation in the labour force, allowing for deaths, etc.

Only about one in twelve (and probably fewer) of the occupied population had received any sort of sixth-form education or beyond, but about a quarter of those entering the labour force had done so.

By 1980, two out of three of the entrants to the labour force will have had some education beyond the compulsory period, about a fifth of the forty-year-olds and about an eighth of the sixty-year-olds.

TABLE 2. MINIMUM SCHOOL LIFE (IN YEARS) FOR
PEOPLE OF DIFFERENT AGES

Year	Age in that year		
	20	40	60
1918	8	7	—
1938	9	8	7
1964	10	9	9
1980	11	10	9

A similar table which shows the length of compulsory education
of people of different ages is also revealing, for the majority of
the labour force will have left school at the minimum leaving
age. In 1918, a considerable proportion of the labour force had
virtually no education at all; in 1980, on the other hand, nobody will be working who left school before fourteen (except
immigrants – admittedly a fairly big exception), while everybody over the age of forty-eight will have left at the age of
fifteen or later.

This shift of educational qualifications in the labour force
suggests a considerable rise in the supply potential of the
economy. If we take forty as the age at which managerial
responsibilities are commonly assumed (which is far too late in
any case) it will not be till 1980 that one-fifth of the labour force
at that age left school after the age of fifteen. The radical
improvement of educational attainments takes a long time to
work itself through the economy. Yet the change from 1938 is
sufficiently great (especially in the numbers with degrees) to
hope that a point of break-through may be somewhere in the
offing. (One way to make it so is to lower the age at which top
jobs in industry are given to people and to accelerate the retirement of elderly directors. Recent evidence reported in *The
Director*, January 1965, shows that the younger directors tend
to have considerably higher educational qualifications than
their older colleagues.)

These changes cannot be proved beyond a doubt to have
raised the supply potential of the economy by improving the
calibre of the labour force, but they are suggestive, because
greater literacy and ability is associated with longer school life

and so is a general improvement in what might be called 'intelligence' – that is, in the capacity to cope.

Further, those people with a higher level of education are likely to be able to acquire new skills more easily, especially as the new skills that are to be acquired often have a basic requirement of a certain educational attainment before they can be taught. Evidence seems to be accumulating that there is a tendency for unemployment in the US to be associated with low educational levels. While (contrary to what is widely held there) the cure for unemployment cannot be more education – except in the unlikely case that extra outlays on education unbalance the budget and so, acting through the multiplier, raise employment levels – and the association of unemployment with low educational attainment is probably part of the total poverty syndrome, it is nevertheless true that the rapid shift of the economy towards skill-intensive occupations is likely to lead to relatively greater redundancy among the unskilled. A structural unemployment situation could then develop, where skill shortages coincided with unemployment among the unskilled. The wider spread of education would be growth-inducing because it enabled such structural imbalances to be avoided. It is fair to point out, however, that there are few if any signs of such a situation developing in the UK, though the decline in the rate of growth of female participation rates in the labour force may be due to the lack of skills among women.

Thus, the general conclusion seems to be that education has already considerably raised the growth potential of the economy, and that more education will do still more. There is one other consideration, however, that has been left to last, because it raises some broad issues about the structure of education.

The productivity of education

As the economy shifts into a greater concentration of output in the service trades, so there is a tendency for the overall rate of growth of productivity to fall. One cause of this is genuine – these industries tend to be labour-intensive, and their technologies are relatively stagnant. The other cause is statistical and, in consequence, a misleading impression can be gained. The output of the government sector is, for the most part, measured by its inputs. Thus, by definition, changing technology cannot significantly affect productivity (which is output over input). In the case of education – which took over 1 per cent of the labour force in 1960, and will take over 2 per cent in 1980, and which claimed about a third of those in the labour force with higher qualifications in 1960, and will still have a fifth or so of them in 1980 – this is especially serious. The contribution of education to the rate of growth of GNP is – statistically – to hold it back.

It is, however, an unfair impression to give, since the technology of education has begun to change fairly rapidly, though not nearly (as yet) as fast as that of medicine, where the rate of growth of productivity since 1940 has been considerable. The statistical problems of assessing productivity change in this sector, and allowing for it in growth programmes, may be left on one side. But the importance of orienting education in such a way that its own productivity rises cannot be over-stressed, especially as, for the next ten years, acute shortages of teachers are likely to inhibit the development of the education service.

The other broad consideration is this. The emphasis in this chapter on technical education and on research presupposes a generally adequate education system. All the possibilities of technical advance suggested here rest, therefore, on a broad advance on the whole education front.

SUGGESTIONS FOR FURTHER READING

The Residual Factor in Economic Growth, ed. J. Vaizey (OECD, 1965). This is a volume containing the papers presented to a conference by Balogh, Kaldor, Tinbergen, Svennilson, and other economists, which discussed fully the part that education and training play in economic growth.

International Labour Review, April 1964, contains articles on the economics of manpower forecasting by Hollister and others which throw considerable doubt on the validity of detailed forecasts.

National Institute Economic Review (29), August 1964. 'Long-term growth and short-term policy', by W. A. H. Godley and J. R. Shepherd, discusses the underlying growth trend in the British economy in recent years, which might be said to be due to a 'long-term trend of productivity'. This article is referred to on page 238.

National Institute Economic Review (20), May 1962. 'Research and development, a comparison between British and American industry', by Christopher Freeman, is an analysis of UK and US expenditures on research and development. This article is referred to on page 246.

Charles A. Myers and Frederick Herbison, *Education, Manpower and Economic Growth* (McGraw Hill, 1964), is an attempt to bring together a considerable number of manpower forecasts, and a discussion of the problems (both practical and theoretical) of analysing the part played by skills in economic development, with a view to making policy recommendations (especially in developing nations).

J. Vaizey, *The Economics of Education* (Faber, 1962). A general survey of the subject.

9

RICH AND POOR NATIONS

The most urgent and important problems are rarely those in the forefront of political discussion. Our own immediate interests dominate. Disinterestedness, as well as far-sighted self-interest, are at a discount. Next to the task of preventing nuclear war, the main political task of the next decades is to raise incomes in the poor countries and to enable them to embark on economic development. It is both intolerable and dangerous that two-thirds of the world's population should be miserably poor while the rest of us enjoy living standards twenty times as high. If we care about human equality and brotherhood, the existence of vast poverty and misery must be our main concern.

At one time, both the Left and the Right, from different motives, were more international-minded than they are today. Before the first world war, and before the split of the Second International, socialists thought that they owed primary loyalty to the oppressed in all countries. It was even thought that international solidarity could prevent war. Partly as a result of the split of the Second International, partly as a result of the wars and partly as a result of prosperity and increasing participation in national government, some of the international spirit has evaporated. National solidarity has been achieved at the expense of international solidarity. Labour Foreign Ministers have not yet evolved a radical foreign policy which would lay the same emphasis on international solidarity as on national goals, and the benefits of the welfare state were closely hugged to the national breast. Trade unionists often oppose coloured immigration and favour barriers against imports from poor countries. The Right, too, is turning away from visions of imperial responsibility and feelings of *noblesse oblige* to national consolidation, if necessary at the expense of international obligations. In spite of greatly increased travel and communication, interests and sympathies are probably today directed more at national issues than they were sixty years ago. This is not to deny that we have made progress in giving practical expression to international solidarity, although even there, a closer examination of the·motives for aid will show that these motives are mixed, and that some have nothing to do with international brotherhood. Moreover, there has recently been a wave of disillusionment over international aid and co-operation. Neither the West nor the Soviet bloc have done very much to accelerate development in poor countries.

It is the modest aim of the United Nations Development Decade to raise the annual rate of growth of the poor countries by the end of the decade so as to enable them to double their living levels by the end of the century. By raising annual growth rates from the present 3·5 per cent to 5 per cent by 1970, and allowing for population growth of 2 to 3 per cent per year, the present £25 per head could be raised to £50 after 35 years. It has been estimated that, in order to achieve this growth rate, the underdeveloped countries will have to increase the volume of their imports by 6 per cent per annum. In the 1950s the volume of their exports was expanding by only 4 per cent annually, and as a result of deteriorating terms of trade, the value rose by under 2 per cent per annum. Continuation of this trend would give a trade gap of the order of $20,000m. a year by 1970. Such calculations, even if refined in various ways, are not intended as forecasts, partly because the assumptions are both uncertain and based on a misleading model, and partly because a gap of this size would be impossible. The growth rate would have to be reduced long before the gap materialised. But whatever approach to the calculation of needs is used, whether foreign exchange requirements, savings requirements or 'absorptive capacity' are estimated, a relatively modest development aim is liable to make quite heavy demands on savings and foreign exchange.

The foreign exchange needs can be met in three main ways: by exporting more primary commodities, by exporting more manufactured goods and by receiving more capital from abroad in the form of private investment or aid. The ways in which we in the advanced and rich countries can co-operate in this effort are usually discussed under the headings 'aid' and 'trade', although, as we shall see, the distinction is not an altogether fortunate one. The impact on development will be different according to what form foreign exchange earnings take. The ability to make good use of aid depends itself on the quantity, composition and direction of trade and the ability to trade depends on aid. For reasons of space we shall not discuss here the important contribution which private investment can make to development.

Aid

A rational discussion of the consequences of aid is now greatly handicapped by a confusing way of counting aid. Different kinds of flows of gifts and loans are aggregated, the mixture is expressed as a percentage of national income, and the contributions of different advanced countries are ranked according to this arbitrary percentage. The aim is often expressed as raising this proportion to 1 per cent from its present 0·7 per cent. The present rag-bag, in which soft loans and hard loans, short- and long-term loans, at commercial and subsidised rates of interest are lumped together with free gifts, but where even these principles of inclusion are not consistent between countries, obscures the real contribution to aid and the way in which the cost of aid is shared between the rich countries. Since loans on commercial terms cannot be considered as 'aid', the proper measure would be the nominal value of all forms of aid minus the discounted present value of loan repayments, discounted at a rate of interest reflecting the alternative employment of long-term public capital. In this way all forms of aid are reduced to their value as grant (or gift or subsidy). The longer the term of the loan, the lower the interest rate and the later payments start, the greater will be the aid component thus calculated. There is, of course, some doubt as to what is the appropriate discount rate. Should we use the domestic returns on capital or the commercial international lending rate that private investors would require from investing abroad? The rate would vary from 5 to 10 per cent according to which criterion we employ. Given the imperfections of the international capital market, the sacrifices of the donor will diverge from the benefits to the recipient and different rates are therefore appropriate according to which of these two we attempt to measure: the sacrifice of the donor in granting aid or the benefit to the recipient in receiving it. Mr Pincus has attempted to recalculate aid to isolate the genuine aid component, and found that actual aid given is considerably smaller than it appears now, though the aid given by different countries is reduced in different proportions. Thus, for the year 1962, the United States moves from third place to second, the United Kingdom moves down from fourth to fifth, while Germany moves up from fifth (after Portugal, France, USA, UK) to third (after France and USA). Portugal moves from first place to eighth. At the same time, the aid given by the UK is substantially reduced from 0·72 per cent of Gross National Product to 0·27 per cent, of France from 1·51 to 1·32, of Germany from 0·59 to 0·27 per cent, and of all OECD countries from 0·82 to 0·52. Although we all exaggerate, we exaggerate in different degrees. Since 1962, however, the ranking of the UK has improved, as a result both of greater increases in aid and of interest waivers. It would be interesting to trace the behaviour of aid, calculated on this basis, through recent years. Although the volume has levelled off, if account were taken of the softening of terms, a different picture may emerge.

A serious defect of these calculations is that they take the terms of the loans seriously. Much more difficult than choosing the appropriate rate of discount is to estimate the true prospective rate of repayment and the likelihood of default. It is already clear that much of our past aid will have to be written off. But, since refinancing will count as aid, it will tend to reduce the future flow of new aid.

The results of what little aid was given have been disappointing. Many recipients have put it to bad use or have not been able to use it at all, or have wasted it in other ways. Others spent it on wars or acts hostile to the donor country and its allies, or have sided with the donor country's enemies. Some aid has gone to swell the fortunes of the rich in the poor countries, which often are substantially greater than those of many taxpayers in the donor countries.

In addition, some of the main donor countries have found themselves in balance of payments difficulties and have seen in aid an easy victim. Such reactions in the donor countries are misguided. The proper response to profligacy, waste, corruption, incompetence and hostility in the recipient countries, and to balance of payments difficulties in the donor countries, is not to slash aid, but to evolve an integrated strategy, combining aid with other measures conducive to making aid effective and minimising foreign exchange losses. Such a strategy would have to include a number of provisions.

Since aid consists in the transfer of real goods – machines, spare parts, materials, consumer goods, etc. – and of skills and know-how, international monetary and trading arrangements must not frustrate this transfer but must facilitate it. A system in which a donor fears the loss of international reserves to another rich country, or in which creditors refuse to accept imports from debtors while insisting on repayment and interest, is bound to breed disappointment and frustration. Aid should be related to a rational international trade and payments system.

Aid must be given in a form which avoids the creation of large and increasing debt burdens. The present tendency for high and increasing proportions of export receipts of developing countries to be devoted to servicing past debts is dangerous. Deflationary or restrictive actions, which developing countries would have to take in order to effect the debt payment, would threaten to undo much of the benefit initially derived from the loans. This involves co-ordination between donors as well as international control of commercial debt, for otherwise the soft lenders can rightly complain that their generosity is used to serve the hard loans of others.

Aid should not create or aggravate balance of payments difficulties for the donor countries. Since the underdeveloped countries do not tend to hoard reserves of foreign exchange, this is largely a problem of the distribution of reserves between rich countries. Aid given by one donor may partly be spent on the goods of another rich country, which, in turn, adds the receipts to its reserves.

There are a number of methods of expanding aid which reduce the strain on the donor's balance of payments.

(a) Co-operative international expansion of aid would mean that although, say, some sterling aid will be spent in America, some dollar aid will be spent in Britain. If donors move together, they can eliminate, or at least reduce, each other's losses.

(b) A reform of the present system of international liquidity would enable a donor country to lose some of the purchases to another rich country without suffering a loss of international reserves. The International Monetary Fund would compensate it for the loss by additional accommodation. Since such a reform would be desirable on other grounds than facilitating aid, it should be carried out in any case. But it can also be linked specifically with increased aid.

The Hon. Maxwell Stamp recently proposed a scheme which links an increase in international liquidity with aid to under-developed countries. Mr Harold Wilson's 'Ten-Point Economic Programme for the Commonwealth', published in 1963, also included proposals for combining increased liquidity with aid, which were similar to Mr Stamp's ideas. These schemes attempt to harness the resources of the rich, which may otherwise remain underemployed because of fears of balance of payments difficulties, to the needs of the developing countries. It is proposed to create a new international currency which is issued to the developing countries. These can spend it on imports from whatever country is ready to accept payment in this currency. The issuing authorities would have to consider a number of conditions, of which the deterioration in the terms of trade of the poor countries, and the level of employment and demand in the rich countries might be two. Since deflation in the rich countries of the North and deteriorating terms of trade in the poor countries of the South often go together, the timing of the issues will be normally non-controversial. It may be objected that aid to developing countries should not have to depend on slumps in rich countries and that, in any case, such a scheme could not deal with the problem of key currencies, for there is no guarantee that the developing countries would spend their funds on products from America and Britain. If they went to surplus countries which hoarded the receipts, the sterling or dollar problem would still be unsolved. It can also be argued that aid to developing countries lacks the flexibility that would be required from international monetary policy. But such objections show only that the scheme does not solve all problems; that additional aid will have to be given on other principles and that the maldistribution of international liquidity will also have to be tackled by other methods. They do not detract from the virtues of a scheme which links aid and liquidity without increasing indebtedness.

(c) Another and more limited way of overcoming donors' fears of foreign exchange losses resulting from the expansion of aid would be to institute a system of taxes and subsidies so as to equalise export advantages. Deficit countries would receive subsidies for the aid-financed exports, which would be paid out of indirect taxes levied on the aid-financed exports of surplus countries. In this manner the fear of foreign exchange losses is removed from additional aid, but from additional aid only.

(d) The fourth, and least attractive method of reducing the strain on the balance of payments of increased aid is to tie the aid more tightly to the donor's currency. Tying aid reduces the value to the recipient of the aid given. Not only is his choice restricted, so that he can no longer buy what he wants where he wants, but prices of products financed in this way have a tendency both to be higher and to rise as a result of reduced international competition. This happened when India was invited to receive aid from unemployed British steel mills in 1963, but the prices quoted were 30 per cent above those charged elsewhere. It is also argued that tying aid may prevent the adjustments in the donor country which greater competitiveness in international trade would require: it may help to freeze an existing inefficient industrial structure. But against these considerations it can be said that in the absence of better methods of dealing with the balance of payments problem, tied aid is better than nothing, particularly if the terms are sufficiently generous to compensate for the higher prices.

Ordinary tying does not avoid all foreign exchange loss. Such loss may occur for either of two mutually exclusive reasons. First, UK exports may constitute additional output and therefore have an import content. Secondly, aid-financed exports may be secured partly at the expense of other exports. But *all* increases in production have an import content and this is not a valid argument for cutting aid rather than, say, office-building, unless the import content of aid is particularly high. If, on the other hand, the increase in aid-financed exports is at the expense of some other activity, no additional imports are required unless the import content of aid is higher than that of the displaced activity.

Aid-financed exports may reduce commercial exports either to the aid-receiving country (known as *switching*), or to third markets (which may be described as *frustration*). Switching will tend to increase as the proportion of tied aid increases and if it were considered wise to tie our aid increasingly, the problem of preventing or reducing switching would become even more serious. There are a number of ways in which switching can be reduced, but all the arguments against tying apply with even greater force to these methods. The remedy for frustration is proper planning, so that domestic rather than foreign purchases are cut to accommodate aid. In a badly planned economy, aid may take the form of some vital bottleneck items, such as certain types of engineering goods, which could be exported for cash or used at home with high returns. But in a properly planned economy, aid would replace the demand on resources which has the lowest priority and domestic fiscal and monetary policies would see to it that the economy is not overloaded and exports not priced out of world markets.

Aid should be geared to the development plans of the receiving countries. This does not mean that elegant academic exercises in plan-drafting should be rewarded, but all aid, whether limited to specific projects or not, should be fitted into a development programme and its implementation. An isolated project, however well executed from a managerial and engineering point of view, can be as useless as a luxurious prestige project, if it is not related to other projects and policy measures. The advantage of tying aid to projects is claimed to be that there is a better chance that aid will be used more sensibly and efficiently. But this is often merely an appearance. What may happen is that receiving countries will put up their worthiest projects for aid. This does not mean that they would not be carried out if aid were not received. The aid tied to the top priority project simply frees internal funds which can still be wasted. There is no guarantee that waste will be avoided simply because labels are attached to certain sums. Experience has shown that project aid which does not contain an adequate 'free' foreign exchange component (sometimes called 'local costs') runs into difficulties when the project gives rise indirectly to the need for imported raw materials, spare parts, consumer goods, etc. Substantial waste in the form of unused capacity and unexpended aid or of excessive import bias may arise if essential complementary purchases and the indirect foreign exchange requirements to which they give rise are not covered by the aid.

Gearing aid to development plans has also certain implications for the donor. Not only must he be able to appraise in detail the requested projects in relation to the ability of the recipient country to make good use of the money, but he must also be able to assure some continuity in the flow of aid. The fear of cessation or reduction is bound to reduce the effectiveness of aid, even if in the event it does not cease and is not cut.

Difficult political problems arise if attempts are made to make aid conditional upon certain technical, managerial or economic policies, such as regional integration, land reform, effective taxation, import liberalisation, pricing policies or even birth control. Yet such policies may be essential if aid is to be effective. It will be politically easier to impose such conditions if aid is viewed as a co-operative international endeavour rather than as charity or political bribery. But what may be decried as economic neo-colonialism is a very different thing from political or old-fashioned economic colonialism. It is often a policy of support of the progressive groups in the developing country and strengthens their hand in removing obstacles to economic development.

It is essential to formulate a coherent set of objectives from which criteria for giving aid can be derived. The size, content, form, direction and timing of aid will be different according to which of several objectives is pursued, and how much weight is given to each. Political stability, strategic allegiance, alleviation of misery, acceleration of growth or the reduction of international inequalities may each dictate different and possibly conflicting policies. Confusion of aims is bound to breed disappointment and disenchantment. This does not mean that policy may not have to strike a balance between several aims. But the objectives must be clear: clarity is essential to avoid self-defeating policies. If aid is intended to oust Communists, it will be withdrawn when Communist aid is accepted. If it is intended to promote political stability by raising economic performance, Communist aid will be welcome. Again, British export promotion and the acceleration of development may lead to different policies. There is everything to be said in favour of promoting British exports. But it should not be confused with promoting development. The result of such a confusion may well be that neither is achieved. It is not for economists to select one or several objectives – not even accelerated economic development, itself not an unambiguous objective. This is a political choice. But the economist can point out inconsistencies and he can draw attention to the costs of pursuing strategic, political or humanitarian objectives. He can show that there are conflicts between progress and equality; that the chances of reducing the gap between income per head in the rich countries and in the poor are very slender and that effective aid policies may actually increase this gap, as well as the gaps between different underdeveloped countries, and that choices have to be made between raising consumption now or later and between raising consumption of the very poor with little development potential and the less poor with more development potential.

The aid burden should be distributed fairly between all donors. Recipients should be aware that they, in turn, should be or may become donors. Since development is a process and since different countries have reached different stages in this process, each country can benefit from the experience of those ahead of it and contribute to the experience of those behind. Although the provision of capital may be reserved for the richest countries, teaching the lessons learned from elementary education, family planning and land reform can be done much better by countries which have recently gone through these experiences. Thus aid, instead of being seen as charity from the rich to the poor, would become a co-operative international effort.

Particular problems arise from the fact that agricultural productivity is increasing in the rich North beyond its ability to absorb the surpluses. It seems sensible to channel these food surpluses to the poor countries. Such schemes should not reduce the ability of the recipient countries to improve their own agriculture, should not disrupt existing supplies of agricultural products and should share the burden of aid fairly between different rich food-producing and food-importing countries. It is true that these conditions complicate the administration of 'Food for Peace' programmes. They also raise other problems, such as storage facilities, matching the particular types of food of which there are surpluses and the types which are acceptable and needed by the ill- and under-fed. If these difficulties could be overcome, it would be possible to distribute the food surpluses of the North to the undernourished and ill-nourished South without damaging their indigenous agriculture, without hurting commercial suppliers and without putting an excessive burden on rich food importers.

Trade

Since the underdeveloped countries earn six times as much foreign exchange from trade as they receive in the form of aid and investment, no solution can be effective without increasing their opportunities to trade. The remarkable trend in the fifties and sixties towards freer and more extensive trade has been largely confined to trade between rich countries. What can we in the advanced nations do to enable the poor countries to earn more through exports? The following recommendations have been made:

(a) we should raise both the level and the rate of growth of our demand for their products;

(b) we should, in the first place, remove discrimination against their exports; we should then go further and discriminate in their favour, as well as encouraging them to discriminate against us;

(c) we should stabilise and raise the prices of primary products.

Let us consider these recommendations in turn.

Anything that raises the demand of advanced industrial countries for the products of the developing countries and keeps it growing, will help them to earn more foreign exchange. Deflation and stagnation in rich countries reduce the earning power of the poor. So much is clear, though it is less clear for which products in particular demand would rise most with expansion and whether these are the right ones from the point of view of the developing countries.

An accelerated rate of advance in the rich countries, moreover, is not an unmixed blessing for the poor. It may affect adversely their primary exports in three ways: it may speed up the introduction of synthetics; it may be associated with greater economy in the use of raw materials; and it may lead to a shift in the pattern of demand away from products which use a high proportion of imported raw materials. It may also increase the gap between the level of techniques in advanced countries and that appropriate for underdeveloped countries. It may make it more difficult to sell manufactured exports in competition with the new products of the advanced countries. If these detrimental effects of faster advance prevailed over the beneficial effects, greater reliance would have to be placed on import substitution, either within a country if its market is sufficiently large, or by regional unions between developing countries, and on aid from the advanced countries.

Discrimination against manufactures

Whereas we now discriminate in various ways *against* the exports of the developing countries, we should at least remove this discrimination and, if politically possible, aim at discriminating *in their favour*. At present their share of world trade is only 26 per cent. A rise in this share by a few percentage points will make a big difference to their earnings.

Discrimination against the exports of underdeveloped countries takes several forms. First, we protect agricultural production and mining, which affects an important part of the exports of underdeveloped countries. We shall argue that this particular form of discrimination, in spite of a widespread belief to the contrary, may not be so detrimental for the developing countries as is often believed and that rather different considerations apply to temperate zone agricultural than to manufactured products. Secondly, all advanced industrial countries impose special restrictions upon the labour-intensive manufactured exports of underdeveloped countries. In Britain we impose special restrictions on the import of cotton textiles, in the form of restrictive agreements with the producers of

Hong Kong, Pakistan and India. The USA has similar agreements and Continental Europe buys hardly any of their manufactures. Thirdly, all advanced countries impose higher tariffs, the higher the stage of processing foods and raw materials. We thus discriminate against their higher-valued exports, make it difficult for them to process their own raw materials and impede their industrialisation.

The removal of the discrimination against cotton textiles and jute would damage Lancashire and Dundee in Britain, and powerful vested interests in Germany and the USA. But we could set up industries which would supply the developing countries with the engineering goods which they require, and absorb the workers released as a result of larger textile and jute imports. Whether this or some other scheme of retraining and re-employment is adopted, our national expansion should be planned so as to provide for the acceptance of many more exports from the poor developing countries, particularly of manufactured goods, which will play an increasing part as these countries develop and industrialise. Britain has been much more liberal than either America or Europe in admitting products from developing countries. But this generosity should not be used, as it sometimes is, as an argument against doing more now. And Europe should begin to open its markets to the semi-processed and manufactured products of the developing countries. If all advanced countries were to admit manufactures from underdeveloped countries more freely, Britain would be likely to increase her exports by more than the additional expenditure on imports, as long as she remained generally competitive. For underdeveloped countries would spend all their additional receipts and our share in their additional imports is likely to be larger than our share in their additional exports.

But we should aim higher than merely at removing existing discrimination. The infant industry argument for tariffs could be extended to an argument for *infant industry preferences* and infant export industries' subsidies. Low-cost products like cotton textiles can already compete with British products if Britain removes protection. But more complicated products like light machinery, radios, etc., would have to be given preference over similar imports from richer countries. These would have to be accompanied by market research and sales promotion of various kinds, even if it hurt vested interests at home.

Another form of discrimination in favour of poor countries, or rather against ourselves, would be the encouragement of, and assistance to, the formation of regionally integrated unions between them, which would discriminate against our manufactured exports. Such integration would help in the establishment and growth of industries which could fully exploit available economies of scale and counteract the structural changes in developed countries which militate against the poor countries' power to earn more through exports. But these schemes are at present impeded by the rules of GATT. Countries must grant each other 100 per cent preference or none, they must extend free trade to all goods and they must never raise tariffs without counter-concessions. These rules have good practical reasons for unions between advanced countries, but the case for preferences of less than 100 per cent and partial freeing of trade is much stronger for trade with and between developing countries.

The GATT rules should be revised for regional unions between developing countries so as to permit:

(a) regional and, where appropriate, many-tier preferences of less than 100 per cent, i.e. mutual tariff reductions which do not have to be extended to all GATT members;

(b) partial tariff reductions on certain goods only which do not have to be extended to all goods;

(c) the ability to raise the external tariff without having to make counter-concessions. The economic arguments against such a revision are now well known but are based on assumptions which do not apply to conditions in these countries.

The arguments for granting preferences to the exports of the underdeveloped countries, permitting them to use export subsidies and encouraging them to form regional unions are logical extensions of the infant industry argument for tariff protection. The same arguments can be used to support a double exchange rate in the developing countries (which would have additional merits): one low rate for manufacturing exports and luxury imports, the other high for primary exports and necessary imports.

Agricultural protection

So far we have discussed the exports of manufactures of under-developed countries. It is often said that the rich countries should help the poor countries by giving up their agricultural (and mining) protection and thereby raise their demand for those exports of the poor countries which are substitutes for the protected products. But there are certain drawbacks to such policies. In the first place, it is not certain that abolition of protection would raise world prices of primary products. It may simply give an additional impetus to the already rapid pro-ductivity growth in agriculture in the advanced countries. While men are transferred from agriculture to industry, unit costs in agriculture will fall as a result of increased efficiency and total production may increase. Secondly, if abolition were to raise the world prices of agricultural products, this rise may not benefit the producers of these products, but increase the profits of foreign companies or large landowners. Thirdly, whether it benefits the producers or not, a price rise harms those poor countries which import these foodstuffs and benefits the exporters of these foodstuffs in rich countries. Fourthly, the abolition of protection would accelerate the shift of resources into manufacturing industry in advanced countries. Their already strong superiority would further increase, because these industries are subject to economies of large-scale production. Since an important objective of development is to raise the proportion of the national income generated by manufacturing industry, and since industry initially suffers from high costs which can be reduced only with expansion, an accentuation of the comparative advantage enjoyed by the rich countries would handicap this process. In any case, it is inconsistent to com-plain *both* that the rich, through their trade policies, keep the poor down to remain 'hewers of wood and drawers of water' *and* that the rich do not buy enough wood and water from them because they protect their own hewers and drawers. It would be very nice if the rich countries paid higher prices for the poor countries' primary exports (as long as they accrue to the poor producers), but if this can be achieved only by reduced ability to sell the still small but increasingly important share of manufactured exports, the proposition is less attractive.

Against this, three arguments could be advanced. First, though it may be admitted that the abolition of protection in advanced countries would reduce the profitability of industrial exports of the poor countries, it would, if it were successful in raising the prices of primary exports, increase their means to industrialise. And since these countries are so heavily dependent on these earnings, this is an important consideration. Secondly, it may be said that there is still wide scope for international specialisation within the industrial sector. Thirdly, one could argue that, although the present system of agricultural protection may help industrialisation in the poor countries, it also slows down the rate of growth of the rich and the benefits of growth may conceivably more than offset the damage from increased industrial competitiveness (although this view cannot easily be reconciled with advocacy of narrowing the gap between rich and poor). These arguments may weaken, but they do not refute the case against abandoning agricultural protection. The first one points to the need for providing the means to industrialise in other, more effective ways than by raising primary prices. But there may be serious obstacles to these. The second argument assumes, perhaps wrongly, that all manufacturing industries can be lumped into one category. The third is double-edged. The effects of faster growth induced by a shift into manufacturing are not all beneficial for the developing countries. The introduction of synthetic substitutes, economy in raw material use and a switch to less raw-material-using products may be speeded up, if extra external supplies are less than the reduction in domestic production. If it is argued that this would restore the comparative advantage of the poor countries in industrial products, the argument ignores the already great difficulties and costs of adaptation in conditions of increased uncertainty and continual change.

This conclusion is not generally accepted, and rests on four assumptions, each of which can be doubted:

(a) that agricultural resources in the advanced countries would flow into industry;

(b) that industry is subject to increasing returns to scale;

(c) that the industry in question is directly competitive with the industry of the developing country;

(d) that the benefits from accelerated growth in the advanced countries do not outweigh the damage from retarded industrialisation in the developing countries.

In any case, it appears that the case for buying more manufactured goods from the poor is stronger than the case for accentuating our superiority by abolishing agricultural protection.

Commodity agreements

The problem of primary products, which form the bulk of the exports of the underdeveloped countries, is twofold. The prices of these commodities in an uncontrolled market tend to fluctuate violently. In addition, these prices have shown a downward trend, relative to the prices of manufactures, during the 1950s, though they have recently turned up. The low income elasticity of demand for the commodity exports of primary producers, combined with their high income elasticity of demand for manufactured imports, has manifested itself in balance of payments difficulties for the developing countries. These difficulties are a manifestation of the way the terms of trade would tend to move if balance of payments equilibrium were established.

A number of theoretical arguments have been put forward why we should expect deteriorating terms of trade to be a persistent long-term trend. Empirical evidence has also been adduced for this trend over decades to support the theoretical arguments. But the theoretical arguments are not entirely convincing and the existence of the long-term trend can be doubted. On the other hand, for some of the arguments it is not necessary to predict the future trend of the terms of trade between primary and manufactured products. It is possible to admit ignorance and to base policy on evaluating the harm done by an adverse trend compared with the costs of having insured against it unnecessarily. The policy conclusions might be similar, without the dubious theoretical and empirical premises.

There is a variety of ways in which the prices of primary products, and with them the incomes of their producers, can be stabilised and raised, which score different marks with respect to international equity and efficiency. *Stabilisation* against short-term fluctuations is an unmitigated benefit, for short-term fluctuations in commodity prices are at best useless, at worst harmful to the improved allocation of resources. Uncertainty disrupts development plans, discourages efficient planned production in the industry concerned, and efficient planning of use by the buyers of the commodity. The best way of dealing with instability is a buffer stock. Given adequate foresight, independent administration and low storage costs, buffer stocks could, like Joseph in Egypt, do good and do well simultaneously.

International commodity agreements, which *raise* the prices of primary products and support them at levels higher than they would otherwise be, have the advantage of improving both the balances of payments and the terms of trade of the primary exporters. But they suffer from certain drawbacks. First, price increases do not always benefit the poor producers, but may accrue to middlemen, companies or rich landowners. Second, not all primary-producing countries are poor and not all importers of primary products are rich. A rise in the prices of some primary products will therefore benefit some of the richest countries like America and Australia, and harm some of the poorest. Third, the burden of support falls most heavily on those who import most. There is no reason why those who admit primary products most generously should shoulder most of the support burden. Fourth, they encourage the production of products for which demand may not be expanding sufficiently. To include quota restrictions in the agreements would, even if administratively and politically possible, prevent the most efficient producers from meeting demand. Fifth, high prices will tend to accelerate the introduction of synthetic substitutes, economy in the use of raw materials and a switch away from raw-material-intensive products, in industrial countries, and thus reinforce the trend of falling demand for the poor countries' exports, without providing sufficient incentives to high-cost producers to move out of the production of these goods and to diversify. There is much to be said for stabilisation, and something may be said for raising the prices of certain foodstuffs, for encouraging their efficient production at the higher prices, for buying up the excess of supply over demand, and for distributing the surplus, subject to certain safeguards, to under- and ill-fed people. But there are a number of objections to international commodity agreements which raise the prices of primary products, although the case for such agreements has to be examined separately for each commodity.

Price compensation schemes

The dilemma in manipulating the prices of primary products is that policies which benefit certain groups of producers may be bad for the allocation of resources, and policies that lead to efficient allocation may have bad effects on income distribution. Restriction schemes may improve balances of payments and terms of trade, but they reduce the scope for using prices as a means of allocating resources. It is the intention of schemes of price compensation to separate these two aspects by permitting the pricing system to fulfil its allocative function, while compensating for the damage done to distribution. The use of prices must not be identified with *laissez-faire* and free markets. Prices can be used as an instrument of planning. Their beneficial effects can be separated from their harmful effects and the latter can be eliminated. If it were thought that trade in primary products should be conducted at world prices in order to prevent over-production or production by high-cost producers, or wrong allocation between buyers, it would still be possible to safeguard the balance of payments, the terms of trade and the national income of a country exporting these products by paying it the deficiency of their actual prices below an agreed level of prices. The payment could be either a full compensation or on some agreed sliding scale. The agreed standard price could be adjusted from time to time. A standard quantity – perhaps that of a base year or of an average of past years – to which the standard price applies would also have to be specified. Otherwise it would pay the country to increase supplies. Such a scheme would be a component of international aid which is geared to losses suffered from falling export prices. There is no need to ask a poor country to make up the difference if the price rises above the agreed level (though symmetrical schemes could be arranged for rich exporters). In this way, balances of payments, terms of trade and national incomes could be stabilised, but it would be left to the receiving government to decide what to do with the deficiency payments. It may wish to compensate some of the producers for their losses or it may wish to subsidise diversification, or it may use the funds for the general purposes of development.

One's opinion of such a scheme will depend largely on one's view on the efficiency of price policies in underdeveloped countries. In many of these, prices do not respond much to demand and supply, and neither productive factors nor demand respond to prices. Reactions may even be perverse and low prices, far from discouraging production, may encourage it. Price differentials are certainly not a sufficient condition, perhaps not a necessary one, and possibly even an obstacle to shifting resources in the direction required by development.

Compensatory finance

The merit of the price compensation schemes discussed above is that they are fairly easy to administer and are appropriate for commodities that are subject to reductions of demand. But their drawback is that they apply to price only and not to volume – whereas it is the product of price and volume that we should try to stabilise. If the fluctuations result from local conditions of supply, like a bad harvest, or even from world conditions of supply, a price compensation scheme may not be appropriate. Another type of scheme is intended to compensate, not for the fall in the prices of certain commodities, but for the fall in total export earnings of an underdeveloped country, whatever its cause. A number of such schemes of compensatory finance have been proposed. Professor A. G. Hart has proposed a Development Insurance Fund which would entitle a country to draw automatically on currencies to compensate for all or most of the shortfall of its export proceeds compared with the average of the preceding three years, repayments being contingent on recovery. This type of scheme is better adapted to deal with the problem of instability of particular countries than a price compensation scheme, although the two can be used in conjunction. If certain prices were successfully stabilised there would be less to do for the Development Insurance Fund. The proponent of this Fund does not, however, answer the question how a country can be prevented from adopting policies which would lead to a decline in the value of its exports if it knew that it would receive compensation for this decline.

It is possible to borrow from the International Monetary Fund for short periods if export earnings decline as a result of fluctuations in exports of primary products. At the United Nations Conference on Trade and Development, the Secretary-General in his report *Towards a New Trade Policy for Development* (United Nations, 1964) suggested schemes for longer-term compensatory finance and the British Government put forward proposals to supplement short-term by long-term finance where a prolonged fall in export earnings disrupts development.

So far we have assumed that the schemes are multilateral. Either groups of countries or international institutions could adopt them. Britain should try to persuade other advanced countries to adopt the appropriate schemes and to implement them by the appropriate international institutions. But if this proved unsuccessful, or until it proved successful, there are certain things which we could do ourselves, in co-operation with the underdeveloped countries. We could enter into long-term contracts and bulk-purchase agreements or we could arrange for bilateral inter-governmental deficiency payments, either of the price compensation type or of the export earnings compensation type, as described above. There is nothing in these schemes that would prevent them from being applied as between two or a small number of countries, although the effects on our balance of payments would, of course, be more favourable in a multilateral scheme.

UNCTAD

In March 1964 the United Nations Conference on Trade and Development, at which 122 governments were represented, assembled in Geneva and sat for three months. Its Secretary-General, Dr Raul Prebisch, has been one of the chief exponents of the need for a new type of analysis of, and a new deal for, the underdeveloped countries. During the conference's sessions and in its resolutions, the voices of a large number – 75 and later 77 – of underdeveloped countries joined in asking for more determined action on the part of the advanced nations to help to meet the large and growing needs of the underdeveloped world. A considerable number of proposals were discussed, but little agreement was reached. As for trade, the demands for ending protection in the advanced countries were particularly opposed by the French. It was agreed that tariffs should be altered so as to encourage processing of their own raw materials in the underdeveloped countries. There was hardly any progress with respect to infant export preferences. With regard to aid, Britain proposed the already mentioned scheme of supplementary finance for falls in export earnings, which goes beyond the short-term arrangements of the IMF. The target of 1 per cent of national income to be given in the form of aid was reaffirmed (with a definition of 'aid' wider than the one used in this chapter), four years after the United Nations had set it up for the Development Decade. The approach via the 1 per cent target was complemented by greater emphasis on aid requirements of developing countries. Costs to donors can thus be related to benefits to recipients in a more general analysis. It was agreed to study the reduction of the debt burden of the poor countries, which had grown from $8,000m. to $20,000m. A Trade and Development Board of 55 countries will prepare the next conference.

Different people will see a different significance in the outcome of this conference. It has been compared, at the international level, with the rise of the trade union movement. The following appear to be some of the lessons:

(1) Measures that benefit both sides, like mutually profitable trade and investment, are no longer the 'engines of growth' that they were in the nineteenth century. Partly for this reason intergovernmental aid has played an increasing part in promoting development in the underdeveloped countries. This raises an important question: to what extent does the failure of international policies for development turn upon lack of international solidarity and to what extent upon the absence of the appropriate mechanism and institutions to express whatever solidarity exists?

(2) The GATT philosophy, which has presupposed equality of nations, has serious limitations in dealing with trade as a means to development. Unequal treatment is appropriate for the relations between unequals, and the precise forms it should take need careful thought.

(3) On these grounds, as well as on the ground of including

the Soviet bloc in an institution which will exercise pressure to adapt policies to the needs of the developing countries, the establishment of a new world trade organisation is desirable, which should not supplant but complement GATT.

Conclusions

The discussion of aid and trade has suffered from a number of confusions. One is the juxtaposition of aid and trade as alternative means of promoting development. Another is the excessive preoccupation with the provision of resources at the expense of so-called non-economic measures which trigger off or accelerate the complex development process.

Trade and aid are not alternatives: not even at the margin. In many circumstances aid is the precondition for trade and trade the only way in which aid loans can be serviced. One of the functions of aid is to enable developing countries to build up their economies and their export trade. To see in aid an alternative to trade is to reject its ultimate purpose. Of course, it would be possible to give away cumulatively more and more free grants and to refuse to buy more. But such a solution is neither practicable nor desirable. The proper use of aid funds depends upon successful development and this in turn entails the ability to participate in the international division of labour and to earn more by trade. It is to be hoped that eventually we shall see a system of international taxation and subsidies on the same principles as those which we now accept within a developed national welfare state. But even in a welfare state the principles are (a) to prevent anybody from falling below an adequate minimum, and (b) to assist people in making the best use of their talents. Both principles provide conditions in which individuals, by their own efforts, can improve their lot. Moreover, if aid is given in the form of loans, repayment is only possible if the donors accept more imports. Trade and aid are interrelated in a number of complex ways which are obscured by the slogan 'trade versus aid'. Perhaps a more useful distinction, if not for bargaining at any rate for clear thinking, would be that between measures that should be judged by commercial criteria, whether they are purchases of goods and services or whether they are commercial loans and private investment (a very important subject, of which we have not said anything in this chapter), and those that should be judged by other criteria. The first group comprise mutually beneficial economic trans-actions, while the second group involve an economic sacrifice of the donor. Most practical policies, including aid loans and price support schemes, will be packages containing both elements, but this is not an argument against distinguishing between measures where economic interests coincide and those where political, moral and other considerations enter.

The other and related point worth making is that neither the provision of funds nor improved opportunities to earn foreign exchange by trade are enough for development. In order to make sensible use of the money lent, granted and earned, the developing countries need a growing number of skilled admin-istrators, engineers, agronomists, veterinarians, health workers, teachers, etc. By helping to train and educate these people we can ensure that money given in aid is put to good use and that opportunities for mutually beneficial trade and invest-ment are created.

Nor should aid and trade be looked upon exclusively as the provision of resources. Clearly, the developing countries are short of savings in general, and of certain types of sophisticated capital equipment, which only foreign exchange can buy, in particular. Equally clearly, exports can be regarded as a flexible and productive method of transforming domestic resources into much-needed imports. But it is nowadays generally recognised that lack of resources is not the only, and at early stages of development not the main, obstacle. If it were, countries with rich oil revenues would have no difficulties in developing. Development is a complex process in which the provision of additional resources interacts with changes in social and cul-tural institutions and human motivation and attitudes to work and life. Unless aid and trade make an impact upon these inter-related factors, they will run to waste. If, on the other hand, they are applied where these conditions are favourable, their impact can be substantial. There are political difficulties in making aid contingent upon the required changes in institu-tions, skills and attitudes, and there are intellectual difficulties in knowing just what these changes ought to be. But unless we shift the emphasis from resource allocation to social transformation, disillusionment will be the result. As important as the exports of goods and services is the transformation of institutions and attitudes. Otherwise charity, even if dispensed abroad, remains an escape by which we may save our consciences but not the developing countries. Attempts to attach to aid such conditions as the pursuit of effective birth control, land reform, changes in educational structures and the formation of larger regional integrated areas will be decried as neo-colonialism and neo-imperialism. It may be that channelling aid through international institutions, on which recipients are represented, would avoid these charges, but the donor countries would still have to see to it that these institutions are run by men who can be trusted to insist on the conditions favourable to development. The ultimate test of our policies is their impact on internal social reform, rather than some crude quantitative ratio of aid to national income.

This chapter has been concerned with methods by which the underdeveloped countries can be helped to accelerate their development. We have argued that the distinction between trade and aid is not entirely useful in clarifying the issues, and that much more than the provision of foreign exchange or savings is needed. This would lead on to a number of other issues, which, however, will not be discussed here. In particular, there is the question whether the removal of restrictions on immigration would help the underdeveloped countries to deal with their population problem. As things are, the advanced countries of the West, and particularly Britain and America, are depriving the underdeveloped countries of their scarcest and most valuable human resources, doctors, nurses, engineers, and skilled workers, while preventing the entry of untrained men. Again, we shall not deal with the important question whether education and training are best carried out by bringing the students and trainees here or whether the teachers should go out and train and educate on the spot.

Finally, we can only mention the vast research effort that is needed to enable the underdeveloped countries to make good use of the aid provided. Most research at present is focused on the problems of the advanced countries, on their industries where labour is relatively scarce and capital relative plentiful, and on their temperate zone agriculture. Effective aid should take the form of directing research at the problems of under-developed countries. For industry, research should be con-cerned with technologies appropriate for small markets where unskilled and untrained labour is abundant but the attitudes and institutions, as well as the industrial hinterland of developed countries, are absent. For agriculture, research should be directed at tropical agriculture, soil conditions in tropical regions, reactions to patterns of rainfall, drainage, irrigation, fertilisers, improved seeds, animal stocks, cropping patterns, the use and adaptation of agricultural implements, the prevention of plant and animal diseases, the storage of perishable products, the appropriate irrigation schemes, the use of energy from wind, sun and the tides. In addition, much research is required into the obstacles to acceptance of whatever knowledge is available through extension services and the reasons for the frequent lack of impact of facilities and planning on agriculture. We tend to assume far too readily that the stock of knowledge in existence in the rich North can easily be drawn upon by the poor South. In actual fact, much of its knowledge, far from being trans-ferable or adaptable, can be a hindrance to development.

In spite of the general acceptance of the principles of over-seas aid, technical assistance and removal of trade barriers, many of our actions belie these principles. We give aid, but we often tie it to high-priced products and charge profitable interest; we declare our willingness to supply capital and skills, but we borrow from the poor countries or encourage repatria-tion of private capital and of administrators, whose pensions are charged to the countries for which they no longer work and are counted as part of our aid effort; we in Britain open our markets to textiles but ask the Indian and Hong Kong manu-facturers to exercise voluntary restraints on sales. Continental Europe uses aid as a concealed subsidy to their domestic labour-intensive industries and to inefficient firms which are kept alive by protective tariffs. We staff our hospitals with Indian and Pakistani doctors and nurses who could render immensely valuable service in their own countries, but exclude unskilled coloured immigrants. We send young volunteers overseas, where they find themselves teaching in the boarding-schools of the rich. We complain about the emptiness of affluence and fail to harness our growing capacity to produce for the needs of the poor countries. A programme of practical action should begin by accepting the aim of the United Nations Development Decade to double the personal incomes of the poor two-thirds of the world by the end of the century. Although the 1 per cent target has serious limitations we should try to raise the present pitifully inadequate proportions of our national income which we devote to aid and to relate it to the needs of the recipient countries. Having in the last few years borrowed from abroad and run down our reserves, a good deal of any extra production will have to be used to restore balance in our international payments. There are numerous competitive claims on the remainder of the increase in production. We need more and better schools, houses, hospitals, roads. We are already committed to much of this increase and the pressure to increase our standard of living and comfort will be strong. The outlook is clearly not good for an increase in aid to countries which can be seen to show scant gratitude, which, at best, can be said to have strictly limited 'absorptive capacity' and where, at worst, corruption, absolutism and militarism prevail. It will not be difficult to rationalise our selfishness and inertia as caution and wisdom. Economists will be found who show how detrimental our aid is to development efforts. Our balance of payments difficulties will provide additional arguments against increasing aid and the strength of sterling will be cited as in the best interest of the underdeveloped countries.

In spite of this, it would be both politically short-sighted and morally wrong not to give very high priority to an increase in aid. A strong balance of payments must be the first interest of those who take aid seriously, so that no financial obstacles stand in the way of the transfer of real resources. Then, high marginal tax rates on consumption and a carefully thought-out set of priorities of private investment and of public expenditure are important. If capital aid cannot be increased much, it is all the more urgent that all efforts must go into securing the full effectiveness of whatever aid is given. Technical assistance can play an important role here. The temporary service of skilled experts in underdeveloped countries still runs into too many obstacles here. We are not providing them with the right incentives and we are presenting them with the wrong deterrents. We would need changes in the conditions of employment in business, universities and the civil service so that far from suffering for service abroad, such service would be rewarded and regarded as an integral part of a career.

Finally, there are a number of ways in which modernisation and planning in Britain can be geared to the needs of the under-developed countries: to their need to trade, to receive aid and to repay debt. Such dovetailing of plans would make it possible to reduce the real costs that would fall on the British economy while increasing the benefits that can be bestowed on the recipient countries. Proper planning would have to see to it that bottlenecks are broken, so that aid does not deprive us of scarce items which could be sold for cash abroad. It would make available goods from temporary excess capacity and excess skilled manpower. It could make use of machinery scrapped in the process of modernisation, and could identify markets for one another's goods, in order to ease the transition to freer imports. The co-ordination under a Minister with Cabinet rank of all forms of aid and the co-ordination of all aid with domestic economic planning should make it possible to step up aid, to soften its terms, to make it more effective and to revive the international vision which otherwise might fade in the scramble for a parochially interpreted national welfare.

SUGGESTIONS FOR FURTHER READING

An attempt to isolate the element of pure grant in all aid and to render different forms of aid comparable between donors was made by John A. Pincus in 'The Cost of Foreign Aid', *The Review of Economics and Statistics* (November 1963), pp. 360–7, and by Wilson E. Schmidt, 'The Economics of Charity: Loans versus Grants', *Journal of Political Economy* (August 1964). A survey of British aid is given in the White Paper (Cmnd. 2147, September 1963) and in *British Aid – 1, Survey and Comment*, published by the Overseas Development Institute in 1963. On technical assistance, Sir Andrew Cohen's Henry Morley

Lecture 'New Work and Ideas in the Field of Technical Co-operation' is lively and informative. There are a number of well-written and useful studies published by the Overseas Development Institute and by the OECD Development Centre in Paris. Particularly valuable is Göran Ohlin's survey *Reappraisals of Foreign Aid Policies* (December 1964). Mr Maxwell Stamp's scheme of linking a reform of international liquidity with aid to underdeveloped countries was originally published in *Moorgate and Wall Street* (Spring 1961), and a revised version in the Autumn 1962 number of the same journal.

On trade problems, *New Directions for World Trade*, proceedings of a Chatham House Conference in 1963, has a number of valuable contributions. Dr Prebisch's report as Secretary-General of the United Nations Conference on Trade and Development, *Towards a New Trade Policy for Development*, contains the general philosophy of UNCTAD, calculations of aid requirements based on prospects of exports and import needs and a discussion of possible solutions of commodity problems. Documents of UNCTAD are collected in the British Blue Book, Cmnd. 2417, *United Nations Conference on Trade and Development, Final Acts with Related Documents* (July 1964).

Professor A. G. Hart, in his contribution to *New Directions for World Trade*, discusses the scheme mentioned on page 280. For other proposals of compensatory finance, see United Nations, *International Compensations for Fluctuations in Commodity Trade* (Report by a Committee of Experts, New York, 1961); Organisation of American States, *Final Report of the Group of Experts on the Stabilisation of Export Receipts* (Washington, D.C., 1962). On present borrowing facilities from the International Monetary Fund, *Compensatory Financing of Export Fluctuations* (Washington, D.C., 1963). On the tendency of the terms of trade of primary producers to deteriorate, see Prebisch's Report mentioned above, and for a different view, A. Maizels in the *National Institute Economic Review* (May 1964). The general literature on development problems is vast and growing, but John Kenneth Galbraith's *Economic Development* (Oxford University Press, 1964) is a lively and stimulating introduction by one who combines theoretical acumen, practical wisdom and wit.

INDEX